broken pieces

ALA Editions purchases fund advocacy, awareness, and accreditation programs for library professionals worldwide.

broken pieces
a library life, 1941–1978

michael gorman

American Library Association • Chicago 2011

© 2011 by Michael Gorman. Any claim of copyright is subject to applicable limitations and exceptions, such as rights of fair use and library copying pursuant to Sections 107 and 108 of the U.S. Copyright Act. No copyright is claimed for content in the public domain, such as works of the U.S. government.

Extensive effort has gone into ensuring the reliability of the information in this book; however, the publisher makes no warranty, express or implied, with respect to the material contained herein.

ISBNs: 978-0-8389-1104-4 (paper); 978-0-8389- 9302-6 (PDF); 978-0-8389-9303-3 (ePub); 978-0-8389- 9304-0 (Mobipocket); 978-0-8389- 9305-7 (Kindle). For more information on digital formats, visit the ALA Store at alastore.ala.org and select eEditions.

Library of Congress Cataloging-in-Publication Data
Gorman, Michael, 1941–
   Broken pieces : a library life, 1941–1978 / Michael Gorman.
       p. cm.
   Includes bibliographical references and index.
   ISBN 978-0-8389-1104-4 (alk. paper)
   1. Gorman, Michael, 1941– 2. Librarians—United States—Biography.
3. Librarians-England—Biography. I. Title.
   Z720.G68A3 2011
   020.92--dc22
       [B]   2011011676

Cover design by Karen Sheets de Gracia.
Interior design in Adobe Garamond by Adrianna Sutton.

♾ This paper meets the requirements of ANSI/NISO Z39.48–1992 (Permanence of Paper).

Printed in the United States of America
15 14 13 12 11   5 4 3 2 1

This book is dedicated to Louis and Bess Gorman and Leo and Finn Singer, my beloved grandchildren.

We look back on our life as a thing of broken pieces, because our mistakes and failures are always the first to strike us, and outweigh in our imagination what we have accomplished and attained.
—Johann Wolfgang von Goethe, *Maxims and reflections*

I learned that to remember is, at least in part, to imagine, and that the act of transposing memory into written words is a creative act that transforms the memory itself . . . is becomes was in the blink of an eye and memories are shadows.
—Joel Agee, "A lie that tells the truth"

We are all fools whether we dance or not, so why not dance?
—Japanese proverb

It's all right now, I learned my lesson well.
You can't please everyone, so you've got to please yourself.
—R. Nelson, "Garden party"

contents

acknowledgments • xi
preface • xiii

Chapter 1   Et in Arcadia Ego, 1941–1945 • 1
Chapter 2   London, 1945–1947 • 11
Chapter 3   On the Move, 1948–1952 • 19
Chapter 4   Finchley Catholic Grammar School, 1952–1957 • 35
Chapter 5   Hampstead Public Library, 1957–1960 • 51
Chapter 6   Paris and Afterwards, 1960–1962 • 75
Chapter 7   Marriage and Library School, 1962–1966 • 99
Chapter 8   BNB, Children, Cataloguing, and a Crisis, 1966–1969 • 115
Chapter 9   BNB, the British Library, 1970–1974 • 139
Chapter 10 Illinois, 1974–1975 • 157
Chapter 11 Back to England, the University of Illinois, 1975–1978 • 175
Chapter 12 The Anglo-American Cataloguing Rules • 191

epilogue • 205
notes • 209
index • 223

acknowledgments

I have many people to thank for their help. My wife, Anne Reuland; my friend and careful reader Anne Heanue; my brother Timothy Gorman for much information about our family, for careful reading of the text, and for checking many facts; Anne (Gillett) Gorman for many memories of the events told here; Jonathan Oates, the archivist of the Ealing Local History Centre; Bob Usherwood, the editor of the newsletter of the CILIP Retired Members Guild; and the compilers of the countless numbers of printed and digital sources I have consulted. I would also like to thank Don Chatham, Chris Rhodes, and Jenni Fry of ALA, copy editor Johanna Rosenbohm, cover designer Karen Sheets de Gracia, and book designer and compositor Adrianna Sutton.

Nothing in this book is derived from Wikipedia or from the use of Google.

preface
o, lucky man!

I have been lucky all my life—lucky in being at the right place at the right time; lucky in the jobs and tasks to which I have been appointed. Lucky in love and in being born in the times in which, and into the family into which, I was born. Lucky to have been relatively unscathed by the many failures, wrongs, and hurts for which I have been responsible (I wish I could say the same for the many people involved in those failures, wrongs, and hurts). I have been lucky in reaping the rewards of the far fewer things that I have done right. So much, in retrospect, seems to be the result of happy accident and happenstance that even someone who believes in rationalism above all, as I do, must acknowledge that luck is a powerful force in my life.

In my early life, almost the only things that I really cared about, apart from a very few people, were books, films, radio, and cricket. As I grew older, I developed a keen interest in politics (British and U.S.) and in the practice of librarianship—one as an amateur, the other as part of my life's work. I have despaired of politics for many complex reasons (not related to the venality or supposed inferiority of today's politicians) that I will not describe in this book, and I have ceased to be active in most aspects of librarianship, for reasons that I will explain partially in the final chapter. So here I am, focused on family and a few friends and back to books, films, radio, and cricket for inspiration and solace. Time's arrow has becomes time's circle. This book is about a major part of that circle.

Michael Gorman
Chicago, 2008–2010

1

Et in Arcadia Ego, 1941–1945

I walked up the steps of the Central Library of Hampstead Public Libraries in Arkwright Road, London NW3, on the first day of my job as a junior assistant—September 1, 1957. The effective date of my retirement from the position of Dean of Library Services at the Madden Library of the California State University, Fresno, was August 31, 2007. With brief gaps of which I will write later, the fifty years between those two events were spent as a library employee.

The former Hampstead Central Library building is a solid brick and stone structure with high-ceilinged rooms. It was designed by Arnold Taylor and opened in 1897—a durable manifestation of the seriousness of the public library movement in Britain in the late nineteenth century, a seriousness that is still evident even in its current use as the Arts Centre of the London Borough of Camden (an entity that came into existence in 1972 when it swallowed the historic boroughs of Hampstead, Holborn, and St. Pancras). The building was refurbished in 2004 by the architect Tony Fretton. In 1957, the reference library was on the left, the music library on the right, and the central lending library straight ahead. In my mind, I can see each of these tall rooms and the children's library (added to the original building in 1909 and with a separate entrance) on the semi-basement floor below as clearly as I saw them then—the wooden floors, sunlight illuminating the ranges of books, people working, studying, and writing in the muted light of the low library lamps. I remember too my first meetings with many of the staff of the library and the cordiality and great kindness with which they greeted a socially inept 16-year-old on the first day of his first full-time job, a position necessitated by my having been kicked out of school. I was utterly without training or qualifications and was relieved to find this did not appear to matter much to anyone.

My library life started years before—in the late 1940s in the northwestern London suburb of Golders Green in the neighboring borough of Hendon (absorbed into the London borough of Barnet at the same time that Hampstead ceased being a municipal entity and became simply a state of mind). My reading life began even earlier, sometime in 1944 in a small school in the Oxfordshire countryside. I write "sometime" because I cannot remember not being able to read or even puzzling over letters and words. My mother, as part of the war effort, worked in a munitions factory and since, in those far-off wartime days, there were neither preschools nor kindergartens, I had to go to the only place available—the local elementary school. I suppose I learned my alphabet and words there and not at home but, whichever it was, my earliest memories involve reading and my precocious start led me to reading long books at an earlier age than is usual. (I read my first Dickens—*Barnaby Rudge*—when I was 8 and living in Golders Green in northwest London. I knew almost nothing about Dickens and less than nothing about the Gordon Riots and eighteenth-century England.)

I have always thought that my early adeptness in reading was a cause of a phenomenon of which I have never read or heard in the case of anyone else. I see words as pictures that speak their meaning visually. To me, the word *sly* has a slinky, winking quality and the word *broad* an inherent spaciousness—in short, they *look* sly and broad. In the same manner *memories*, *munitions*, and *elementary* (all words used in the preceding paragraph) look like their meaning just as much as they convey that meaning intellectually or phonically. It is a difficult thing to describe, but it has shaped my life as much if not more than many of the objective facts of, and people encountered in, that life. Poetry has always had a special effect on me as the words are loaded not only with mental and aural meaning but also a visual meaning akin to that of an Asian calligraphic and pictorial scroll. I have studied and practiced (with modest success) calligraphy for many years and am convinced that this one attempt at artistic expression is tied to the way in which I perceive words. Perhaps to compensate or as part of a neurological balance, I have an undeveloped visual sense. This is a great handicap in a world in which more and more information is conveyed visually in a reaction to globalism and the decline of literacy and the rise of aliteracy in the Western world.

FAMILIES

Much of what follows concerns my family, where it came from and how it was formed, and how it has affected my life. It seems to me that one of the central dilemmas of modern life is that, on the one hand, the family is regarded as a central component of society and that a "good" (i.e., loving) family is the model of how life should be lived. On the other hand, it is demonstrably true that the family is a major cause of psychological distress. The waiting rooms of psychiatrists are full of people who, rightly or wrongly, blame their neuroses and other psychic dislocations on their family life in early years and currently. We grow up being told that perfect families are attainable, but we all live in imperfect families and most of us suspect that *our* family is uniquely imperfect and that, consequently, we are doomed to failure. I have always been wary of political theories built on extending the "family" into the public sphere, from the sublimity of the Jeffersonian ideal of families extending to communities to the ridiculousness of Thatcherian economics that equates national budgets with those of "families gathered around the kitchen table," not to mention the fatuity of using the club of "family values" to enforce conformity.

I had a good war. My father, Philip Denis Gorman, who was born on April 25, 1903, in a house in Regent's Park Road, Primrose Hill, to Thomas and Maggie (née Kiernan) Gorman, joined the British Army as a private soldier on May 31, 1921, and was engaged in the British effort in World War II in the Middle East and North Africa. He had married my mother, Alicia Felicia Barrett, in 1940. She was born on November 18, 1918 (exactly a week after Armistice Day), in Wood Green, a north London suburb, the fourth child of Joseph and Alice (née Kitchen) Barrett. Though my father was present at my conception in the summer of 1940 and I know he was in Britain in 1941 (a small black-and-white snap of him in his khaki uniform beaming bemusedly at a baby—me—in a high old-fashioned perambulator), he was in far-off places, including North Africa (he participated in the pivotal battle of El Alamein), for all I can remember of the first five years of my life. What must have been often lonely, frightening, deprived years for him were relatively easy years for my mother and idyllic years for me.

Margaret Barrett, Philip Gorman, Alicia Gorman (née Barrett), Billy Craigen, March 2, 1940, Wood Green

My mother's family on her wedding day. Front row (left to right): Tony, Alice, Jack. Back row: Margaret, Alicia, Mary.

They are all dead now—the people who gathered in front of a north London Catholic church on March 2, 1940, after my parent's wedding. The black-and-white photographs show my mother, then 21 years old, in a smart pale-colored dress with padded shoulders and a knee-length skirt, standing next to my father, his hat in hand and wearing his coarse khaki army uniform, his dark wavy hair shining. He was then less than two months shy of his 37th birthday. Others present at the wedding were all my from mother's family or connections of that family—her severe, disapproving, black-clad mother; her brother Tony, then a Jesuit seminarian; her brother Jack; her dramatic-looking, unsmiling sister Margaret; her winsome younger sister Mary in her Women's Auxiliary Air Force (WAAF) uniform; and my father's "best man," 21-year-old Billy Craigen (had my father ever met him before that day?), the son of the Barretts' solicitor marcelled and dashing in his RAF officer's uniform. Almost all you need to know about the Barretts and Gormans can be found in these dramatis personae.

My father was the seventh of 14 children (though only 10 survived past infancy and, of those, his brothers Charles Stewart Lawrence Gorman and Desmond Thomas Gorman died in the Kaiser's War, aged 23 and 19) and his mother, who lived well into her 90s, was alive and kicking at the age of 70. His surviving brothers and sisters (David, Kathleen, Aileen, Thomas, Terence, Norah, and Hugh) and their spouses all lived in the London area. It is hard to believe that, even in wartime, not one of his family could attend his wedding, even harder to believe that he had no male friend available to be his best man. The fact is that the Gormans were working-class London Irish tribal Catholics. My grandfather, Thomas Gorman (born in Burnley, Lancashire, of Irish and Welsh parents in 1866), was a copperplate printer and died in his 60s in the 1930s (of prostate cancer). My grandmother (born Mary Margaret Kiernan in Dublin, Ireland in 1871), worked as a domestic servant (she was described as a "nursery governess" in the 1891 census) when young and a char (housecleaner) later in her life. She was still working in her 80s. She had, when young, red hair that she could sit on—a point of great pride to my father—and there is a family legend that she was a servant in the house of either James McNeil Whistler or Walter Sickert (all such stories are improved by an artistic vagueness) and there is a drawing of her called "the Irish Girl" or "Girl with Red Hair" by one of those artists in the National Gallery in London—a legend with no basis in fact that I have been able to discern. My father was a noncommissioned officer (i.e., and crucially, not a commissioned officer) in the army and his brothers worked in various occupations connected with motorcars—chauffeuring and the like. The Barretts, in contrast, were middle-class London (by way of Liverpool) Irish (on my grandfather's side—his father was born in Cork and his mother Margaret, née McLaughlin, was born in London of Kerry-born parents), and practicing Catholics. Joseph Barrett was an engineer and successful businessman—founder and co-owner of Barrett & Wright, a central heating and air conditioning company that was still in business until the late twentieth century (when it merged with a large Swedish engineering firm). He was proud of his barefoot Irish heritage and of the fact (or myth?) that the last man hanged in public in Britain—Michael Barrett, convicted of complicity in the Fenian outrage in Clerkenwell Gaol, London—was his uncle, cousin, or some other familial connection. A man called Michael Barrett was, indeed, the last man hanged in public in Britain—in Newgate Prison, London, on May 26, 1868. His name is inscribed on the Cenotaph in Dublin with the other Fenian dead. He was a Fermanagh man, and my grandfather's father—Patrick Philip Barrett—was born in Cork in 1855, and his grandfather—Joseph Barrett—in Cork in 1801, so it may be that there is no familial connection. The imprecisions in this story are due to the facts that my grandfather died in 1936 and that the Barretts are a family with a developed gift for mythologizing. My mother's cousin, my dear late friend Katherine Burgess, a "literary lady," described them as "fantasists"—neither the first nor the last to have their roots in Ireland. In any event, the Barretts lived a comfortable middle-class life in prosperous Wood Green and knew themselves to be superior to the likes of the Gormans. Class differences were more important than heritage and their shared Catholicism (though the latter burned much less ardently in my father and his family), and I am sure that my mother's siblings, with their rags-to-riches sensibilities, looked down on the career soldier Phil Gorman. I know her mother did as she referred to him as "your poor drunken father" more than once to me (I was 8 or 9 at the time). My mother's sisters made marriages that were, in the Barrett's view, far more suitable than an alliance with the rough soldiery—Margaret married a Jewish doctor called Benjamin Roditi and Mary the dashing RAF officer Patrick Donnelly, scion of another respectable Wood Green Irish family.

My mother had opened a tea shop (called, wincingly, "Ye Olde Corner House") in a small house off North End Way next to Hampstead Heath (almost opposite a famous public house—the Old Bull and Bush) in 1939; the purchase of the house and shop was financed by my grandmother. It is not clear to me whether my parents lived there after their marriage or in married quarters in the Middlesex Regiment barracks in Mill Hill—another north London suburb. Unfortunately, the building was destroyed by a German bomb in 1940 (probably in October), fortunately while they were not there. The story they told afterwards was that the people they knew in the neighborhood had assumed that my parents had been killed (a lot of people died anonymously in London and other English cities in that first wave of mass bombing) and were taken aback and, one assumes, greatly pleased when my father strolled into the saloon bar of the Hare and Hounds (the Old Bull and Bush's smaller next-door neighbor) two evenings later. My mother, pregnant by now, moved to Lidstone, Oxfordshire, to live with my grandmother, who had moved there in 1940; my father, presumably, resumed his war work (probably in Mill Hill Barracks training new conscripts).

Much has been written about the evacuees (women and children) whom the government caused to be moved from London and billeted, with varying degrees of hospitality, on the inhabitants of rural England and Wales. The staff and resources of many institutions were also relocated to safer parts. This was true of Queen Mary's Maternity Hospital, Hampstead, which, early in 1941, relocated to a building called Freeland House near Witney, Oxfordshire, a town in the Cotswolds famed for the quality of the blankets that were made there in the years when the quality of English wool was unmatched in the world. Thus it was that I was born in the premises occupied by the staff of the Hampstead hospital on March 6, 1941. I have never been to Witney since. Most people I know have a clear picture of the place in which they were born—the suburb, city, town, or village, if not the actual building—but I have no idea what Witney looks like, though I have seen a picture of Freeland House. Is this a lack that has contributed to my later rootlessness or just another fact of life for a war baby?

I was the first of six children born to my parents and the first of the 19 grandchildren of Joseph and Alice Barrett. (It is symptomatic of the distance from my father's family that my mother imposed and enforced that, despite my father having numerous siblings many of whom had children, I never knew any of my paternal cousins, am not sure how many of them there are or were, and do not even know the names of all of them.) Had it not been for the Second World War, I would probably have been the oldest of nine or ten children, since my siblings were born with some regularity after my father returned from the war in late 1945. My brother David John was born in Hampstead's New End hospital on May 4, 1946 (he died, sadly, on November 4, 2005), my sister Philippa Mary in Queen Mary's Maternity Hospital, by then back in Heath Street, Hampstead, on April 10, 1948, my sister Joanna Susan in Edgware General Hospital on June 30, 1950, my brother Timothy James on June 15, 1952, and my brother Paul Justin on December 17, 1959 (our maternal grandmother's 71st birthday), the latter two in the Hospital of St. John & St. Elizabeth in Grove End Road, St. John's Wood—now the hospital of choice for pop stars, sheiks, models, actresses, and the similarly rich and vacuous. My father died there in June 1980 after a stay of several months, something that would be impossible for him to afford today; so he, like Oscar Wilde, died beyond his means. Adolf Hitler was responsible for the five-year hiatus between my birth and David's. One can only speculate on the last seven-year hiatus, but it ended when my mother was 41 and my father 56.

My memories of the war involve no personal privations or deprivations. They are fragmentary, of course. I was only 4 years old when VE Day (in May 1945) and VJ Day (in August 1945) arrived, but those memories I have are vivid and, with one exception, uniformly pleasant. It seems the sun always shone on the treed, hilly Cotswold countryside (still my favorite scenery in the whole broad world), and its Cotswold stone buildings still glow golden in my memory. I remember being in a hay cart after the harvest in 1944, late in an evening that still held traces of daylight as some adults sang, "Run, rabbit, run." I remember geese with their small, orange, evil eyes in my grandmother's garden of her cottage in Lidstone—a tiny village at the foot of a very steep hill leading down to the River Glyme and a place surrounded by tumuli, barrows, and other ancient remnants. I remember well the adults muttering about a death—the death of a young man who had tried to ride his motorcycle down Lidstone's hill, ending up smashing into the Cotswold dry-stone wall at the foot of the hill—a peculiarly pointless death in the middle of a world war. I remember the low rooms in the cottage in Heythrop with its small mullioned windows, a cottage that was near Heythrop College (a Jesuit college in which my Uncle Tony was a seminarian). I remember seeing an aeroplane spinning down dark against the sky and the dark smoke that rose from the fields beyond the stone walls after it crashed (I still dream of it with some regularity). I remember the bookshop in the main street of Chipping Norton (we all called it "Chippy") and my grandmother insisting on buying no more than one book when I wanted three. I remember the long line of blue-clad Italian prisoners of war (dark-haired, mournful-looking men) trudging back to their camp after working all day in the fields. I remember the American soldiers, huge and cheerful, in Chipping Norton and one glorious day when one of them lifted me high in the air to see the inside of a tank. He was African American and I have no idea what the tank was doing there in an Oxfordshire market town but

I can see his smiling face and remember his spontaneous kindness to a little boy to this day. Above all, I remember the security and happiness of living with, and, I am sure, being spoiled by, three women—my mother, my grandmother, and my Aunt Mary (I thought her very pretty in her WAAF uniform and still like its soft "RAF blue" color very much). We were never short of food (other early memories are of shelling peas from a local garden, of eating eggs taken from the chickens that lived in the garden, and of apples picked moments earlier), and I never then felt deprived of love. The only men I saw were the older inhabitants of those small villages and the market town, Chipping Norton, the Italian POWs (and them from a distance), American soldiers, and the boisterous Jesuit seminarian friends of my uncle. When I read of the miseries of life in wartime London and other British cities, not to mention the carnage and suffering of Europe during and after WWII, I realize that mine was a privileged and fortunate existence and that fortune smiled on me then—not for the last time. I often wonder if I blundered into library work (the circumstances that led to my walk up the stairs of the Arkwright Road library seemed haphazard at the time) or if my early life steered me toward a working environment in which four out of five coworkers are female. That early life has most certainly shaped my ways of life and temperament, for good and bad.

CINEMA

The first film I ever saw was *Bambi*. This was not an auspicious start to a lifetime of watching, liking, and, at times, being obsessed by the cinema. The film was released in England in August 1942. It was shown in Chipping Norton in 1943 or 1944. My mother took me one afternoon. I have only fragmentary memories (I must have been 3 ½ at most) but recall the bright colors and the fascination of being in the dark and, most vividly of all, being terrified by some scene—perhaps the arrival of the hunters or of Bambi's mother's death?—to the point at which I started screaming uncontrollably and we had to leave the cinema, much to my mother's annoyance. At some point when we lived in Golders Green, my father's younger sister Norah, who, though then single, had a child called Frances without benefit of clergy and stayed with us for a period of time. I have no idea how or why my mother's mandated wall of separation between our family and the rest of the Gormans was breached but thus it was for some months if short of a year. Auntie Norah was fond of the cinema and promised to take me to see *The third man* at the Ionic. This was shortly after the film was released in September 1949. The alternately hypnotic and maddening zither theme (by Anton Karas) was played all the time on the BBC Light Programme and I, who had never heard of the zither, still less actually heard one, became consumed with the idea of seeing the film. I invented a holiday, told my parents and Auntie Norah that there was no school on the Thursday of that week and that I would be available to accompany her to the Ionic. I remember almost all of the film, including the many parts that I did not understand, but especially the scene in the Ferris wheel between Harry Lime (Orson Welles) and Holly Martins (Joseph Cotten). I also thought then, and still think, that Anna Schmidt (Alida Valli) was one of the most beautiful women who ever lived. Thus it was, long before the *Cahiers du cinema* boys aestheticized films, that a work of art showed me a new way of looking at life and the possibility of understanding through what was, though I did not know it at the time, a mind-altering experience of art.

....

2

London, 1945–1947

In my own living memory as a child after the Second World War, Catholics in Britain, apart from the recusant aristocratic families, were regarded as second-class, ignorant and peasant-like—largely because of the example of the priest-ridden (as they then were) Irish who suffered from having too many children in each family.

—A. C. Grayling

There is a black-and-white snap of me with a mass of dark curls, smiling shyly in a sleeveless Fair Isle sweater and short flannel trousers. I am standing on a path in Chipping Norton between tall hedges on either side and holding a piece of paper in my hand. I have a memory of that path and the errand I was on but, alas, cannot now tell if the momentousness of the occasion has fused in my mind with that picture or if the picture is a record of the actual event. Whichever it is, I have a vivid memory of running along that path with a message for my mother that had been given to me by . . . by whom? In the story I have in my mind it was a postwoman who asked me to take a telegram to my mother. It is possible, but I was only 4 years old and, even in those safer days, that seems rather young to be running around unsupervised with important pieces of paper. It was the telegram that told us my father was coming home from the war—a message that was greeted with tears that I now know were not entirely those of joy. I remember being very happy, not least because I assumed that life would go on much as it had done only with no War and a father to be a lively and friendly companion. I was grievously mistaken and realize with the hindsight of more than 60 years that my poor father was as much a victim of the changes that were to come as I, and not the malignant deus ex machina that I perceived him to be then and for many years after.

The day of homecoming arrived some weeks later. My father was "demobbed" (demobilized) on November 12, 1945, and, though not entirely released from his army obligations (he finally retired from the army in 1951) was on Civvy Street for the first time in twenty-five years. He was

42 years old and had spent his entire adult life in the army as a private soldier and then noncommissioned officer. His highest rank was staff sergeant, which accounts for my mother's nickname for him, Staff (he called her Tom—her family's nickname for her that derived from her being a tomboy). He had joined the army (in the Middlesex Regiment—the "Diehards") in 1920. His first trip overseas was to Ireland, then in the grip of the struggle leading to the Anglo-Irish Treaty of 1922 that led to the Irish Free State—one can only conjecture what his feelings were—"Patsy" Gorman patrolling the high-hedged Irish roads and lanes in the service of the English imperialists. After that, and before World War II, he was stationed in Germany, India (for more than six years), Sudan, Egypt, Singapore, and China. He spoke about his military life very rarely and usually dismissively. He was a handsome man, about 5 feet 9 inches tall (a little shorter than my tall mother), with a clipped military mustache that he wore for most of his life; thick, dark, wavy hair (to which he applied Brilliantine or, in leaner times, what he called Metropolitan Water Board Hairdressing); and a Roman nose. He was wiry and athletic (legend had it that he played for the British Army team in field hockey when stationed in India in the 1930s—there is a snap of him posing with a hockey stick in shorts and the classic half-kneeling athletic attitude). Though I mostly take after my mother and see her face every morning in the shaving mirror, I inherited his skinny arms and legs—the latter earning him the nickname Sparrowlegs from his army friends. He was, as I now realize far too late, a shy man whose lack of self-confidence manifested itself in the affectation of confidence. He had left school at 14 and had almost no education though he, too, was fond of reading, had an almost magical gift with numbers, and had military virtues of which I knew nothing. His commendation on his demob called him "a thoroughly reliable and efficient N.C.O. with a strong sense of initiative. [He] has the gift of handling men and getting the benefit out of them. Of the greatest assistance both in administration and discipline." When I saw him, for the first time that I remember, on a wintry afternoon in late 1945, he was standing in the door of my grandmother's flat in Chipping Norton in his rough khaki uniform. He was smiling broadly, so deeply tanned by the sun of North Africa that he appeared to be black, and carrying a small bunch of bananas (a fruit I had never seen). I immediately started to scream and cry and to try to run from the room. Was this because I recognized the change to come that was embodied in this black stranger? Was it hysteria induced by the announced momentousness of the occasion? Was it his strange appearance and the unknown fruit he was carrying? Whatever it was (and I assume a

Freudian would have a field day with the incident), our relationship (which never had much of a chance) never recovered from his homecoming.

At some point shortly thereafter, we moved to London. I assumed, when young, that this was a decision both my parents made. Many years later, after my father's death in June 1980, my mother told me that she had not wished to leave Oxfordshire and, by implication, did not wish to be married. She too had a good war living an independent life, working in the munitions factory with all the other turbaned, aproned women listening to *Music while you work*, flirting and drinking safely with the seminarians and, perhaps not as safely, with American soldiers, and accompanying them to the flicks, safe from money worries, and with a curly-headed little boy on whom to dote. My Uncle Tony (the Rev. Fr. Joseph Anthony Barrett, S.J.) told me later that he, his mother, and my grandmother "made" my mother stay with my father and go to London with him. I am not sure which combination of moral and religious suasion and economic pressure accomplished this, but I know that it was, in many ways, a disaster for her. She was not a natural mother (I think she was bored by children) and, for the rest of her life, was consumed by financial worries. She was still a young woman (26 at the time), hopeless with money, and already prone to her family's penchant for alcohol. My father, though 42 then, had led the feckless life of a single soldier for all his adult life and was hardly the reassuring paterfamilias who might have made a good life for both of them and the family they begat.

I think that my mother did love my father and he her, but the loveless, emotionally cramped nature of her Barrett family life, their tendency to engage in feuds and bitter quarrels that escalated into long estrangements, and the psychic blow of her father's death when she was 15 had created someone who was needy and emotionally unscrupulous and prone to dwelling on the slightest of slights. This latter trait, a dominating feature of her life, resulted in great part from the fact that she had a quite severe speech defect due to an untreated cleft palate. (Her older brother Jack was similarly though even more gravely afflicted.) Her family were not always kind and she was mocked by children when a child, and laughed at by adults in later life—adults without the excuse of childish innocence of the effects of words and actions. I was completely unconscious of her speech defect until I was told, at the age of 6 or 7, by fellow school children that "your mother's voice is funny." I suppose young children accept what they are used to and, for the rest of her life, I had to strain my ears, usually quick to note accents and speech patterns, to hear the ways in which her speech differed from others.

I think that the incident that marked her psyche and set her on the course that she took for the rest of her life occurred when she was 14 or 15. She told me of it a number of times late in her life—when in her 70s and a widow for more than a decade—always with eyes full of tears. It seems that her older sister Margaret was being honored with a dance (for her 18th birthday?), an event to which my mother was regarding with happy anticipation. Quite late in the day, unpardonably late even given the generally unpardonable nature of his action, her father called her into his room and told her that she could not attend as she was an embarrassment to the family because of the way she spoke. I am convinced that, coming from the father she adored (she always spoke proudly and fondly of him), this inflicted emotional wounds from which she never recovered.

My mother was incompletely estranged from her mother by the time she moved to London in 1946. The pressure on her to go there with her husband, and her mother's refusal to support her should she refuse to do so, undoubtedly led to the intensification of this estrangement. My mother never had any time for her husband's family, the snobbery about the Gormans being the only remnant of the comfortable prewar Wood Green life; as a consequence there was no extended family to support my parents' endeavors. So there they were, completely unprepared (in completely different ways) for the practicalities of family life, staying in a flat in an old house in St. John's Wood (84 Avenue Road, NW8) between Swiss Cottage to the north and Regent's Park to the south. My father had no trade or expertise and was looking out for himself and his family, for the first time in his adult life, in his early 40s.

I hated London and hated my father. I hated the privations of the feckless penury of our lives. I hated the attention paid to my new brother. I hated the fact that my father had insisted of having my head shorn of its copious curls—of which my mother had been very proud in those halcyon days that I knew, even at the age of 5, were gone, at least for the duration of my childhood. I remember little in detail about the flat in the house in Avenue Road. It must have been a handsome house before it was divided into several flats. I remember a huge mulberry tree in the communal back garden, Regents Park at the southern end of the road across Prince Albert Road and the views of the London Zoo from outside, and a family called St. Leger who rented another flat in number 84. Horse racing was an enduring interest of my father's, and he was greatly impressed that these people were related, even if in some distant manner, to Lieutenant General Anthony St. Leger, an Irish soldier who was the creator of the last and longest of the five "classic" British horse races, the St. Leger, run in Doncaster, Yorkshire, each year since 1776. I also remember my first sight of an escalator, in the Woolworth's in Finchley Road near the tube station, and my passionate desire to own a red, rounded penknife with three blades on sale there for one shilling. We went there fairly often and the knife drew me across the slotted wooden floors each time to view its red perfection. Perhaps a shilling was beyond their means; perhaps they thought a knife inappropriate for a 6-year-old. Whichever it was, I have wanted few objects (other than books) with the passion elicited by the red penknife in Woolies'.

My father's first civilian job (he was a reserve soldier still, but that affected only two weeks a year) was with a furrier in the City of London. I have no memory of what he did there and what his relationship was with the mysterious people called "Margolis" and "Pollard" of whom he spoke each evening with some disdain and derision. I suppose they were his bosses and, free from the rigid hierarchies of the Army, his natural antiauthoritarianism came to the fore, expressed in his characteristic "sod them!" dismissiveness. I visited the furrier once with him and was shown many pieces of fur, black dry leather on one side and coarse hair on the other. One specimen was of a repulsive fur called "Persian Lamb." The tight whorls of the dyed black fur were singularly unpleasant both in appearance and to the touch. In London in the 1940s, a lot of women wore furs of various kinds. I was always fascinated by the sight of the common (in both senses) fox tippets worn by women with erratic lipstick and peroxided or hennaed hair. These "tarts' tea cozies," as they were known, consisted of an eviscerated fox, eyes replaced with red glass and neat black-tipped feet dangling coyly on the usually ample and lightly powdered bosom of the ruby port or "gin and it"–drinking wearer. The tippets had a ghastly allure, but the stiff swatches of the fur of other animals in the establishment run by Margolis (or Pollard? or both?) lacked appeal, as did the nasty animal smell of the room. At some point after a year or so, my father walked out on the job and was unemployed for a fair stretch of time. Sod them, indeed!

We did not stay on Avenue Road very long. Some complex and changing mix of penury, a growing family, and Barrett family intervention led us to move five times between 1946 and 1953. Our next stop was a second-floor flat in 13 Langland Gardens, a street off Finchley Road that runs parallel, and next, to Arkwright Road and lies on the lower slopes (geographically and in class terms) of the glory that is Hampstead. In these days of property price hyperinflation and the transcendence of the North West 3 area, 13 Langland Gardens is a most desirable residence. Then it was, at best, genteel.

A family called the Outlaws lived in the basement of the house—the two sons performed some vaguely janitorial duties. I was fascinated both by their rakish name and their life in the basement. I used to go there every day to read the *Mirror,* a newspaper that was anathema to my mother on the damning grounds that it was a strong supporter of the Labour Party and that it was "common." I was oblivious to the first and rejoiced in the second. My favorites were two cartoon strips called "Jane" and "Pip, Squeak, and Wilfred." The former featured a buxom blonde—the eponym—who had been credited with enlivening the morale of Britain's fighting men during Hitler's War, even stripping off in one widely welcomed panel. Even at that young age, I was far from immune to her charms, and "Jane" added a frisson of the forbidden to those sessions at the Outlaw's kitchen table, drinking tea provided by Mrs. Outlaw whose kindness to me belied her, to me, somewhat frightening appearance. She wore, at all times, a floral pinafore that she called a "pinny" and often the kind of turban that working class women wore in those far-off days. She had an aura of gin and lipstick but that alone cannot have been frightening—perhaps it was just my always active imagination spinning a character out of nothing more than her name. Of Mr. Outlaw there was no trace. "Pip, Squeak, and Wilfred" were, respectively, a mongrel dog, a penguin, and a baby rabbit. This unlikely trio acted as humans (only more comically) and had a human Uncle Dick with whom they lived in a house in London, together with his pretty maid, Angeline. The strip about this very odd ménage ran in the *Mirror* from shortly after World War I until the mid-1950s. I became the proud owner of a prewar *Wilfred's annual,* which I believe was given to me by one of the Outlaws. I also read the articles in the paper and, though I was not conscious of the fact, it could be that I absorbed from them some of the Labourite ideas that flowered in my midteens. My mother was an unrepentant Tory all her life and, though I suspect my father had voted Labour in the postwar election that threw Churchill and the Tories out of government, he had the wisdom to express his Labour sympathies only in muttered expostulations triggered by my mother's wilder political pronouncements. When one considers she was in her late 20s at this time and he in his mid-40s, it speaks volumes about the strength of her personality and the domestically appeasing nature of his.

For a whole autumn term, I walked every day up the hill from 13 Langland Gardens, across the wide boulevard of Fitzjohns Avenue, and down a long and overgrown alley between houses to a school on Rosslyn Hill (south of Hampstead tube station) called, mysteriously to me then, Bartram's—a name that matched in grimness the tall Victorian brick building surrounded by a high brick wall. It was a long walk (at least a mile each way) for a 6-year-old across two very busy roads, but I have always liked walking and those were different days. Today there is a hostel of sorts for young women called "Bartram's Hall of Residence" in the same area, so I imagine that the old school has been converted to that purpose. I hope the 18–35-year-old women who reside there temporarily find more joy than I did in their surroundings.

It must have been some time during the term that I attended Bartram's that I conceived and carried out the crime of stealing and burying my father's military medals in 13 Langland Gardens' scruffy back garden. He had a number of these—all dull and/or tarnished metal—commemorating his service in Germany, India, and other countries in the 1920s and 1930s and his activities during the war (including the Africa Star). They were kept in a tin box that had once held cheroots. I recall the damp earth and the mud on the lettering and images, the tangle of wet leaves and roots at which I scrabbled to create a shallow hole, the sense of triumph as the medals vanished from view, and the edgy elation with which I climbed the stairs to our flat. Again, this is an incident replete with Freudian implications, as is the fact that I have no memory at all of what ensued. I believe they were never recovered and I remember no discussion of the event. Perhaps my father was more of a mensch that I ever gave him credit for and simply did not care about the medals that documented the military career of which he almost never spoke.

It was also around this time that I decided to run away from home. I planned this trip without a destination carefully. The planning involved collecting several crab apples from the tree behind 13 Langland Gardens and putting them into my emptied school satchel together with the book that I was reading at the time. I told my mother I was leaving. In retrospect, her laughter at the announcement was more an indication of the robust ideas on child rearing of the time than of indifference, though our closeness of the war years had begun to fray under the strain of her daily life in London and was never to be recovered. I well recall walking down Langland Gardens in the midafternoon, past the low walls and privet hedges of the tall houses, to the stir and bustle of Finchley Road, turning right and walking up the incline, crossing Heath Drive, Croftway, and Platts Lane, to the bench outside the Congregational Church—no great distance but it seemed like miles to me. I sat there alternately reading a little and looking at the traffic on Finchley Road and, opposite, heading down Fortis Green Road to the hidden realms of West Hampstead. I looked at the furniture shop and the baker's on the other side (the latter with "Tell me where is fancy bread" stenciled over the door), ate a couple of the sour, mushy, mottled crab apples, read my book, and waited for what I remember as two hours, certainly until it began to darken, before deciding to leave the bench. I did not want to go home but my planning did not stretch beyond the arrival of the dark, so I decided to postpone my new life until another day. It was wet, as it always seemed to be in postwar London, and I think the reason why this episode has endured in my memory is the image of the forlorn little boy walking past the gaslights, from one pool of amber light into the wet dark and another pool of light beyond, down Finchley Road and up the steep incline of Langland Gardens. That image is the perfect encapsulation of that time in my life. I was always alone in my memories of that time; always escaping into the far better world of books; always outside looking in on other lives lived behind the lighted windows or lived in the infinity of bookish worlds. It seemed natural at the time though there must surely be ways of growing up that lead to happier lives.

3

On the Move, 1948–1952

I spent a single term as a pupil in Bartram's—months of which I remember only my solitary walks to and from the school, the cheerful postman to whom I said hello every morning until warned not to talk to strangers, the cracked black playground within the high wall, and the high-windowed classroom. I was then enrolled in a Catholic school, St. Mary's in Fitzjohns Avenue, run by nuns of the Institute of the Blessed Virgin Mary (now affiliated with the Congregation of Jesus)—otherwise known as Mary Ward nuns, after their founder. The school was and is in a huge and handsome house with long, grassy gardens on which thousands of crocuses bloomed each spring. In contrast to Bartram's, the school was warm in temperature and furnishings, full of light, and avowedly religious. My favorite place in the school was the small chapel—a golden, warm haven glowing like a jewel. More important to me, the majority of the pupils and all the teachers were female. It was and is a private school with high fees that were completely beyond my parent's means. It remains a mystery to me how I, and three of my siblings, were able to attend without, as far as I know, any money changing hands. Most of the pupils were the children of upper-class and affluent middle-class Catholic families and, even at that young age, I was conscious of the fact that their speech patterns and ways of life were very different from mine. I spent two plus mostly happy years there—my only happy years at school. The best was the last. Boys had to leave the school at the age of 8. Largely because of my precocity in reading and, hence, writing, spelling, etc., I was a year ahead of the other pupils and, therefore, spent my last year in a class in which all the other members were girls. Naturally, I enjoyed every moment of my time in that year, apart from the agony of wrestling with the compulsory knitting and its scruffy, mauled results shamingly pinned up (with "Mickey Gorman" written underneath) next to other, much more accomplished work. There were two other pupils called Michael when I arrived at the school. They were known, for reasons of distinction, as "Michael" and "Mike." In the interests of the same convenience, the nuns decided I would be known as "Mickey." Less than ten years later, I lived in dread of the nuns coming into Hampstead Central Library (their local library) with their inevitable cries of "Mickey Gorman, how you've grown!" Since they met me when I was 6 and I was now, at 16, six feet tall, my growth was a less than surprising finding, though deeply embarrassing to me.

I achieved a certain measure of fame in the school one day in 1947 when, after borrowing a book from the small library maintained by the nuns, I walked down a corridor head down reading the first pages and so engrossed that I collided with and broke a glass door with my head. Much blood ensued and I had to be taken to a local hospital to have the wound on the top of my head stitched. I believe there is a residual scar from this adventure in reading and hope to live long enough to discover if it is still there under my increasingly thinning hair.

Convents, then, were harbors for laywomen who found the outside world difficult. St. Mary's was no exception and sheltered various "Misses" who assisted in teaching, did housework, cooked, and otherwise made themselves useful in return for bed and board. There were loud, hearty, tweeded Misses and shy, skittering small Misses—all lifers in an environment that did the Lord's work in providing them with a family of sorts. Not the least of my regrets about the modern dissolution of the convents is the fact this kindly version of social work is no longer available. As children do, I accepted their considerable eccentricities of behavior and appearance without question.

My father had grown up in a house near Hampstead Heath, the more than 700-acre open land of meadows, heath, ponds, and woods that covers the highest of London's hills. I imagine he and his brothers and sisters ran wild on the heath that lay all around their house off the road that leads from the top of the Heath to Golders Green. He was very fond of Hampstead, and the trips from Golders Green and Hendon up the hill to the Whitestone Pond were among the very few happy family-related events I remember from that period. It was not so much the pond and heath but the activities that took place there—most especially the donkey rides, the Punch and

Judy shows, and the sellers of such delicacies as candy floss, toffee apples, shrimps, and winkles. The happy few would float toy boats on the pond for the rest of us to watch, and there were almost always kite fliers on the southern slope away from the pond. We could stand on the pavement across the road from the pond and look down over the sandy, rabbit-pitted heath and the kite fliers to a prospect of London shimmering in the smog if the sun were shining. I loved the peaty smell and shaggy, docile presence of the saddled donkeys, paddling in the shallow pond, and carrying a bag of shrimps on the bus home. There was a bench outside the huge pub near the pond—Jack Straw's Castle—and I would sit there with a glass of lemonade and packet of salty crisps (Smith's) that my father brought out from the bar for me before going back in to enjoy his pints and to buy a bottle of Worthington White Label beer for my mother in an attempt, invariably vain, to propitiate her. (She always suspected that our trips were a cover for visiting his family—an activity that had been proscribed.) It was usually sunny, as it seems to me now, and this was the 'Appy 'Ampstead celebrated in Cockney music hall songs, not the abode of toffs, artists, and intellectuals that it has come to be. Hampstead is interwoven with my early life and is, with one or two others, a lost world preeminent among all the worlds from which I am exiled forever.

The time came when, in 1949, I had to leave the nuns, and the Misses, and the posh little girls, one of whom, red-haired Priscilla Richardson, a beauty two years older than me, was my first love, unspoken but no less passionate for that. We were living, by then, in a house that my parents had purchased with the bitterly resented help of my maternal grandmother. She was now resident in Palmers Green, a North London suburb made famous in literary circles by the poet Stevie Smith, who lived there with her Aunt Madge ("The Lion Aunt"). The house to which we moved, 14 The Grove, NW11, is in Golders Green, an area noted for its Jewish population. We were one of two non-Jewish families living in that short street, though it terminated at Limes Avenue, opposite the side of a convent of Catholic nuns—the La Sagesse sisters. One day in the summer of 1949, my father and I set off by bus to visit my future school in North Finchley. I remember it well, as it was one of the few times we went anywhere other than Hampstead together and the only time that I recall him taking any part in my increasingly erratic upbringing. We ended up, as I suppose could have been predicted, at the wrong school (it had "Woodside" in its name and the intended school was in Woodside Lane). Somehow or other, we arrived late at St. Alban's Catholic Preparatory School and, somehow or another, I was enrolled as a pupil. I spent the next eight years at schools in Finchley, a suburb well suited to be the longtime parliamentary constituency of the appalling Margaret Thatcher.

THE SMITHS

One accepts things in childhood that seem strange when remembered as an adult. One day in the summer of 1951, I spent most of the day, as usual, in Hendon Park—a large open space that was about a mile from Bell Lane. On this occasion I had a cricket ball as well as a book to pass the time and was bowling the ball at a tree while pretending to be whichever English bowler I then prized (Bob Appleyard? Johnny Wardle? I cannot remember). I had done this for many days that summer and on previous summers. A boy of about my age (he was in fact about 10 months younger) came up to me. He was carrying a precious possession—a cricket bat. He asked if we could play together and we spent a considerable amount of time bowling and batting until both of us were tired. He told me his name was Vincent Smith. I cannot remember why I decided to brave my mother's wrath and invite Vincent back to my house. We walked along Queens Road to West View to Heriot Road to Brent Street and then down Bell Lane, my apprehension mounting. It was justified; my mother was angry, as ever, at the intrusion of strangers, even a well-behaved, well-spoken 10-year-old boy. She asked Vincent where he lived (in Second Avenue—a short distance from Bell Lane). Then something surprising happened: just when I was thinking she would tell him to go, she asked about his parents and it soon emerged that his mother—Daphne Smith—had been to the same school as my mother when both were in their late teens. I have no idea how that was discovered. Vincent was a name given mostly by Catholics, so perhaps it was some enquiry about church. In any event, however it came out, it was a fact that my mother knew his when she was called Daphne Abram. A visit was paid to Second Avenue and diplomatic relations were soon established. It turned out that they not only each had four children at that time, but Vincent and I were of an age; Damian Smith was about the same age as David; Barbara Smith as Philippa; and Helen Smith and Joanna were both babies. The next year, both women gave birth to boys, Howard Smith and my brother Timothy. My mother was given to enthusiastic friendships with women that always ended in tears in the short or long run. Her friendship with Daphne lasted longer than most as did the twinning of our families. Vincent's father Ernie worked in a garage in Golders Green. He and my father were deemed to be friends and would meet every Sunday for drinks in the pub before lunch. The four of them embarked on a marathon of card-playing—solo whist—every Saturday night for a number of years, alternating between the houses and accompanied by sandwiches and bottled beer. It is still my favorite card game and, in the early days, I would enjoy watching them and listening to the lengthy post-mortems of each hand along the lines of "I had a perfect *misère* but you spoiled it by going *abondance*," fascinating and alluring to me at 11, the stuff of comedy a few years later. In the fashion of the time and of our kind of people, we called the adults "Uncle" or "Auntie" and I have fond memories of Auntie Daphne's kindness, especially as I barely knew the numerous women who were my actual aunts. The families had holidays together, but I have no memory of them so they may have been after I dissociated myself from family life. Daphne's father lived with them. He was a retired coal miner from Whitstable, Kent, and an ardent trade unionist who had been on a delegation to the Bolshevik government just after World War I. He was very bitter about the British and American interventions on behalf of the White Russians in the Russian Civil War of 1917–1923 and showed me numerous pamphlets on the topic, explaining that the ruling classes had suppressed the truth of those events. Daphne's sister Barbara ("Auntie Barbara," naturally) also lived with them for a while. She was rumored to have had a fast life in one of the African colonies (Kenya?) and had some carved masks and so on that induced in me an irrational and enduring dislike of primitive art.

....

St. Alban's shared a plot of land with two other schools. All three were founded by Canon Clement Henry Parsons (1892–1980)—a looming presence in the eight years I spent in two of those schools. St. Alban's is situated on a large estate, the main house of which was once owned by a Mr. Derry, the co-owner of the famous Derry & Toms department store. Canon Parsons, who must have been something of a pedagogical entrepreneur, began his scholastic empire with eighteen pupils in 1926 and had, by the time I arrived at St. Alban's, acquired several houses and constructed other buildings on the estate. The complex, in 1949, housed a school for boys up to the age of 11—St. Alban's—Finchley Catholic Grammar School, and the newly added Challoner (a "secondary modern" school)—both for boys aged 11–18. In postwar Britain, a cruel system separated children at age 11 by means of the "Eleven Plus"—a glorified IQ test designed to distinguish the intellectual wheat from the trade-school chaff, the former to the grammar schools and the latter to the secondary moderns. The Eleven Plus can be blamed on the crackpot theories about, and, as it turned out fraudulent research into, "intelligence" of one Sir Cyril Burt that, essentially, stated that only the most "intelligent" 20 percent of children could benefit from a good education and that the 20 percent could be distinguished at or about the age of 11. As all such endeavors do, this system favored the well-off and the lucky. I suppose it was lucky for me that my last two years of "preparatory" schooling amounted to cramming for the Eleven Plus and I was able to pass it and go on to a grammar school, but, even then, I suspected that working on distinguishing which shape of five did not "belong" and like tomfoolery was not an enriching educational experience. There were also less loopy verbal and arithmetical components of the Eleven Plus, and those posed no difficulty to me.

The Eleven Plus was almost three years in the future on the day I arrived for my first day at an all-boys school. I enjoyed the long trip from Golders Green on the 125 bus, but that was where almost all joy ended. I loathed the absence of acceptable females, the company of brawling, pointless 8- to 11-year old boys, the petty hierarchies of the playground, the classes that were on topics that were either already very familiar to me from my reading or bored me to tears—sometimes literally (science, for example)—and the unremitting awfulness of the food. Something about a boiled onion repels me to this day and I attribute my herbivorousness to the ghastly manifestations of scrag mutton and the like that we were forced to eat in a long dark room dominated by a colored depiction of the infant Jesus smiling in defiance of his external bleeding heart on prominent display.

The school was presided over by a formidable presence known to all as Mrs. Hawkins. Lilian Hawkins was, at 60 or so (she died in 1983 at the age of 94), a hawk-nosed, lipsticked presence with dyed, permed hair. A boy told me that the glass of water on her desk was, in fact, neat gin, but I was familiar with the smell of gin and doubted this, as much as I wanted to believe it. The other teachers were a job lot. I remember Mrs. Hawkins's son, who was known as "Broady" Hawkins (the boys believed his nickname derived from Broadmoor—the infamous hospital for the criminally insane—in which he was reputed to have been housed). He was very tall and narrow, with tight curly black hair, 1940s round black-rimmed spectacles, and long yellow teeth. He was, I believe, the games master and he always seemed to be around and grinning in the changing rooms after our football games, played in the mud with atrociously heavy leather balls, and, worse, cross-country runs. I have loved cricket since my early years, but did not enjoy even that game when played on the tufted, lumpy grass of St. Alban's playing fields. A severe Miss Geoghegan ruled her classes with terror, and Armel O'Connor, a kindly faced, blue-eyed, white-haired Irishman with a soft voice and very soft hands gave us music lessons. I remember the tears in his eyes as he led us in singing "Swing low, sweet chariot" after telling us that he wanted it played at his funeral. His niece, a red-haired, stylishly skirted young woman with a lovely Irish accent—Miss O'Connor—was a light in the darkness for one term and then was gone. In my imagination I can still see her tripping lightly along the low wall at the edge of the asphalted playground, humming to herself with her thoughts clearly far away from the scrum of boys fighting, throwing paper airplanes, and chalking squares for hopscotch in the largely unsupervised, feral world of the playground. My parents never talked about sex, still less sought to acquaint me with the "facts of life" (surely the grimmest three words about the glories and possibilities of sex), and my keen interest in Miss O'Connor was not informed by any realistic understanding of what lay beneath her oatmeal tweed skirts and woolen twin sets. This lack of understanding did not prevent her being much in my thoughts. There must have been other teachers but they are never present in my fitfully vivid memories of St. Alban's occasions great and small.

I had few friendships at St. Alban's and none that endured. The sad fact is that I remember an older boy called McLeod (I can see his face and almond eyes as I write his name) because he once spoke kindly to me and picked me up after I fell and cut myself (we never spoke again) and no others. My mother was an increasingly remote and physically frightening figure. We lived in something approaching penury, made worse by the need to keep up the pretense that we were living a middle-class life, and it was a constant struggle to provide food and clothing to the growing family. The worst manifestations of our poverty to me were the occasions when I was sent to answer the front doorbell to tell a debt collector or bailiff that there was "no one at home" while my mother stayed quiet in a back room behind a shut door, or when I was sent to the butcher's shop to ask for meat "on tick," a deeply humiliating procedure. I rarely made the mistake of inviting a boy from school home as my mother invariably became enraged—I think because she was embarrassed by the lack of food to share. We moved from Golders Green to a smaller, meaner house—96 Bell Lane—in Hendon because of some unspecified money crisis. It was scarcely big enough for our family (then two parents and four children) but we had to let one room to a "paying guest" (a succession of gloomy men in temporary jobs) to make ends meet. The one shining thing about the little house was that it faced a school—Bell Lane Elementary—once attended by the great cricketer Denis Charles Scott Compton (the "Brylcreem Boy") and his brother Leslie. Their mother was reputed to be still living in the neighborhood (this was long before the days of millions being paid to sportsmen) and my mother once pointed her out to me, though the little old lady in a dark coat could have been anybody and probably was. I did a paper round for a newsagent's shop opposite and used the money I earned to buy a bicycle so I could wheel around in the early morning with the heavy canvas sacks of *Mails, Mirrors, Expresses, Telegraphs, Times* (for those with pretensions), and, on Fridays, the *Drapers' Record.* Just before Christmas, I would knock on every door to which I delivered newspapers and ask for a "Christmas box." At one address, a man in a shirt without a collar left the door slightly ajar as he called out to someone unseen "It's that paperboy with the posh voice," proving that my determined attempts to acquire a Cockney accent had not yet borne fruit.

My father, after leaving the fur trade and after a subsequent period of unemployment (lean years) started the job that he held for the rest of his working life. It was being a salesman for a company that sold net and lace curtain materials to the numerous drapers' shops of London and its suburbs. Every "respectable" house in Britain then had, in addition to thick curtains to be drawn at night, net or lace curtains that covered the windows at all times. Most women made those interior curtains themselves. There was, therefore, money to be made in selling yards of the material, even wholesale. For some reason, I was ashamed of his work and thought the sight of him trudging off to work with his large, flat, black portfolios of samples of curtaining partly shameful and partly ludicrous. This silly snobbery would have been there if he were anything short of a Lloyds' underwriter or merchant banker (those were honorable professions in that distant time) but, in long retrospect, there was something heroic about the way he faced his hard life without complaint and set off every day for his wide-ranging journeys wrestling those portfolios on and off buses in all kinds of weather. I am sure he liked the independence, not being in an office all day, and meeting different people in different places all over London.

One of the people he met was a man whose last name was Frank. These were days in which many foods were still rationed and, to buy eggs, butter, milk, etc., one needed the coupons from the ration books that were issued to both adults and children. I was given the job of traveling, each Saturday morning, for what seemed like a long time, to a street in Finchley Central to deliver ration coupons (I suppose, being a large and growing family, we had coupons to spare or, if not, to sell) and sometimes some butter to Mr. Frank and his wife. I enjoyed these excursions very much. First, I was out and alone with a book and an envelope with the coupons inside. Then, there was something of mystery and a whiff of illegality (what we were doing was, in fact, illegal) about being the courier in such an enterprise. A bonus was the fact that the bus to and from the Franks went past the "Naked Lady" statue at Henley's Corner between Temple Fortune and Finchley Central. I was, even at that age and like many a schoolboy then and since, fascinated by the Lady's taut, shiny, bare body. Last, the Franks were very hospitable. They lived in a small flat in a house at the end of a long road that led to the tube station. The flat was overfurnished, replete with lace doilies, stuffed chairs, bibelots, and framed pictures. Mr. Frank was a tall, silver-haired, well-dressed man with bright blue eyes and a strong German accent. Mrs. Frank was also very German and always, at least on Saturday morning, wore a floral pinafore over her frock. The *gemütlich* comfort and quiet of their flat and themselves contrasted starkly with the ramshackle house in which I lived and the racket of my daily life. Mrs. Frank would give me a plate of home-baked biscuits with little sugar sprinkles. These too were unknown in my house. As I ate them, Mr. Frank would sit in his armchair and talk to me in his quiet German voice. One day, I asked him whence they came. To my surprise he produced a passport issued by a place of which I had never heard—Lichtenstein, the tiny Alpine principality between Switzerland and Austria that was neutral in World War II. I have no idea why he showed me (I was 8 or 9 at the time) the passport, if he had acquired it before, during, or after the war, if they were among the very small number of natives of Lichtenstein, if they were German Jews, or other Germans fleeing the debacle of Germany in the 1940s. I asked my father who Mr. Frank was, and he said he was in the "rag trade," a description that covered a wide range of occupations, and that he had never heard of Lichtenstein. Sometimes, when I left for home, the Franks would give me a coin—sixpence, a shilling, or, once, a florin—which made my Saturday morning even better.

In the 1940s and 1950s, London suffered from frequent dense fogs in the autumn and winter, naturally occurring because of the topography of the Thames Valley, and rendered lethal by the concentration of coal and coke smoke in the great city. It would be hard for someone who knows London only in the late twentieth and early twenty-first centuries to visualize, but in the middle of the twentieth it was a grimy black city with what we had not yet learned to call smog a threat to the lungs of all its citizens, and with dark smoke billowing from countless chimneys in every area. Coal (or in our case, a low-grade coal, coke, or dusty black stuff called "nutty slack") was delivered regularly by men with blackened faces wearing strange medieval-looking garments—a species of cape with a hood made of thick leather that protected the coalmen's shoulders and the sides of their faces as they hoisted the filthy sacks to carry them from the van (often horse-drawn) to the coal hole in front of the house. I remember three days in the early 1950s when the sun was never visible, when I first saw people wearing gauze masks, and when it was possible, as I did, to lose your way in well-known streets. The dirty gray air stung the throat and lungs and made eyes water. Those were also years of holes in shoes and socks, of not having all the components of the school uniform (blazer with striped piping and school badge, gray trousers, striped tie, gray or white shirt, and despised navy cap), of almost complete friendlessness, and of our small house into which my parents, four children, and lodgers squeezed. It was also a time in which the public library—at first the Golders Green branch of Hendon Public Libraries and then Hendon's Central Library—became the center of my life and my escape from the petty miseries of my increasingly alienated existence.

When we lived in The Grove in Golders Green, I was a near daily visitor to the local branch in Golders Green Road (about a fifth of a mile from our house). The branch is still in existence as one of the libraries of the London Borough of Barnet. I was allowed to borrow three books at a time from the children's library and to use the reference books if I made myself unobtrusive. My first involvement with the shortcomings of library economy came in the summer holidays when I occasionally borrowed three books in the morning and read them by the afternoon. The charging system they used (almost certainly the simple marriage of a book ticket and a borrower's ticket known as the Browne system) meant that one was forbidden to return a book on the same day it was borrowed, so I had to wait until the next day when all the tickets would have been sorted.

One of the few advantages of the move to Bell Lane, Hendon, was that the local library was now the central library of the then Borough of Hendon (it is now the Hendon branch of Barnet libraries). I made the half mile or so walk or cycle ride up Bell Lane, along Brent Street to the post office, along Brampton Grove and its big posh houses, to The Burroughs—the collection of municipal buildings that included the town hall and the central library—many times a week and every day during school holidays. The building is a handsome, high-ceilinged structure of the "municipal imposing" school, designed by T. M. Wilson, FRIBA, and opened by Lord Elgin in 1929. (It was refurbished in the early twenty-first century at a cost of 1.3 million pounds and is still in use.) The children's library, a large, airy room with high windows, was presided over by a woman known to all its users as "Miss Colwell." It rapidly became my favorite place in the world, mostly because of the wide range of books it made available to me, but also because of the way in which the children users were engaged in the life of the library. For example, children were given a star that was advanced up one rung of a paper ladder for each book read until it was replaced with a gold star with his or her name on it when the top of the ladder was reached. I was also eager to be a "monitor" doing various minor tasks, including the thrilling employment of the date due stamp (my first official act of library work) when issuing books. There were also story hours, puppet shows, and many other activities that encouraged reading and the love of books. I loved the place but took it all for granted, as children do so many good things. It was not until many years later, when I was in library school, that I discovered that "Miss Colwell" was the famous pioneer of children's librarianship called Eileen Colwell (1904–2002), who had come to Hendon in 1926 and practically invented modern British children's librarianship in the period between then and her retirement in 1967. She was a lecturer in Loughborough University after that before retiring for good when in her 70s. I wrote an article sometime in the late 1990s about her and other famous librarians I had known, and sent it with a note of appreciation to her at her retirement home. I treasure both the letter she wrote back and the signed copy I have of her 2000 autobiography.

Grahame Swift has written that we read so as not to be alone. Perhaps that was why I read everything that I could get my hands on. I remember stories about highwaymen (the Captain books by Eric Leyland were a particular favorite); Arthur Conan Doyle's Sherlock Holmes stories and novels as well as his historical romances such as *The white company* and *Sir Nigel;* the *Little grey men* books by "BB" (Denis Watkyns Pitchford); tales of smugglers and pirates such as *Treasure Island* and its many imitators, particularly the Dr. Thorndyke novels by R. Austin Freeman; *The Scarlet Pimpernel* and other books by Baroness Orczy; Alison Uttley's *A traveler in time,* set in my still-remembered Oxfordshire; Zane Grey's westerns; travel books by the prolific H.V. Morton; books about boxing, cricket, and athletics; Johann Wyss's turgid *Swiss family Robinson;* war stories by the likes of Douglas V. Duff and Percy F. Westerman; Edwardian fantasies like Anstey's *Vice versa* and E. Nesbit's books about the Bastables; everything by H. G. Wells and John Buchan; historical novels by Harrison Ainsworth and Doyle (I read Dickens' *Barnaby Rudge* because it belonged to that genre rather than because it is a Great Novel); *Alice through the looking glass* and *Alice in Wonderland;* sea stories by C. S. Forester and many others; the *Magic box* by John Masefield; the "Biggles" books about a flying ace by "Capt." W. E. Johns; *Kim* and *The jungle book* by Kipling; Rider Haggard's books, especially *King Solomon's mines* and *She;* an oddly compelling book of verse, *Fightery Dick* by Derrick Lehmer; Arthur Ransome's *Swallows and Amazons* books, stories by Enid Blyton, particularly those about the Famous Five (though even in those uncritical years, I thought them a bit soppy); Hugh Lofting's *Doctor Doolittle* stories; the *Billy Bunter* books and a large number of other school stories (I still possess one of my favorites, *Pepper's crack eleven* by Rowland Walker). The latter were all set in fee-paying boarding schools populated by children of privilege and were an odd obsession for a poor child enduring a mountingly unhappy education as a day boy in a state school (unwisely, Britain provided and still provides state support for religious education—"faith schools," in the current weasel phrase). Above all, I read everything by my beloved P. G. Wodehouse that I could find in the library or in secondhand shops. I had amassed more than twenty books by PGW by the time I was 10, almost all of them published by Herbert Jenkins, and still possess four shelves of those mostly orange, green, and red clothbound volumes with the trademark centaur with wings in black on the spine. Below them is another shelf of books about the master.

When I look over that list and think of all the other books I read before I was 11, I am struck by the mixture of the enduring and the unimportant and of authors whose names ring down the ages, authors once famous but now unknown (who now reads G. A. Henty, Captain Marryat, or Thomas Hughes's *Tom Brown's schooldays?*), and authors whose names barely registered even then. Also, how easily I moved from the lightweight to the "difficult to read" and back again without being conscious of the transition. I am sure some of the books I read would not pass any test of merit, but I am glad to have lived a time in which the great and the mediocre mingled in the great web of words that engaged and enriched my mind and led me into the infinite worlds of reading.

A widowed mother and her 40-ish unmarried son lived two doors down from 96 Bell Lane. Their surname was Angel. (I suppose it is a result of the quirks of English nomenclature but it seemed odd, even to me at the time, that we lived above the Outlaws in Langland Gardens and near the Angels in Bell Lane.) Those were less suspicious times and my mother took no steps to prevent me spending time with Mr. Angel. He had what seemed like a large collection of books in glass-fronted bookcases in the Angels' back room, of which all I remember were the green leather-bound collected works of Dickens with darkly marbled endpapers. I was overjoyed when he offered to lend me these, one at a time. He also had a stamp collection, held in large ledgers which he opened with reverence of the green chenille-covered living room table. On one occasion, he and a male friend took me to the Farnborough Air Show. It was September 6, 1952. I was excited to go on the train into the Hampshire countryside, awed by the huge crowds and deafened by the noise. The air show ended in tragedy that day, when John Derry, the test pilot who was the first British person to fly at more than the speed of sound, and 26 others were killed when his DeHavilland 110 test plane crashed. In memory I saw it break up in midair, though that may be inaccurate, and I know I put my hands over my ears to muffle the screams of the crowd. It was the second time in my life I had seen a plane crash—an event that, already awful as it was at the time, was to haunt me 15 years later.

It was sometime in the summer of 1951 that I went, with whom I cannot recall, to the Festival of Britain site on the South Bank of the Thames. It was a hundred years since the Great Exhibition that celebrated the glories and military and technological superiority of the British Empire, but this festival was held in a country that was dispirited after the Second World War by six years of privation and dreariness, privation ameliorated only by the tremendous betterments in society brought about by the Attlee Labour government, the greatest in British history. I remember the splashes of color in the pavilions, the "Scandinavian" modernity of design, the Dome of Discovery and the Skylon, and most of all, seeing and boarding the first Routemaster bus—the red double-decker that dominated London's streets for the next half century.

My favorite place to be was, of course, the library. When not there, I frequented secondhand bookshops and junk shops (the latter for books and coins—I once owned a silver thaler issued by the German state of Hesse in 1826 that I found in a bowl of coins in a junk shop in Hendon and for which I paid a penny), looking for bargains, and visited parks in the local area. I still have some of the small volumes of the complete fifteen-volume set of Thackeray's novels that I bought for fifteen shillings (about three dollars at the rate of exchange then) from a shop in the arcade (now long demolished) at Swiss Cottage sometime around 1950 or 1951. I had almost no money—often no money at all—but was quite used to traveling on the buses and underground trains for a few pennies or walking long distances. It seems a completely solitary and unusually unsupervised existence but it suited my temperament and circumstances very well. I would travel at weekends and in the holidays to Golders Green and Hampstead, to Clitterhouse Park and Basing Hill Park on either side of the Hendon Way, and spend hours in Brent Park at the bottom of Bell Lane. I always carried a book on my journeys and could always withdraw into whichever worlds were on offer in what I was reading. At home, I was, as my father said often and dismissively, "wireless mad." Radio, in those pre-television days, was as good a way of escape as reading. Above all, I loved the dramas and serials provided by the BBC, but also looked forward to the regular comedies and music request programs. We had a large wooden Marconi radio with a dark mesh behind the fluted art deco front and dark brown Bakelite knobs. Behind and strictly forbidden, the Mullard valves glowed amid the wires until they broke and the radio was silenced—a fairly frequent occurrence. I remember building a "crystal set" with the help of a fellow pupil called Damian Murphy (his help must have been substantial as I was then and am now almost completely manually inept) and lying in the dark fiddling with the "cat's whisker" to pull in the scratchy, patchy reception of the BBC Home Service. I have now acquired an iPod Nano which I use to download programs from BBC Radio 4 (the successor of the Home Service) so that I can listen to them in the dark hours of the early morning. *Le plus ça change* and all that, but I must admit the reception is better.

....

HORSE MANURE

My father was an enthusiastic, if largely ineffective, gardener. The mean, narrow garden of 96 Bell Lane had a crazily paved walk down one side (on which I used to play one-man cricket—a game of my own invention involving a baldish tennis ball and a wooden box), a rectangle of scrubby grass in the center, and depressed flower beds around the edges. He planted tomatoes in these and spent hours tossing stones to scare the half-feral cats of the neighborhood away from them. There were also a wide selection of weeds and some scruffy brambly plants that bore loganberries. It seems almost incredible now, but in those days the milk (from the Express Dairies) was brought around each day by a milkman with a horse and cart. The milk bottles were topped with foil, the color of which denoted the fat content of the milk—"gold tops" contained Jersey milk with the butter-colored cream occupying the top third of the bottle. Our milkman, who wore a vaguely nautical white cap trimmed in blue and a short white coat, was called Mr. Churchill, something that amazed one of my mother's PGs ("paying guests," or lodgers), a young Frenchman. I thought that was funny at the time but I suppose I would have found it odd if I were staying in a French town and the milk was delivered every day by someone called M. de Gaulle or M. Giscard d'Estaing.

Mr. Churchill left the milk each morning. The horse left its manure. My father believed the latter to be just the thing for his tomatoes so, on occasions that I dreaded, I was enlisted to go into the street and scoop the manure into a wide shovel while he, reverting to his staff sergeantness, imperiously held up any passing traffic. I have always been squeamish about such things and the double embarrassment of retrieving manure and my father's traffic-directing insouciance became almost too much to bear.

....

4

Finchley Catholic Grammar School, 1952–1957

I took the Eleven Plus in February 1952 in a room in St. Alban's Preparatory School. It was a two-day affair, punctuated shockingly by news of the death of King George VI. We were taken from the examination room into the playground, given sheets of music, and led in the singing of "Dies irae" by Mrs. Hawkins and Miss Geoghegan while Armel O'Connor supplied the piano accompaniment. I am sure the spirit of this tribute was not vitiated by the appalling execution by ragged lines of boys whose knowledge of Latin was confined to the (imperfectly understood) words of the Mass. I am no monarchist but most people were saddened by the death of the shy, stuttering king who, it was felt, had risen to the occasion during the war (had certainly done far better than his fascist-sympathizing brother—the man who was briefly Edward VIII—would have done). In the end, the examination was finished and I, and 75 percent of the other boys in my class, passed it, as we should have done after two years of cramming. In the autumn of that year, I was admitted to Finchley Catholic Grammar School and the worst five years of my life began.

My arrival at the school, in the autumn of 1952, was delayed as I had rounded off a summer holiday in Gloucestershire by contracting chicken pox. The holiday was at Hans Hill Farm (near the small Cotswold villages of Longborough, Blockley, and Sezincote and the larger villages of Moreton-in-Marsh and Stow in the Wold) and off the road—the A424—that leads to Broadway and its honey-colored Cotswold stone buildings. The farm was occupied by the family of my Uncle Jack—my mother's brother John Barrett. He was often away in London, visiting mostly during fraught weekends and changing the mood from the tranquility and cheerfulness induced by his wife, my Auntie Mavis, to one of tension and raised voices dominated by him. I was frightened of him, especially of his annoyance when I could not understand his cleft-palatal speech, but also fascinated by his cavalier manner, displays of learning, and gentlemanly pretensions—he insisted on polishing his dark brown brogues with black polish to make them more suitable for a gentleman and waved his long fingers while telling gentlemanly stories. Hans Hill Farm is hundreds of years old, its stone walls four feet deep, with stone flags in the kitchen and a twisting stair leading to the little rooms upstairs. At that time, it had no electricity. My aunt ironed clothes using one of eight smoothing irons that were lined up on the long, black coal-fired range until it cooled and she had to take the next. Best of all, light at night was supplied by oil lamps with tall curving glass cylinders. The sensual pleasure of reading in that soft golden glow lingers with me to this day. Even the chickenpox and its irritations and humiliations (Uncle Jack dabbed each pock with calamine lotion every day and I was, even then, squeamish about nakedness in the presence of men) cannot take away from the pleasure of reading *The Pickwick papers* for the first time (skipping only the ghost stories embedded in the story) safe behind those thick walls in the dead, dark silence of the countryside.

NATURE

Despite my early childhood in the Cotswold countryside, I have lived a largely urban life and have scant familiarity with nature, the names of flowers, trees, etc., and the habits and lives of wild animals. I do remember two incidents that impressed me deeply and are with me today after many decades. At some point in my teens, I believe after I started work in 1957, I went with my friend Vincent Smith to stay with my uncle Jack's family in Hans Hill Farm for a week. One evening, Vincent and I walked to a local pub that served Flowers beer (then a highly prized local brew). As we went down the long farm road to the paved road that leads to the pub in Sezincote, I was suddenly conscious of the deep silence, the velvety blackness of the moonless night, and the uncountable numbers of stars that seemed to blanket the night sky in a manner that is inconceivable in light-polluted urban areas (I wonder if it possible even in the deep Cotswolds today?). It was a transcendent moment of silence and light.

In the early 1960s, I set off in the spring with my school friend, Bryan "Mac" McEnroe, to walk the Roman Road between Salisbury and Dorchester. The road (part of the Portway that ran from London to Weymouth) ran straight from Old Sarum (the Romans' Sorviodunum) to Dorchester (Durnovaria). This was an ill-planned venture that resulted in blistered feet and many cuts and scratches engendered by scaling walls, finding a way down paths between thorny, scrubby bushes, and all the other hazards of trying to follow a 2,000-year-old abandoned road with a small map. One evening, however, we saw something that I can scarcely believe to this day—six or seven hares dancing in a circle in a moonlit field. Superstition has it that hares are devotees of Epona, the Celto-Roman goddess of horses and dreams, and their dancing, chasing, and boxing behaviors on spring moonlit nights are manifestations of possession by that interesting party. Those behaviors account for the Mad March Hare, found in the *Alice* stories and elsewhere. Be that as it may, it did happen on that night in the silence of a Wiltshire spring late evening, and I was privileged to watch it for five or more minutes.

In the years since, I have visited many areas of natural beauty—Yosemite Valley; the islands between Sweden and Finland; the Lake District of the English northwest; the Alps between France and Italy; the Renaissance backdrop of the hills around Lucca in Tuscany; the Hungarian countryside near Esterzgom; the Painted Desert in Arizona; the lovely border country of Scotland; the Buddha-haunted hills above Pusan in Korea; the Ring of Kerry and the Vale of Killarney in Ireland; the open empty countryside of *la France profonde*—but nothing has ever equaled those two evenings in the English countryside long ago.

....

The chicken pox delayed my return to London by bus and I was a week late showing up at FCGS. Worse, my parents had been unable to obtain the regulation school blazer—a black affair with gold and blue piping and the absurdly pretentious school badge—and I went for that first day in a sky blue blazer, two sizes too big, that my father had obtained from a connection of his. My sense of alienation, already strong, was intensified by the derision of the boys and the reprimands of the masters. I was used to my solitary journey on the 125 bus that meandered the byways of Mill Hill (passing the entrance to the Middlesex Regiment barracks in which my parents lived when first married) and Finchley before joining the Great North Road at North Finchley. I would trudge down Woodside Lane to the complex of buildings housing the schools (the Grammar School lay to the west of St. Alban's). I have always been an early riser and took a bus every day from the Bell Lane stop in 1952 and early 1953 and the Church Road stop thereafter, that had me arriving at school at least an hour before classes began. This had several advantages. I left my house at the earliest possible time, the few boys who lived along the same bus route boarded later buses so there was no danger of them interrupting my reading or daydreaming, and I enjoyed the solitude of the almost deserted school. Odd, I suppose, in an 11-year-old boy but that was the kind of boy I was and remained for the next five years.

It is very hard for me to write about FCGS with any detachment even fifty years after I left there. To begin with, it was, as were many postwar grammar schools, a parody of an English public school (the misleading name given to elite private schools in Britain)—institutions with which I was familiar through my reading of many snobbishly silly yet endlessly fascinating school stories. FCGS was replete with the infrastructure of the public school: preposterous uniforms and rules about uniforms; "houses" (I was in Bourne House—named after the onetime cardinal-archbishop of Westminster—despite the fact that we were day boys and there were no physical houses; these were virtual houses long before virtuality became a universal phenomenon); prefects and monitors—the whole feudal structure that pitted boy against boy; trumpery elitism manifested in such things as a "Sixth Form Lawn"; and, worst of all, beatings with canes, straps, and an instrument called the Tolley (a long tongue-shaped strap attached to a wooden handle that Canon Parsons was alleged to have invented). I was then, as I had been for a few years, physically afraid of my mother, whose anger and disappointment frequently and unpredictably manifested itself in violent acts against her children, and the ritualized violence of school did not sit well with me. The combination of physical fear at both ends of my ride on the 125 and my deep-seated resentment of authority made for many wretched days and left marks far more enduring than any created by the beatings. Were the schoolmasters as awful as I remember them? It seems unlikely but there are clearly remembered incidents involving well-remembered words and faces that seem scarcely credible today. All that being said, I was, especially after my second year, something approaching a juvenile delinquent and not anybody with whom I would like to deal, or even know, today—but then I have never even dreamed of being a schoolteacher, someone who is paid, and, one would hope, trained to deal with adolescents, even surly and recalcitrant adolescents.

My first year was spent in Form 1W, the "W" being a reference to the form master, Mr. Willingham (I am not using any of the masters' real names to protect the mostly guilty), who stood out for a number of reasons. He had prodigiously bushy eyebrows which he combed into alarming upward wings. He seemed to actually like the eleven-year-old boys (his motivations were not then, as they later became, entirely clear to me) and invited us to his flat to feed us black treacle sandwiches and play bridge. He ran the Bus Ticket Club, the only association of which I was a member until I joined the Peace Pledge Union seven years later. A prospective member had to recite, without notes, each stop (including the "request" stops) along the length of three London Transport bus routes (I knew the 125 well and added the 13 and 2 by riding on them and memorizing the stops at weekends) and to have an extensive collection of the, then, colorful and distinctive London bus tickets. He also kept a small leather strap—called a drossi, after a boy (D'Rossi?) on whom he had first used it—with which he would whack the hands of boys who committed infractions in class (one of mine was using the word *Esquimeaux* in a written paper because I had read it in a book set in Canada and loved the pretentious look of it). It stung and it hurt but, in the end, seemed like a joke and tells you more about the times than the man.

The level of physical abuse that we took for granted then is hard to believe in these more enlightened days. I was amused when I read one of the masters of my time described as "the legendary Eric Scrope" in a newsletter from the school. This legendary individual was displeased by my insertion of a feeble joke in an essay on the Russian Revolution (I had written that Leon Trotsky's nickname was Fox). He expressed his displeasure by walking silently down the aisle between our scuffed, etched, ink-stained, graffitied desks until he came to mine and, without saying a word, dropped the marked paper on the desk and hit me so hard on my left ear that I fell to the floor, suffered an earache for a week afterwards, and experienced tinnitus for longer. He was a loose-jointed, lantern-jawed, sallow, pocked individual who was said to have been a good cricketer, which goes to show that there is some good in everyone.

My fellow pupils were mostly of Irish descent (Lenihan, McEnroe, O'Hanlon, Fitzgerald, Murphy, Mahoney, Powers, etc.) with a sprinkling of Balts, Hungarians, Italians, and other Catholic results of the displacement caused by the war. There was also a Jew called Lipitsch who, brave lad, left the classroom during prayers. I still have no idea what his parents were thinking and how he endured the year or so of school attendance in a pervasively anti-Semitic atmosphere. The masters were another kettle of fish entirely. What would you make today of a skeletal priest with all the appearance of a Goya Christ in extremis, a complexion that skirted gray and green, wearing a rusty black soutane, with fresh, presumably self-inflicted, deep cuts on his forehead and cheeks, a constant smell of garlic, and an odd manner of holding his long-fingered hands askew at the same sinister angle as his tilted head? To the pupils, he was simply Father Ignatius Loyola ("Dick") Dunn—a caricature to be savored and accepted—but it is hard to imagine him in any other setting than this imitation public school, home of the dispossessed and the cowed. (He died in a conflagration in his bedroom some years later.) What of the huge, big-knuckled Dominic ("Shag") O'Shaughnessy who, under the guise of teaching science, indulged his emotional and physical sadism in mocking and beating the most downtrodden of the boys? I once saw him, in a science class, point to a red-haired boy with a shambling gait and make him cry as he derided him as the modern manifestation of the Missing Link. The one public beating in the five years I spent in this establishment—held before the whole school of eight hundred or so boys in class ranks in the "playground"—was administered by Shag on the person of someone accused of stealing cigarettes from a master. The silence that greeted this extraordinary event was broken after the fourth or fifth stroke of the cane by a boy called Wolfe who broke into hysterical laughter and was dragged from the scene by a monitor—an older boy acting in an official capacity. What of the behavior of Albert "Bum" Blackwell one early morning? (He was called "Bum" because the boys had noticed with the withering accuracy of such observations that his cleft chin exactly resembled the buttocks of a miniature baby.) I had arrived more than an hour before the school's opening and was sitting on a step reading an essay in a copy of Macaulay's *Essays and Lays of ancient Rome* that I had bought from a bookshop in Hendon the previous weekend. In truth, I was entranced more by its half leather binding and elaborately marbled endpapers than its text, though I greatly enjoyed the rollicking meter of the *Lays* and was memorizing *Horatius*:

> Lars Porsena of Closium
> By the Nine Gods he swore
> That the great house of Tarquin
> Should suffer wrong no more.
> By the Nine Gods he swore it,
> And named a trysting day.

Bum walked slowly by, stopped, and then turned to ask me what I was reading. When I told him, he informed me that I was a liar and incapable of reading such a book. It was more than fifty years ago and I do not suppose he remembered that incident for more than minutes but, even then, it seemed to me extraordinary that someone involved in the education of children would quash a nascent interest so casually. It was the last time I associated the secret life of the books I read of my own volition with attendance at school and the "education" I was administered.

The years 1952 to 1957 dragged on in fear and loathing as the spreading effects of puberty added to my wildness and disinclination to learn. In 1953, we moved to a larger house in Hendon—105, Sunny Gardens Road, NW4. The road was spectacularly misnamed. It was rarely sunny and the gardens were mostly scruffy exiguous affairs, realms of weeds, mud, cement statues and plaster gnomes and cats behind privet hedges and low faux stone walls. Its sole saving grace was the nearby Sunnyhill Park—a large expanse of hilly green space that bordered on yew-crowded Hendon Churchyard and overlooked the historic Hendon Aerodrome. 105, a much bigger house than 96 Bell Lane, is a strangely rambling, semidetached affair on at least seven levels. You entered the narrow hall with a staircase leading upstairs on your right, two large rooms (dining and living) on your left, the latter with French doors opening on the scruffy cement patio that lay below the garden; down two stairs to the kitchen and down another stair to the scullery beyond. The cellar/coal hole brooded in the dark and harbored terrors down yet another flight of narrow stairs. The second floor contained three (two large and one small and narrow) bedrooms, with stairs going down to a lavatory and a bathroom and another bedroom, and stairs going up to a bedroom on the third floor, which, in turn, opened on an enormous, slope-roofed attic. This eccentrically capacious dwelling was the home not only of my parents and their five children, but also "paying guests" that included, in addition to the middle-aged depressed clerical workers of yore, a procession of foreign students. One of the latter was a perfectly lovely young woman called Arabella with immaculately combed and cared-for dark hair. She was from Piacenza in Italy, which I assumed must be an enchanted place. Others over the years included two blonde German women (one mousy, one brazen); two athletic young German men who my father (by no means a Germanophile anyway) hinted darkly might be homosexual and thereby rendered even more interesting; an indeterminately Levantine woman called Natasha Vangelatou whom my mother befriended, patronized, and squabbled with in roughly equal amounts; a young woman called Strawinsky who was said to be, and may have been, Igor Stravinsky's granddaughter. There was also a Portuguese girl with large, darkly limpid eyes who taught me, at 15, more of life than I had known up to that time (completing what the brazen blonde German—Marie-Louise—had started). This could have been a hazard since her father, a gentleman in a double-breasted suit, had visited our house before allowing his daughter to stay there. In conversing with my father, he had told him that their family was well connected and that he had "the ear of Salazar." The vision of a Swan Vestas box containing the *dictador*'s severed ear tucked into one of the pockets flashed through my mind. A young French art student called Didier dazzled me with his cosmopolitan worldliness (or what I took for such) and dazzled us all by bringing his friend Michael to the house. Michael Chaplin was a strikingly handsome dark-haired young man whose parents were Charlie and Oona (O'Neill) Chaplin. He was quiet and shy, but his was glamour of an order absent in Hendon.

The center of our religious lives was Our Lady of Dolours Catholic church in Egerton Gardens presided over by a tall priest called Canon Coote—a remote and somewhat condescending figure—assisted by the short, fierce, bald Father di Felice. Every Sunday and every holiday of obligation we were assembled for the march down Sunny Gardens Road across Church Street and, via some alleys and small roads to the stone church with its gray slate pitched roof, its dark Irish Catholic Gothic interior, its sooty high-back pews, and somber stained-glass windows commemorating deceased Catholic worthies of Hendon. The church was built in 1863 and extensively refurbished in the 1920s. The march to church always seems to involve rows, recalcitrance, savagely brushed hair, the search for clean clothes, slammed doors, the quest for and doling out of pennies to put in the collection plate, and one or more children in tears as my mother led the way, stony-faced, for us to do our duty. My father always accompanied us but with a marked lack of enthusiasm. Once at the church, we would pass the people selling Catholic publications such as the *Universe* and Irish newspapers—the one I remember was the *Cork examiner*. Those were days when Catholic families with five children or more were not uncommon and, therefore, the search for empty pews to accommodate the whole family was often unsuccessful. I remember one occasion in which I was kneeling on the hard almost inconspicuously padded red kneeler that swung down from the back of the pew in front, with two or three of my siblings and behind my mother and father with another. My father was also kneeling and I could see the scuffed bottoms of his immaculately polished shoes and, protruding from the bottom of his fawn gabardine trousers, the striped ends of his pajamas. Did he dress so quickly that he had not noticed or was it a silent sartorial symbol of his protest? I never knew. Father di Felice was famous for two things—chain-smoking and his impassioned denunciatory sermons, the most memorable of which was on the topic of those who gave insufficient amounts when the collection plate was passed. Its title was "Confessions of a Penny-in-the-Plater" and it painted a vivid picture of the terrors waiting in the afterlife for those exhibiting parsimony toward Holy Mother Church in general and Our Lady of Dolours and Father di Felice in particular.

THE KIDDER

My father had been badly scalded in a kitchen accident when he was quite young and had an extensive scar down the side of his face, his left arm, and the left side of his body. It was not very visible but the skin was shinier there and he could not grow a beard on that side of his face (not that he ever wanted to, as far as I am aware). He never spoke of what must have been a traumatically painful event, any more than he spoke about his wartime experience. I had a broken nose from the age of 13 and, knowing how I, if few others, perceived it as a crippling deformity for many years, cannot but believe he saw that extensive scar in similar terms. However, he never mentioned it, exhibiting a stoicism that I now, if not then, find quite admirable. This was very different from my mother's cleft palate, which was a forbidden topic to the rest of us, but frequently referred to by her usually in extremely combative terms as in "Cleft palate I may have, but if she thinks she . . ." followed by some dark thoughts on the danger of underestimating her—very real dangers, as I had ample occasion to know.

My father's stoic demeanor was the facade of someone who loved to tease and kid. When he returned from the war, he told me that he had brought a camel back from Egypt for me and that, because of lack of accommodation where we lived, was housing it temporarily at the London Zoo. This camel, in which I believed with all my heart for a long time, bore the name of "Mickey." I do not know what gave the game away but I can remember the keenness of my disappointment after all these years.

When my father was working for the furriers, he was a frequent patron of a tobacconist in the area. He smoked Senior Service cigarettes and cheroots called "Winterman's." The latter smelled vile when ignited but came in small, rectangular, embossed cardboard boxes that were ideal for holding the coins I collected. One morning, the tobacconist remarked on the fact that he was returning after having been there the previous morning. My father assumed an air of puzzlement that appeared to clear up as he said "Oh no, I wasn't here. That must have been my twin brother." He kept up the fiction that there were two of him for months on end and would say things like "Has my brother been in recently?" leaving the tobacconist at a loss for words. He had a remarkable ability to keep a straight face throughout these impostures. I was in a pub with him years later when he walked over to three men playing dominoes for small change and inquired with a blandly innocent face "How do you play this game?" They proceeded to show him and then to lose money to him. He was, of course, an expert and longtime dominoes player and walked back to our table half an hour later with a faint smile, jingling the coins in his pocket in a supremely self-satisfied manner.

....

I played truant from school occasionally but only when my fear of the consequences of what I had done or not done the day before overcame my hatred of being bored. I doubt that there has ever been anything more empty and pointless than the day of a penniless adolescent hanging around in the rain in the charmless environs of North Finchley and Hendon in the pinched 1950s—a day fit to be chronicled by Samuel Beckett or Jean-Paul Sartre. I always carried a book, but where to read in safety and comfort? My favorite places were parks and libraries, but I feared being caught by a truant officer if I spent any time in the latter, so the park it was, moving from shelter from the rain to benches when dry as the minutes plodded slowly toward time to catch the bus home.

I joined a Catholic youth club at St. Edward's Catholic Church halfway between Golders Green and Temple Fortune when I was 13 or 14. The idea was to provide a "wholesome" place for young men and women to play ping-pong and the like and take part in other group activities. It had two attractions, apart from the ping-pong. The first were the fascinating Irish male adolescents—all working (mostly in construction) and leading independent if chronically penurious and feckless lives—who made the youth club their social center on weekday evenings. They were all older than me and I loved their swagger, brogues, and bolshie attitudes. I yearned to share their raffish escapades in the Irish pubs in Camden Town and Kilburn that were the locale for their weekends and even more their (I now realize exaggerated) sexual exploits on Hampstead Heath with wild Irish girls. One, Paddy Reilly, implied that he had gone "all the way" with a girl called Carmel McKeown. It probably was not true but I rejoiced in my shameful awe at his prowess. The other, greater attraction was the girls who mostly giggled in gaggles as we tried to impress them with feats at the ping-pong table. One of them, a darkly pretty and slender girl called Katie Lothian, was my first "girlfriend," in the sense that she allowed me to hold her hand and even kiss her on occasion for a few brief weeks until she told me abruptly that she did not want to see me anymore. I had no money to take her out and our "dates" consisted of me meeting her near the bus stop at Staples Corner, a wasteland of factories, office buildings, and apartment buildings near the North Circular Road, to this day a miserable, if wide, thoroughfare, and walking hand in hand to the flat in which she lived with her mother and her mother's "friend" Ivan. The latter was a short, stout Russian who always wore a short, tight leather jacket. Her mother was very friendly but worried looking. I was very surprised to find out later that she was not only a prostitute (and Ivan her "manager") but had also nearly been a victim of, and actually was a key witness against, one of the most notorious murderers of the early 1950s. We would sit and have tea and chat, Katy allowing me to touch her hand the while, until I had to leave and she and I could walk back to the bus stop—never more than three kisses allowed and sometimes none—for me to board the bus. I would sit, a moody would-be Romantic figure, alone in a seat on the top deck of the bus, until we came to Hendon Central and it was time for my trudge home in the invariable rain. One day, Katy told me that she didn't want to see me anymore, and that was that. Such glamour as there was had gone from my life—until, that is, I enrolled in the Sydney Francis School of Dancing in Hendon Central and learned to jitterbug with several of the shy girls lined up against the opposite wall to where the Brylcreemed youths lolled against the "boy's wall" until the music started.

I will not dwell on the remainder of those years at Finchley Catholic Grammar School; of the seemingly endless drab and humiliating months; of the hatred of the hearty masters (all tweed jackets and pretension) who were what passed for normal among their certifiable peers; of the boil of sexual feeling, romance, and love—of all of which I knew nothing (until the last year of my school attendance) except what I had read in books; of the slender girl in the green school uniform who boarded the 125 bus in Woodside Park every morning and sat seats away from me for the ten minutes that remained of my journey, seemingly unconcerned by my daily and unremitting ardent and idiotically obvious stares (she bore, as I discovered a few years after and as a blow to the heart, a striking resemblance to the young woman in the photograph by the American photographer Elliott Erwitt in the "Family of man" exhibition who is shown lying on a bed gazing lovingly at her baby); of the humiliations, fights, and beatings—the latter a matter of twisted pride and, as I realized far later and far too late, a thrill that lingers. Those were terrible times of lost opportunities, times in which I learned nothing but what I learned from my incessant and solitary reading. It is said that an autodidact has a fool for a teacher, but the books I read were no fools and I am grateful now as then for their instruction and guidance.

I was so unhappy in those years that I mulled insane ideas—of going to what was then Rhodesia as a policeman; of lying about my age to join the British Army at the time of Suez crisis of 1956; of running away to "ride the rails" in America. These ideas came to me at the time when I was coming to realize that I was permanently against the grain and my politics, such as they were, were of the left and opposed to militarism, Conservatism, authoritarianism, and all the other boots coming down on human faces. I was entranced by the romance of the Hungarian Uprising in 1956 and by the oratory of Aneurin Bevan against the Suez affair (despite my mad idea of "joining up"—possibly the only thing I could have done that would have pleased my father). Nye Bevan was my only pure political idol and there will never be another, just as the image of the girl on the 125 bus is unalterably and uniquely forever with me.

My career as a student at FCGS came to an ignominious and whimpering end in 1957 and a series of events, none reflecting any credit on me, took me from thence to the steps of Hampstead Public Library in a few short months in 1957.

I worked in the mailroom of a company called J. D. Laing in Mill Hill in the summer of 1956. I and three other hobbledehoys worked under the benevolent eye of an elderly man (probably far younger then that I am now) who was keen on cricket. I remember us all listening to the radio all day during the great Oval test match against the Australians during which Surrey's Jim Laker took 19 of the 20 Australian wickets (the other being taken by his Surrey colleague Tony Lock)—a feat never accomplished before or since. I quite enjoyed the work and appreciated having a small income. For reasons I cannot now recall, I thought that J. D. Laing would be a good place to work—this despite the fact that I had no interest in their business.

My last year at the grammar school was an unmitigated disaster. I did not study, I did none of the assigned homework, and was punished for that. I was constantly in trouble for fighting, for dumb insolence, for outright cheek. My thoughts were all of girls and romance, sacred and profane, and my waking hours were filled with the misery of my home and school life interweaved with the romantic and sexual fantasies of a 15-year-old boy who was acquiring his first scant experience of either outside the covers of books. I was estranged from my parents and my much younger brothers and sisters. I had just two friends and spent most of my time outside school alone in parks and libraries. That "fifth form" year was supposed to be spent in studying for the "O" (for "ordinary") level examinations that were intended to perform yet another cull of the less deserving of those who had passed the Eleven Plus. This time, the cull was aimed at weeding out those who would not profit from two more years of school spent in preparing for university entrance A level examinations (for *Advanced*). Those who fell at the O-level hurdle were destined for white-collar drudgery—grammar school boys with bad O levels were employable as clerks in banks and building societies, in offices and in shops, or as trainees destined for middle management in a variety of enterprises. Five or more O levels with good marks would get you into the "sixth forms" and on the road to university; anything less was a ticket out. Early in my fifth year, I was hauled into the office of the deputy headmaster for corporal punishment for some infraction. Malleson was an officer type with the short man's swagger, an unpleasantly pointed nose, a mustache that was more of an affront than a facial decoration, and a well-honed line in sarcasm. After the by-now-routine thrashing, he asked me what I was planning to do in the next year. I had no goals in life and no idea of how I might earn a living. I had vague thoughts of winging my way to a decent haul of "O" levels and thus postponing all decisions. I told him that I thought I would come back to the sixth form if I did well enough in the examinations. "Hmmnn," he said, "no, I don't think so," and with that and very few more words, told me that I would not be welcome back. I have no idea why I was surprised by the news, but I was. The foolish optimism of youth had persuaded me that you could defy the bastards and get away with it; that my intelligence and reading would get me through—they always had up to then. So, I was not expelled from school dramatically but allowed to finish the year and to take the "O" levels. I often wonder what would have happened if I had applied myself and received good "O" level results—making them reconsider would have been the most effective defiance—but I did the opposite and, in what I now realize, as I did not then, was an echo of my father's "sod them" antiauthoritarianism, did almost no preparation for the examinations and passed just four subjects (only in one, English, with good marks). Not too bad for someone who was just winging it, but by no means enough to make the school to change their minds. What was then Finchley Catholic Grammar School is now Finchley Catholic High School—"A Business and Enterprise College" (one imagines Canon Parsons revolving in his grave) and, I trust, a more enlightened and effective institution.

I left the school without a backward glance in June of 1957. I was sixteen and penniless, with no skills, no qualifications, and no particular interests apart from reading, motion pictures, cricket, and sex. The Queen's Shilling was not on offer (see "The power of prayer" below), fortunately for me, as I had already decided I was a pacifist and the system was not kind to conchies. My father was eager for me to work and to contribute money to the house; my mother had more or less given up on me. I took a job for the summer with J. D. Laing—this time in an office, writing sums of money into large ledgers and adding them up. I have always been quick with figures and did this repetitive task quite well. My supervisor thought I showed promise and should continue to work there and, eventually, study accountancy by correspondence courses. The prospect appalled me. Work on the ledgers was the merest drudgery and I thought I had a soul above accountancy, a soul born for poetry and rebellion, for romance and *la vie sexuelle* in all its infinite variety. On the other hand, I needed money and had no other source. I was saved by a miserable little farce of my own contriving. A combination of boredom and daydreaming led to me being well behind with a particular task with a deadline. To put it simply, I cooked the books. I wrote in plausible numbers with plausible totals and, to all appearances, finished the job on time. The following week, my fraud was exposed. Worse, profiting from my life experience at home and in school, I lied about it and the lie came out. No more prospects of clerical toil and correspondence courses stretching over the coming decades. I was allowed to work for the rest of the week, to collect the few pounds they owed me, and to shake the dust of J. D. Laing off my feet in what proved to be a providential deliverance.

There I was, loafing about in the house having been kicked out of school and expelled from a contractor's accounts department, the possessor of ignominious examination results, no money, and a seriously defective attitude to life. Indirectly, one of the nuns from the IBVM convent in Fitzjohns Avenue came to my rescue and set the course of my life. She, Mother Joanna, had maintained a friendship with my mother and, in response to my mother's complaints about my indolence and lack of direction is reported to have said, "Mickey likes reading; why doesn't he work in a library?" Told this, I realized I had no idea what such work involved (I probably thought it involved reading books—a common misconception for most of us) but also that the work environment might be congenial and would probably involve working with, and certainly involve meeting, girls. I was enthusiastic for once and decided to apply for a junior assistantship in Hampstead Public Library—Hampstead being a much more intriguing place than Hendon, the deadly adjacent suburb in which I lived. I cannot remember the interview at all—place or the people involved—but it must have been less than inquisitorial and not challenging enough to live in my mind. However the interview was, it had the satisfactory result that I was offered the job and began to work at the library in Arkwright Road on September 1, 1957.

THE POWER OF PRAYER

Sometime not long after the war, my mother, a devout Catholic all her life, decided that it would be a catastrophe if her first born son were to be "called up" for National Service—i.e., conscripted into the British armed forces—as were all men over 18 at that time. Her early days with my father had given her a jaundiced view of military life. That and the inherent dangers convinced her that I should never be a soldier (remember she was still nursing illusions about my character—the curly haired boy of the glorious War years still lived in her memory if decreasingly in actuality). She became determined to prevent the catastrophe and came up with a Catholic solution—she would do a novena each year dedicated to keeping me out of the army. A *novena* is a special devotion for Catholics—nine days of prayer asking for a special grace or gift of God. There are prescribed prayers, adaptable to almost any circumstance. My mother did a novena every year for a number of years as I grew from that outgoing curly-headed boy into a sullen lout. At some time in the early 1950s my mother discontinued her novenas, having come to the conclusion that two years of National Service could be my salvation and, in the nauseating phrase of the time, "make a man of me." Alas, such is the power of prayer that, although National Service did not come to an end officially until December 31, 1960, it had been decided earlier that no one born after September 1, 1939, would be called to serve. God moves in mysterious ways, and who is to say that my mother's piety was not instrumental in saving me from the horrors and boredom of enforced military life or imprisonment as a conchie?

....

5

Hampstead Public Library, 1957–1960

Hampstead ... a place of ghosts, enchanting ghosts. Wordsworth used to walk to it across the fields from London; Keats was inspired by it; D.H. Lawrence fled from it ... George Orwell was bombed out of it ... There is no end to Hampstead's celebrity. Shelley sailed paper boats on a pond by the Vale of Health; Constable painted its sky; John Galsworthy, too ill to travel, was awarded the Nobel Prize in his house in Admirals Walk. When she married, Katherine Mansfield went to live "in a tall grave house with red geraniums and white daisies in the garden at the back," and Virginia Woolf came to tea.

—Kenneth Roy

It would be very easy for me to romanticize my experience at Hampstead Public Library. It set the course of the rest of my life, gave me the education which I and the system had conspired to deny me, introduced me to worlds and ideas of which I had known nothing, and provided me with a congenial social milieu for the first time in my life. I am still amazed at the way in which these well-read, kindly people did more than welcome me and seemed to see something in an insecure, unqualified youth. More, it gave me confidence that I could work with adults and interact with them as an equal. The shelves of the library held great riches and, though the work I did there did not involve reading, I read incessantly on the bus to work, at lunchtimes (more often than not, cheese and pickle sandwiches in the shabby staff room with old bound volumes of *Punch*), on the bus home and deep into the evening. I read even more promiscuously than before—classic novels, English and in translation; travel books; histories; biographies; books on the cinema and on cricket; poetry and plays; best sellers with, for the time, advanced sexual content; and the few books on sex to which I had access. The latter were a necessary and valuable correction to the massive misinformation I had received from fellow pupils at Finchley Catholic Grammar School and the repressed, twitchy priests who lectured us on the evils of masturbation there (to not the slightest avail).

Hampstead Central Library, c. 1950s

It was not easy to gain access to those books on sex because they were mostly sequestered. The deputy borough librarian, Ernie Knowles, had thick white hair, stained yellow in the front from his incessant smoking and brushed straight back from his broad red forehead. He had the keys to a locked cupboard in his office in which all the books deemed too "advanced" to be on the open shelves were stored. These included books on sex, photography books of or containing nudes, and racy novels. The latter included, incredibly, *Forever Amber*. Knowles had joined Hampstead library in 1911 and, unlike the other young men who worked there at the same time, did not enlist in the armed forces as the country was swept with war fever in 1914 (it may be that he had some condition that precluded military service). This was bitterly resented by those who served and survived because they came back to their entry-level jobs while he had advanced into the Library's administration. That bitterness was often expressed to me by the otherwise cheery Mr. Jones, with whom I worked later in the Kilburn branch library forty and more years after the Great War had ended.

The borough librarian—Stanley Butcher—a large man with a booming voice, was a remote but genial presence who, in all probability, did not know my name. I discovered later that he was an influential person in the Library Association and, at one point, headed the committee that oversaw professional examinations. He would often be seen in and about the library chatting to councilors and the like. He also came among us to play on the staff table tennis table, often with one of the porters, a man called Mac, who was perfectly bald and spoke in a strangely tremulous, bleating, high-pitched voice except at closing time, when his stentorian bellows (of "OUT!") could be heard in all parts of the library. Mac suffered from a variety of unnamed ailments that precluded almost all the work that porters usually do. One of the two other porters had a "bad back," so the third—a diminutive Cockney sparrer called George who was rumored to be a "Brown Owl" for a local Brownies troop—regularly staggered around bearing heavy boxes of books under the supervision and watchful and benevolent eyes of the other porters.

I was assigned, early in my time at the library, to a then-advanced piece of library automation. The cards for the library's catalogues were printed from metal plates onto which embossed letters were typed using a fearsome cast-iron machine (an Adana) that resembled a massive spinning wheel. This was operated by a woman called Dorothy Thorold, who came from a very old West Country family and who was the artist Piet Mondrian's landlady when he was in exile in London during the Second World War (she had a delicate pen drawing of a flower in a vase made by Mondrian hanging on a wall near her desk). She was a cataloguer—the first I had ever met—and did her cataloguing directly onto the metal plates with her whirring, clattering wheel. I thought this a very fine thing and, thus, had my first glimpse into the kind of librarian I was destined to be. I remember talking to her for a few minutes before lunch, during which time she spoke of catalogue entries and their headings (*access points* in modern speak). I was, though, three steps removed from actual cataloguing there in the basement of the old library building. First, Miss Thorold would crank out the plates, each bearing one or more of the following letters—CBHKW (for Central, Belsize, Heath, Kilburn, and West—indicating whether the book was located in the Central library and/or in one or more of the four branches). Second, I would take the shiny plates to Valerie Hammond, a dark-haired, zaftig, pretty woman— whom I thought very sophisticated and who was amused by my youth—who would feed them into a printing device from which the cards would emerge complete sets of main and added entries (the first time I had ever heard of these categories that would preoccupy me for some years later) for however many libraries owned the book, plus two extra sets for the Hampstead union catalogue and for the London same. My jobs were to sort the cards, ensuring that each destination had a full set; to clean the plates which were both inky and oily; and to file them (in alphabetical order) for future use.

I worked next and briefly in the interlibrary loan section, in which I learned about the verification of bibliographic information by checking the readers' requests in the catalogue and various printed sources (bibliographies, indexes, etc.). This was a valuable, if disorganized, lesson in the organization of knowledge. I also came to appreciate the variety and complexity of the needs of library patrons. One requested "The tyranny of the org," and I was able to match the request with Wilhelm Reich's famous book despite the requester being, apparently, unable to bring himself to write the word *orgasm*. Another asked for Irving Stone's "The angony and the ecstary"—a Joycean construction that, somehow, expressed the drama of Michelangelo's life better than the actual title. Someone told me that, in the past, a request had been made for "The Saurus," but that may have been apocryphal.

The area that I most enjoyed was the public desk. It faced the double doors at the entrance to the lending library, which was directly in front of the corridor leading from the stairs. It was a combination of information and circulation desk (the reference desk was inside another set of double doors within the lending reading room and book collection), and I met the great variety of patron that Hampstead boasted uniquely among the boroughs of London. Writers, clergymen, journalists, secretarial college students (all young women), wealthy people with cut-glass accents and wealthy people without, all of London human life was there—mostly the better-off and more-educated part, though there were the usual eccentrics and lonely people for whom the library is a refuge, a sanctuary, and a substitute for a social life. A one-eyed, lean, and tattered man who wore an eye patch or did not wear a patch according to his whim lived in a "Rowton House" (a home for the homeless and lost) somewhere in the vicinity and spent many hours every day in the central library. On one occasion he stood patchless and frightening in the middle of the lending library, waved his dirty tweed cap in the air, and shouted, "Je suis le dernier Christ!" very loudly several times. He resisted suggestions that he leave before being semidragged to the entrance by one of the library's three porters. He was in the next day, reading the local newspaper as coolly as a literate cucumber.

The library was on the posh side of the Finchley Road with the less exalted West Hampstead and the decidedly down-market Kilburn stretching on the other side toward the nameless wastes of Willesden—a suburb that only John Betjeman could love. The people who flowed in and ebbed out of the library all day were fascinating but not, to me, as alluring as the characters who worked there. This was my first exposure to people who led "fast" lives, followed the leading critics of the day assiduously, queued up to see foreign films, went to the theater and the ballet, talked (mostly left-wing) politics, and lived, loved, and drank red wine in Hampstead bed-sitters with bull-fighting posters on the walls. This was heady stuff to an impressionable boy from Hendon—a place that knew not such things—and I fell irrevocably head over heels in love with a way of being that is with me still, mutatis mutandis.

If I cast my mind back more than fifty years, I can see them as clearly as if I had seen them yesterday. Christine Haynes had femme fatale good looks and elegant airs (good clothes and cigarette holders) and was proud of the fact that she had been "sent down" (expelled) from Sussex University for witchcraft. She told fortunes using cards. There was a married man in her life whose name was said to be "Dr. Sax"—though since this is the title of a novel by Jack Kerouac, a writer of transcendent interest then to those of us with literary pretensions, it could be that he was a Dr. Sachs, a less glamorous moniker for an important person in the life of the glamorous Miss Haynes. Anthony Babington—a Buddhist with a matinee-idol profile, deep-set, compelling eyes, long brown wavy hair, a resonantly deep voice, and the same name as the hero of *A traveller in time*—was given to deep breathing and often stood on his head in the staff room during lunch breaks. He eschewed the local public baths in favor of swimming in the Hampstead Ponds (immortalized in *The Pickwick papers*) because he wanted to be at one with nature. As a result he often had colds and coughs. Margery Evans was a tall, attractive woman with a long white neck and sleek short hair who wore bright red lipstick and emphasized her large eyes with colorful eyeliner, mascara, and carefully applied shadow. She smoked cigarettes in a long red holder with considerable élan. She had been a ballerina and, consequently, all her moves were elegant and enhanced by the fashionable floating clothing she wore. She was the only person I have ever known who could shelve books gracefully, displaying the fluid movements of a member of the corps de ballet. Frank Atkinson, who ran the lending library—a post of considerable authority—was a handsome, dark, sardonic man of middle height whose glamorous characteristics included having markedly left-wing views and living on a houseboat in the Regents Canal with a woman not then his wife. He had a long-running feud with another senior librarian, called Roger Donald. This poor man had the misfortune to have had his name misprinted in the local paper as "Roper Donald," and was, from that time, called Ropey by Frank and his numerous allies, of which I think Ropey had none. Christine Haynes was in the habit of sitting on Ropey's desk, swinging her long legs and showing some frilly underthings. It was said that she did it out of devilment, but I suppose it could have been a spectacular example of barking up the wrong tree. Atkinson was, as were many of his generation of English librarians, a former Communist Party member but had left because, I believe, of the events of 1956. It was a thrill to discover that there were many current and former Party members in this new world and, even more to find that Frank and others would talk to me about politics, books, films, and the other Hampstead topics as if I were their equal in knowledge and not the callow, insecure, largely ignorant youth I knew myself to be. He taught me a lot about libraries without ever appearing to do so, and I will always be grateful for his tolerance, patience, and kindness.

There was John Staley, in appearance the epitome of the bespectacled pipe-smoking absent-minded scholar, in fact a deeply eccentric junior staff member—a constant reader with a knack for being involved in bizarre incidents and deep, if transient, enthusiasms. It was when in the grip of one of these that he proposed to one and all (including the Governor General of the BBC, by letter) that the popular daily radio soap opera *Mrs. Dale's diary* (a dreary middle-class farrago) should be replaced by a serial based on *The diary of Vaslav Nijinsky*—something that would have revolutionized popular culture in the 1950s. Malcolm Bagnall was a small brown man who was best known in the library for participating in a study based on waking people who were sleeping rough on Hampstead Heath and conducting questionnaires—with predictably mixed results. He brought a cardboard suitcase to work with the materials for his lunches: tins of baked beans. Another farouche luncher was Alan Ronalds, who was in the habit of eating full-sized Swiss rolls (a type of cake rolled around jam and powdered with sugar) whole from their wrappers as if they were giant bananas.

I cannot remember when I first met my friend John Garforth. It was, I think, in 1959 when he came to work in the library. He had already led an interesting life, which included working as a solicitor's clerk in Lincoln's Inn Fields and as a milkman, involvement with the left-wing Unity Theatre, and a two-month stretch in the notorious prison Wormwood Scrubs for being an unrepentant conscientious objector to the National Service that I had so narrowly escaped. He had attended a public school and had the consequent accent but was inspired more by his hero John Osborne in his hatred of the class system and wide-ranging rebelliousness. John, seven years older than me, had already written a novel and two or three plays and lived in a furnished bed-sitter in South Hampstead with his tall actress wife, Doreen, and small daughter in a bohemian clutter that I found wildly exciting. We took to each other and to the pubs of Hampstead with equal enthusiasm.

JOHN GARFORTH

The following is from John Garforth's now inactive website (consulted July 9, 2009).

In 1959 I joined Hampstead borough council as a library assistant. I suppose this was when I became the person I now am. I have never believed there is such a thing as the real me, for anyone, but this was when I learned to play the part of the John Garforth I wanted to be. I worked for the first few months at the central library in Finchley Road. I became friends with Peter Hoggett, who came from Sedgefield and moved in thespian circles with people like Peter Schaffer and Victor Spinetti—he lent me the scripts of several Peter Shaffer plays which have never as far as I know been staged and one, Royal Hunt of the Sun, which was staged by the National some three or four years later and made Peter Shaffer famous. Peter Hoggett seemed to think I was well read, amusing and intelligent. He kept me away from the gay thespians but involved me with Maureen Sullivan, who was away at library school at the time, and her new husband Phil Johnson-Laird. He involved me with Michael Gorman, a bohemian genius who worked at the Kilburn branch library and was regarded as mad, bad and dangerous to know. Peter was the kind of person who held dinner parties and his skill at compiling a guest list resulted in the group which my second wife found an intimidating group of what she called 'Hampstead Intellectuals.' Phil Johnson-Laird was off to University College to read Linguistics, a dropout from public school (they used to play rugby against celeb teams that included Stanley Baker) who took Latin in about three months to qualify. He was the most heavyweight mind I had ever encountered. (We used to play chess, and the only time I ever beat him the game lasted until four in the morning.) Phil was influenced by Karl Popper, who believed in piecemeal revolution. At that time I was a disciple of Sartre, Maureen's inspiration was Albert Schweitzer. Those were heady days. Michael was irritated by the bleeding hearts brigade (Mother Theresa, Danilo Dolci and me) and preferred to talk of Robert Graves and James Joyce. Michael was a poet and a wit; over the years I have used many of his best lines as if they were my own.

I met Anne Gillett on the first day of my employment at Hampstead PL. She was a little older than me, a slender, pretty young woman who had finished her library qualifications at North Western Polytechnic the year before. For most of the period of which I am writing, she was little more than an acquaintance, probably because what seems a minor age difference now loomed much larger when we both were young. She was an assiduous reader and had already read all the books of which I had then heard and many more, noting, as I learned later, each title and the dates read in a notebook. After events that I will describe later, we married on March 6, 1962 (my 21st birthday), at Our Lady Help of Christians Catholic church in Rickmansworth, Hertfordshire.

After doing various jobs in the central library, I was sent to be one of four junior assistants at the Belsize Park branch in Antrim Road. The library was and is a striking modern one-story building, elliptically shaped at one end and consisting, essentially, of one large public room with a staff area attached. Dick Dennis was the branch librarian. He had succeeded Edward Dudley, who had left to teach in the library school at North Western Polytechnic in Kentish Town. Dudley was one of the éminences grises of British librarianship who, until well into his 90s, contributed a column to *Update*, the tritely named magazine of the Chartered Institute of Library and Information Professionals, the gawkily named successor organization of the Library Association. He appeared in the Belsize branch every so often, a glamorous (to me and probably to others) slim man with longish hair who wore denim shirts and red knitted ties at a time when such things were rare and marked their wearers as intellectuals and, quite possibly, revolutionaries. He was a Party member (or, more probably, an ex-Party member) but had confined most of his revolutions to the Association of Assistant Librarians.

Clothes were very different then. I wore a navy suit, white shirt, tie, and dark dress shoes to work every day and was expected to do so. The suits, which were dark, shiny, cheap, and from either Meaker's or Montague Burton (the haberdashers of the lower middle class), were the official clothing of male possessors of few O levels. The other three junior assistants, all girls in their late teens, wore dresses ("frocks"), cardigans, court shoes, and, if daring, colored stockings (an eccentricity that was tolerated in Hampstead, but strictly forbidden in Ealing Public Library, in which I worked in the early 1960s). One of these young women became my on-again, off-again girlfriend. Her name was Isabel Thomson, a girl with a retroussé nose, wide generous mouth, curvy figure, and lovely dark blue eyes. I had been reading T. S. Eliot and told her that her friendly bust gave promise of pneumatic bliss (she certainly was "nice"), but it did not impress her very much. She had a gramophone and a collection of Ella Fitzgerald and Frank Sinatra records—unimaginable luxuries in my house—and lived just across the road in a second-floor flat that she shared with her dourly genial father, a Scottish railway worker, who was either a widower or the relict of a bolting wife. I never quite knew which. I almost never had any money, so we shared infrequent visits to the cinema (sitting in the ninepenny seats), walks in the park, and cuddles on the sofa listening to Ella and Frank. This all came to an end when she decided to go out with a cad called Brian—who was a student of laundry management and a paying guest in my parents' house—finding his ownership of a small open sports car and ability to pay for meals an irresistible draw. He was a Young Conservative and dressed accordingly. I had already conceived a dislike of Conservatives, young or old, and the appurtenances of the type (sports cars, flat caps, Kenneth More–style banter, brightly colored waistcoats, etc.), and the caddishness of Brian cemented those dislikes in my soul, where they still lodge. I was no longer working at the Belsize branch when this brief romantic melodrama occurred, and I only saw Isabel twice again, each time fleetingly.

The Belsize branch was the site of an exciting technological innovation—photocharging. This was a circulation system that used a microfilm camera—it was either a Recordak or a Remington—to photograph the accession (identifying) number of the book, stamped in the top right-hand corner of the recto of the first leaf of the book (usually the endpaper), together with the borrower's card and linking the two with a punched "transaction" card (made by Remington Rand) that was inserted in a pocket of the book. When the book was returned the transaction cards were sorted; missing cards identified books that were overdue. The sorting was accomplished by the distinctly low-tech means of inserting long needles into the punched holes and allowing those that were notched at that number to fall off. When the sorting was complete, one could take the list of missing numbers and scroll through the microfilm to locate the name and address of delinquent borrowers. I became quite adept in all aspects of photocharging, up to and including wielding the sorting needle, and was sent to demonstrate the (extremely simple) procedures when it was installed in the other branches.

I remember a post-Isabel pre-Christmas party in the Belsize library in which we brought in food and drink and, after the doors were closed, ate, drank, and made merry to music from a tape player (the first time I had seen such a thing). I kissed all three of the young ladies at different times as the music played on and the evening turned to night and then to early morning.

MG operating a photocharging machine in the Belsize branch in early 1958. From the Annual Report of Hampstead PL.

It was a high old time and the transgressive nature of holding the party on official premises, drinking and dancing, and holding long conversations in corners with the young ladies until the pale light of dawn over NW3 was a thrill in itself. I felt myself, for the first time, to be a true Hampstead bohemian, if only for a night, despite the essential innocence of the event.

In the course of my time in Hampstead Public Library, I worked in the central library and in all four of the branches—two of them, West Hampstead and Heath, only intermittently as a fill-in staff member. The West Hampstead branch sits on the corner of Dennington Park Road and West End Lane. It was built in 1954 as part of a small housing development and had the dreary, pinched look of much of the public architecture of the time. It was the replacement for the original library built in 1901 on the corner of Sarre and Westbere Roads and destroyed by German bombing in 1940. Among its notable features were large double doors that, as it turned out, were made of two layers of glass. One day in the late 1950s, the contrast between the interior coolness and the exterior heat caused this two-ply construction to explode and shards of glass to be propelled with force across West End Lane, luckily without major injuries to those in the vicinity.

The staff activities of the library took place in the basement, reached by steep stairs descending from behind a door marked *Staff Only*. This entirely unremarkable arrangement had one remarkable feature—concert hall–like acoustics. One of the numerous odd ducks who worked in HPL at the time was a twenty-something man called Paul Oddy, the first sighted person I ever knew who wore dark glasses indoors, always wore his suit jacket collar turned up (a raffishly eccentric feature in the 1950s), and who prided himself on his resonant baritone and knowledge of opera (of which my knowledge then was nonexistent and now is minuscule). If he were on duty at West Hampstead (he was rotated around the branches in a vain attempt to find the right niche), he would forever be going up and down those stairs, singing "*Nessun dorma*," "*Che gelida manina*," and the like at the top of his lungs. They sounded all right to me and no one ever objected, despite being audible in much of the public areas.

The branch librarian at the time was a shy person who appeared to be greatly worried most of the time and had a pink, blinking air about her. It was told of her that she was advised by a doctor to get away from all daily cares and take a holiday in which she could forget all about work and relax in perfect peace. Obediently, she signed up for a cruise holiday in which she and the other passengers would be at sea for fourteen days. The story goes that it was a lovely day when the ship sailed from Portsmouth headed south and she was sitting in a deck chair sunbathing and flicking through the first of the books she intended to read on the voyage. A male passenger approached her and asked her if she were "the woman from the West Hampstead library." When she assented warily, he proceeded to launch into a long list of detailed complaints about the collections and services of the library. As the shoreline receded from view, she realized with a sinking heart that she was saddled with this obsessive bore for two weeks.

The Heath branch library in Keats Grove (a short road that goes from Downshire Hill to South End Green and the edge of Hampstead Heath) was built in 1931 in the grounds of, next to, and modeled on the style of Keats House. It is one of the loveliest settings of any library I know. What is now called Keats House was originally Wentworth Place, two eighteenth-century semidetached houses, one of which was rented by John Keats and his friend Charles Armitage Brown from 1818–1820. The other house was rented by the Brawne family. Keats fell in love with and became engaged to Fanny Brawne, and is said to have written his "Ode to a nightingale" under a plum tree in the garden. In 1820 Keats, seriously ill with tuberculosis, left Hampstead in search of a warmer, drier climate and died in Rome in the following year, aged 25. The two houses were knocked into one in the 1830s and saved from demolition by public subscription; that house was opened as Keats House Museum in 1925. The museum is based on a collection of Keatsiana formed by Sir Charles Dilke, the protagonist of one of the great political scandals of the Victorian age.

I worked in that branch library on a number of occasions and have fond memories of its setting and the warm interior light of the central reading room. One time that I remember clearly was a day on which I was asked to look after the museum while the curator had his lunch break. There were no visitors and I had nothing to do while waiting for one to come, so I decided to tidy the sitting room—straighten the chairs and tables, etc. When the curator returned I was chagrined to discover that those tables and chairs had been carefully placed, supposedly as they were on the last day Keats lived in the house. Fortunately, there was a detailed chart of the furniture placement and everything was restored to its disorder without anyone knowing about my mistake.

It was about this time, 1958 or so, when I conceived three abiding passions, inevitably from and for books. The first was for James Joyce's books—in particular *Ulysses,* which I read three times in two years. The second was for Arthurian myths. The third was for the lives and works of the Pre-Raphaelite artists and their times. I read *Ulysses* before reading anything else by Joyce (or indeed anything much about the author). I do not know what impelled me to pick up the fat green Bodley Head volume and to begin with "Stately, plump Buck Mulligan . . ." and read on to the final " . . . yes I said yes I will Yes" 933 pages later with such ardor, but that is what I did. I had nothing like the knowledge and education that would have enabled me to understand the book fully but I never had any difficulty with it and believe with all my heart that it is a "good read" as well as all the other superior virtues it possesses. After *Ulysses,* I read the rest of Joyce's works—even attempting twice (and failing twice) to scale the heights of *Finnegans wake.* I read books about Joyce and *Ulysses,* notably those by Stuart Gilbert and Frank Budgen; studied chronologies of Bloomsday and maps of Dublin; and generally immersed myself in the man and his times. My second enthusiasm was for Arthurian myth (the Matter of Britain). I read Mallory's *Morte d'Arthur* and children's versions of the Arthur stories, not to mention T. H. White's *Sword in the stone,* when younger, and had been entranced but my enthusiasm was rekindled by two books—Geoffrey Ashe's *King Arthur's Avalon* and R. S. Loomis's *Arthurian literature in the Middle Ages.* I read all I could of Sir Gawain and of the Fisher King, of the religious symbolism of the myths, of the historical background (such as it was) of Ambrosius and the last days of the Romans in Britain. I even read Tennyson's *Idylls of the King,* which awoke in me a love of Victorian poetry that had been kindled by Macaulay's *Lays* and, in turn, led to a fascination with the Victorian era and its history. I even conceived the idea of writing a London *Ulysses,* telling of a day in the life of ordinary people that was based on Arthurian myth, but did no more that create an outline of what would have been, in all probability, among the worst novels ever written. I had no knowledge of art then (and have little more now) but my Joycean and Arthurian obsessions led me to the Pre-Raphaelites. I saw prints of their Arthurian and other paintings in books long before I saw the actual paintings in galleries in London and, later, in Liverpool and Manchester. More important, I read William Gaunt's brilliant books on the Pre-Raphaelites and the aesthetic movement in the Victorian age. In some strange way, these three interests merged and such interior visual life as I have is populated by Holman Hunt's and Rossetti's Arthurian and Odyssean visions of knights and monsters and pale, long-necked "stunners."

A DREAM OF KILBURN

Last night I dreamt I went to Kilburn Branch Library again. Jean Smith was there, very little altered, except her hair was now steel gray. Mr.

Jones was there, aged and stooped but quite recognizable. The familiar rooms were now offices of some kind and the three of us were waiting to open the door to let in a group of visitors. There were still a few books left around. The one I picked up was on Christianity and by the bizarre author Ayn Rand. It was signed by the author and by George, one of the porters at Hampstead Central Library. This seemed odd, even for a dream. This was not the first time, nor will be the last, that Kilburn Library has come back to me in a dream.

....

Kilburn is the western part of the old borough of Hampstead. All the books describe it as being a fashionable spa in the eighteenth century," something that was even harder to believe in the time of which I am writing than it is now. Then, it was a run-down working class area of terraced houses in little streets running between West End Lane—the westernmost border of the marginally fashionable parts of Hampstead, which themselves were west of the truly fashionable parts of the borough. It was the home of so many Irish that it was widely known as "County KIL-burn." It was there, halfway down Cotleigh Road, a short street on a hill running down from West End Lane to Kingsgate Road, that I found my ideal library—a place that lives in me today nearly fifty years later as vividly as it did then. The library, built in 1902, is a simple brick one-story double-fronted structure with a basement. You walked up stone stairs to the big wooden double doors, both opened during library hours, down a corridor to the lending/reference library on the left and the children's library on the right. Each had entrance doors and were high ceilinged with tall windows to let in the wan Kilburn light. The library was in operation until 2006, at which point it became the West Hampstead Women's Centre and the library was moved to accommodation in the Kilburn High Road, a much-traveled thoroughfare of little charm. In the year 1957–58, the Kilburn library had 2,597 adults and 1,004 children as registered readers. They borrowed 132,374 adult books (70 percent of which were fiction) and 44,239 children's books. That works out to be 51 books per adult, and 44 per child that year. O, how the world has changed!

When I was posted to the Kilburn branch library in 1958, there were five staff members—the librarian Tom Howard, Mr. Jones, and Miss Huggett (both of whom had worked for the Hampstead library for decades—they were then in their 60s); Jean Smith, who ran the children's library; and me. There was also a porter (janitor) called Mr. Dowley, a short, gnomelike Irishman with a sweet nature, a strong brogue, and a great fondness for

Kilburn Branch Library

drink. He was unmarried and spent, I think, all his leisure hours with all the other unmarried Irishmen in the many pubs in the vicinity of Kilburn High Road. He tended a vast boiler called a Robin Hood, which contrived to be both efficient and unpredictable.

Tom Howard had not been the branch librarian long and was then young. He was the only qualified librarian on the staff but, a quiet and unassertive man, did not make much of a point of that and found humor in the fact that all the regular users of the library thought that Mr. Jones was in charge. One day, he and Mr. Jones were working together at the small central desk in the adult library when an elderly man greeted them with "Morning, Mr. Jones, I see you've got the lad with you." Mr. Jones (I do not believe I knew his first name or ever heard him addressed as anything but "Mr. Jones") had joined Hampstead Library before World War I (I believe in 1911). He still held a grudge against the deputy borough librarian—Ernie Knowles—for not serving in that war as he did and thus, as Mr. Jones saw it, using the time to gain advancement. He was a courtly tallish gentleman with silver hair who invariably wore blue double-breasted suits with white shirts and a pocket handkerchief peeking out of his top pocket. He had one jet black eyebrow and one white eyebrow, a singularity of which he seemed proud. I once heard a child ask his mother in a whisper why his eyebrows were different colors. She whispered "Shhh! You have no idea the trouble that man has seen!" Mr. Jones, who was invariably in a good humor, showed no other signs of a troubled life. He was quite deaf, wore no hearing aid, and often improvised answers to questions that he could not hear. I can see him now, rubbing his chin thoughtfully, and saying "I'm sure I've seen that around here somewhere" when asked if we had the *Encyclopædia Britannica*, the many volumes of which were gleaming on their shelves two feet away. We sometimes went for lunch together in a pub on the Kilburn High Road. I took it for granted then but it is surprising to me now that he seemed to welcome the company of a teenager and was happy to chat over our sandwiches and during the walk to and from the pub. We never drank beer with those lunches and he warned me against the dangers of having alcohol on my breath when dealing with the public. Nevertheless, I was always happy to hear him say, "How about lyonch?" Mr. Jones lived in Cricklewood and was married, but I knew nothing about him beyond his kindly, unruffled Kilburn library life.

Miss Huggett was a staff member of many decades standing who was spending the latter years of her career in Kilburn branch library. She made her lunch daily in the staff room as a result of which the room always bore at least the whiff, and sometimes the strong smell, of boiled potatoes and long-boiled cabbage and Brussels sprouts. She always wore an apron, usually floral, with a capacious pocket in the front in which she was wont to carry the "reserves" (cards that users had filled out to reserve books and request them from other branches). She did not trust the other members of staff with the reserves and would take them to her house when she took her annual two-week holiday. I was surprised that no one complained about the hiatus in the popular service. She retired in 1959, having joined the library during the First World War.

Jean Smith was a bustling, busy woman who ran the children's library, which was heavily used, not least by the teachers and schoolchildren from the elementary school at the end of Cotleigh Road. She was assiduous in putting on puppet shows, staging plays performed by the children, and reading to circles of quiet children in the scheduled story hours. She had a gentleman friend called Jim, who was called "Lucky Jim" behind Jean's back. Jim and Jean had met in a NALGO convalescent home. He was widely suspected of leading a double life, at least, since his appearances were spasmodic and his leavings frequent. He made Jean very happy and she was always girlish and lipsticked in the fur coat that he had given her. They were excellent company when together.

Tom Howard, Jean Smith, Miss Huggett, Mr, Jones, outside Kilburn Branch Library, c. 1956

The great English playwright, Joe Orton, and his companion Kenneth Halliwell were serial abusers of library materials (an offense for which they were both jailed). Though I remember seeing them only once—in the Hampstead Central Library—they were users of the Kilburn branch library. Orton had the face of a slightly doughy boy, the pastiest complexion I have ever seen, and a slyly mocking smile. Halliwell was taller, bald, and sinister in black. Most of their vandalism was devoted to decorating their flat floor to ceiling with plates from library books, but some of it was more rococo, such as the book they borrowed from the Kilburn branch, hollowed out so that it formed a kind of box, and left on the shelf containing a chocolate bar and a note saying the chocolate was for the "old trout"—Annie Huggett.

The handsome singer and actor John Gower was a patron of the Kilburn branch library in the 1950s. As a child, he was known as the "Boy Wonder of Wapping," because of his prematurely deep bass-baritone singing voice. By the time I met him, he had already been in a West End musical and was a regular at the Player's Theatre, the revivalist Victorian music hall, but was a friendly library user with no side. The Player's Theatre, under the arches at Charing Cross, was housed in a Victorian music hall called "Joy's" (after a Mr. Joy who owned and ran it). The 1950s and 1960s incarnation was called "Late Joys"—a reference both to its history and the delights of listening to the performers and chorus singing "Swing me just a little bit higher, Obadiah, do," "Oh, Nicholas, don't be so ridiculous (I don't like kissing in the daytime)," and "K-K-K-Katy" while drinking beer at the tables provided to the audience.

The two years I spent in Kilburn as a junior assistant were, in many ways, the formative years of my life in libraries. I learned a lot there, mostly subconsciously and mostly indirectly. There were long tables at the far end of the lending library at which sat, every day and from early in the morning, a number of older citizens who were there to read the many newspapers taken by the Kilburn branch. They waged a fierce competition for the most favored titles, including such unsportsmanlike strategies as the first at the newspaper rack collecting two or three papers and reading one while sitting on the others. This and other maneuvers were the occasion of muttered disputes, evil eye glances, snorts of disdain, and rolled eyes. I played my part in the daily drama by sorting the delivered papers before the library opened and arranging them on the racks in order, before, as the junior person, opening the main doors at 8 a.m. to let the four or five regular newspaper readers begin their unacknowledged race down the corridor, through the double doors of the lending library, and across to the racks to be the first to grab today's *Daily mirror* or *Daily telegraph*. This taught me a lot about the local library as a social center—a place for those who could probably have afforded the cost of their own copy of their favorite newspaper from the newsagent on the corner of Kingsgate Road, but chose the informal community of the daily struggle in the library. Besides, where else would they have gone that afforded light, warmth, a comfortable chair, and a wide table on which to spread their papers? Nothing in life is exactly what it seems, and the library was more than just a purveyor of reading matter to those retired people. The small newspaper-reading crowd was the opening act of the rhythms of the library day. Retired men and women would appear to return and borrow books throughout the day, as would a few of the unemployed (most of them stayed in the library to read for an hour or so and thus pass the weary hours). There were a smattering of women with young children—not as many as one, looking back, might expect in the 1950s, but this was a working-class area, many of Kilburn's young mothers had jobs, and someone with a young child was more likely to be an "off the books" child minder or an older relative than the stay-at-home mother. One of the more irritating assumptions of many in the middle class is that women joined the workforce for the first time in the 1960s and 1970s. Poor and working-class women have always worked, but it was as chars, nannies, factory women, waitresses, and shop assistants—all of whom are invisible to the middle-class retrospective gaze. Then there were the "researchers," solitary men who would spend hours reading reference books and writing in notebooks, usually in green ink. In the afternoons the organized classes from the local elementary school would be brought in by their teachers to listen to Jean's story hour or to pursue the topics of the class; later individual older children would come to the library to do their homework. After five, working people would arrive, and then there was a lull for dinner followed by the late stragglers eager to borrow something to read before closing time at 7 p.m. After the last reader (as we called them in those far-off days) had left, I would straighten the tables and chairs, sort and shelve some of the late returns, tidy the newspapers, turn off the lights, and, careful to lock the door behind me, be walking up the hill to West End Lane and on to West Hampstead Station by 7:25, if I were lucky.

Since it was a heavily Irish area, we had large numbers of books on Ireland—the Lakes of Killarney, Irish castles, etc.—that mostly sat unread while the relatively few books on Australia and other countries flew off the shelves. Observing this was my first lesson in library collection development—that collections should be built on analysis of the real, not perceived, needs of the populations served and that the number of titles collected in each subject should be proportionate to those needs. I also learned that people care passionately about the texts they read and that their interactions with those texts are many and various. There were two shelves labeled "Mysteries," upon which we would put recently returned detective stories—then as now, a very popular genre. The many shelves of general fiction stretched away to their right. One morning, when we had few mysteries returned and the shelves bore only a few books, I heard a woman say to her companion, "They never have any books in this library." There must have been a few thousand books within easy reach, but none of them interested this woman. This taught me that a library consists of a multidimensional myriad of collections, each with a public of one, and not the orderly unitary collection of the librarian's dream. If you looked at the back end leaves of any thriller, romance novel, or Western in Kilburn library, you would be very likely to find a neat row of cryptic penciled or ink (often red ink) signs (say, +, *, ‡, or □). Each of these was the private sign of a reader of that genre. Since there were a large number of titles in each genre and since many of them are similar, the sign was a precaution against taking out a book that had already been read. One slow morning, a woman approached me at the desk and asked me "Who wrote, 'The quality of mercy is not strained'?" It happened to be one of the few things I remembered from my schooling, so I replied "Shakespeare, in *The merchant of Venice*." She was startled and replied, "Not Ella Wheeler Wilcox?" When I shook my head, she asked if she could borrow an eraser, opened the book she was carrying, and began rubbing in the margins. The author had written " . . . as Shakespeare wrote 'The quality of mercy is not strained.'" She had crossed the line out vigorously and written, "NO!! ELLA WHEELER WILCOX!!!!" in deeply scored capital letters. The result was a smudged page with the incised letters still clearly readable after the pencil marks were removed. At least she cared. I learned a great many things from the mundane task of filing cards (received from the central library) into the catalogue. These 5-by-3 white cards with their holes (dimensions and placing of which were, I discovered later, in accordance with an international—ISO—standard) were as familiar and essential a part of libraries then as they are redolent of far-off days now. They were secured in place by long thin metal rods. When learning to file, the tyro was told to put the cards "above the rod" so that they could be checked before the rod was withdrawn and the cards allowed to fall into place. The intricacies of such things as the extended Roman alphabet (even in Kilburn we came across cards containing the odd é or æ or ø), word-by-word as opposed to letter-by-letter filing, and the filing of subdivisions of subject headings were endlessly fascinating to me and I must have been one of the few people who regularly volunteered to file in a card catalogue. One late evening, two boys of 11 or so were discovered in the corridor between the children's and lending libraries, each armed with a metal rod which they had removed from the catalogue in the children's library, re-enacting a fencing scene from *Robin Hood* or one of the pirate films that were then popular. It seemed funny at the time and imaginative on their part, but one shudders to think what might had happened had they not been interrupted.

The days went by for nearly two years. I would take an early 113 bus from Hendon (if I had been home the night before) and then the Bakerloo Line tube train from Finchley Road station for the short ride to West Hampstead and a five-minute walk down West End Lane to the top of Cotleigh Road. I have always been an early riser and prided myself on being the first to the library. I enjoyed the quiet and the mundane tasks before opening the front door at 8. I took a tea break in the little staff room at the back that invariably smelled of Annie Huggett's cooked lunch and left for lunch at noon—occasionally with Mr. Jones in the pub in Kilburn High Road, and occasionally at the restaurant on the corner of Broadhurst Gardens and West End Lane in which a plate of spaghetti Bolognese—an exotic delicacy unknown in Hendon at that time—could be had for two shillings and sixpence. Since my weekly wage was four pounds before tax and other deductions, this was an investment. More often than not, I ate cheese sandwiches in the staff room while reading literature high and low—Dickens, Thackeray, Eliot, Graves, and the like alternating with current best sellers by Morris West, James Jones, Herman Wouk, and all the other American writers of places and events that could not have been further from the Hendon-Kilburn experience if they had been set on one of the smaller moons of Saturn. These were all hefty books—six hundred pages or more of characters, incident, and, crucially, sex. The latter seems mild by today's standard but did not then. Thus it was that American books and films created in my mind an America that was irresistibly alluring and seductive, an America of guns, villains, humor, silken legs, gumshoes, wide-open spaces, sunshine, cocktails, and adultery—all of which were, as far as I knew, absent from North West London fifty years ago. The afternoon would wear on but it was one of the only jobs I remember in which I never once watched the clock.

I spent the evenings, and very occasionally the nights, with various girls, none of who would qualify as "girlfriends," with my friend Mac and with John Garforth, usually drinking in Hampstead pubs, in cinemas and coffee bars, in people's bed-sitters drinking cheap red wine and talking about books, politics, films, and the few other things that engaged our interests in the desultory, ill-informed, dogmatic way of young people who have read too much and experienced too little. It seems a wonderful foreign country now, half a century later, but I was plagued with a sense of things missed and of the pointlessness of life outside books and films. We had all read Colin Wilson's *The outsider* (possibly the most overrated book ever published) and recognized our underappreciated, fascinating, lonely selves in its heady mixture of half-digested philosophizing and superficial erudition. (Wilson himself—the polo-necked Nietzsche of the post-war lower middle class—was in the habit of visiting the library and enquiring about the number of reservations for *The outsider* and the number of times it had been borrowed.) I was writing poetry (of a sort) and had ambitions to write a novel. I was living at home, after a fashion. I did not have a steady girlfriend, though I was often in love, in a way. The women and girls with whom I fell in love rarely requited it and those who did soon tired of me. Though I liked my work, the idea of spending the rest of my working life in libraries did not occur to me—for one thing, I had no qualifications or any reasonable expectation of acquiring them; for another, I felt that I was destined for higher things, the more enticing for being barely formulated. I never had any money—my tiny salary went for a modest contribution to my penurious family, for the dowdy clothes required by the job, for cigarettes and drinks, for cinema tickets and bus fares, and I was always out of money well before the end of the month came round. A better, richer life seemed unattainable, absent some life-changing event. It never occurred to me then that I could have changed my life by doing mundane things such as studying for exams, going on the stage, becoming politically active, or any one of a number of possibilities that were open to a healthy, articulate, intelligent young man with no ties. It was not that I lacked confidence. Looking back, it seems that my social circumstances and lack of drive conspired to make me passive and to wait for something to turn up. After all, I had landed in the library more or less by happenstance and that led me to believing that the best course was to hope for a simple twist of fate. Out of this and my fascination with all things French (born of my reading and seeing French films at the Everyman) came the hare-brained idea that changed my life again.

WAR AND PEACE

War is legalised murder.
—Harry Patch, 1898–2009, the last British survivor of the First World War trenches.

Despite the fact that I am writing more than ninety years after the end of what was then called the Great War, I have a direct connection with that orgy of pointless carnage. My uncles, my father's brothers Charles and Desmond, were killed in that war; their brother Dave was gassed in the trenches and suffered the consequences for the rest of his life. I have read many books on the war and its consequences but have never managed to understand fully how its many lessons were never learned and how "the war to end all wars" was succeeded by an even greater conflict only twenty years later. I decided, when in my late teens, that there is no such thing as a good war; that all wars are, ultimately, futile; that militarism and jingoism are malign and ever-present forces; and that of all the isms that have plagued the world in the past centuries, nationalism and imperialism (nationalism projected on to other peoples) are the most pernicious. In short, I am a pacifist and an internationalist who believes that the oppressed and exploited of all countries are one people with a common struggle against oppressors who have much in common, no matter under which flag they operate. My pacifism was influenced by that of my friends John Garforth and Philip Johnson-Laird; also, I am sure, by some psychological reaction against my poor father's career as a soldier. However, it is a deeply held belief that is rooted in intellectual and historical analysis and in an aversion for George Orwell's bleak warning—"If you want a vision of the future, imagine a boot stamping on a human face—forever." I have lived long enough to have seen the tragedies of Korea, South East Asia, and the Falklands (Malvinas); the continuing debacles of Iraq and Afghanistan; the slaughters of Rwanda, the Congo, East Timor, Angola, and Northern Ireland; and the bloody late colonial wars as Britain, France, and the others shed their empires—all those millions of people dying for nothing, all those societies smashed, and all the famines and other ills with which conflict afflicts the powerless. I will don no uniform, march under no flag, and partake in none of the empty patriotic rituals that sustain wars and turn peoples against each other.

6

Paris and Afterwards, 1960–1962

I cannot now remember how it began, but the idea was born in the early months of 1960. I would leave the library and, with my school friend Bryan "Mac" McEnroe, leave London and England and go to Paris. I am sure the idea came to us when out drinking in Hampstead, and I am sure it came about because of the combination of lack of success in forming a lengthy relationship with a girl (though I had started to go out with Anne Gillett in 1959), my general sense of pointlessness and lack of direction, the vision of life embodied in French films seen at the Everyman cinema in Hampstead and in books about and from France, the sense that I could never become the writer I wished to be in northwest London (though I had no more idea than a newborn bird how to do that anywhere), and the essential heedlessness of youth. Mac was working for the wine shipper Justerini & Brooks in their shop in the West End. Neither of us thought our jobs were leading to careers but neither of us had more than a hazy idea of what going away to Paris would lead to or how it would be when we got there. Thus it was that we spent the evenings of the early months of 1960 talking of Paris and how, on the evening of the 30th of June of that year, we boarded the ten o'clock night train from Waterloo Station to the Gare du Nord, each with a small bag and a very few pound notes. I had resigned from Hampstead Public Library, said goodbye to Kilburn, been wished well by the other staff there, heard the gloomy forebodings of my parents and Mr. Dowley (who had visited Paris once and found it wanting), and, with scarcely a backward look, left for a different and better way of life—all the more alluring for being utterly unknown.

I remember walking along the long platform by the train with increasing excitement and apprehension on that evening of the hinge of the year. We opened a door at random and entered an eight-seat compartment already occupied by three young American men. It turned out that they were students from the University of Washington, that they were called Tom, Bob, and John, and that they were off to Paris for a few days en route to Moscow to witness the Gary Powers trial. Their exotic (to us) origins and their exotic destination combined with their sheer Americanness (they had fawn drip-dry suits!) made them wonderful traveling companions and a peculiarly fitting embellishment of this marvelous adventure. They had a copy of the *Herald-tribune* and, on seeing it, I filched a line from Peter de Vries, opening the conversation by saying "Hark! The *Herald-tribune* sings." That and our pretentious chatter about Joyce, Ingmar Bergman, and Khrushchev (among many others) made them think that we were fellow students and not just two unemployed hobbledehoys off on a lark. I think the lack of comprehension was mutual, as I had only the haziest idea of where the state of Washington was and no idea at all of the lives of middle-class American college students in 1960 (other than what I now know are the erroneous impressions I had picked up from films—mostly Robert Wagner romancing blonde co-eds at "hops" while wearing peculiar two-tone jackets and a greased quiff). The train drew away from the station and out into the dingy darkness of South London and beyond into the Kent countryside and down to Dover, the English Channel, and the waiting ferry. I had never left England before, and the sight of the giant ferry and the gray night sea, the clank of chains and the banging of metal ramps, the salty smell of the night air, the taste of the sandwiches and beer we bought in the train café were, almost literally, intoxicating. It was a thrill to hand my new passport to the palpably bored official in the shed near the sea into which we straggled in long slow lines, to return to the smoky, slightly grubby compartment, and to wait for the moment when the train inched forward amid all the din of metal on metal that attended the stowing of a whole train in the great ungainly boat. After the ferry pulled away from the shore and I had seen the white cliffs of Dover for the first time, Mac and I parted from the young American men, leaving our bags in the compartment, and went to the bar. I had no way of judging, but it seemed to be somewhat rough when we were out into the open sea, the floor tipping and yawing as we learned to steady our pints of beer. We sat in a curved banquette looking out of a porthole at the little there was to see. Shortly after, a man in his 40s, wearing a crumpled beige cotton suit and a dirty looking tie knotted two buttons down from his open shirt collar, sat at the other end of the banquette and drank from his glass of whisky and water. "Off to France?" he said. We nodded. He leaned forward to come a little nearer so that we could see every detail of his grimy, stubbled face. "I am from Nebraska," he said "and I will tell you what I believe." He took a deep drag on his untipped cigarette and blew a sideways stream of smoke with a great air of satisfaction. "Yes, sir," he said, smiling "I come here—Europe—" (he pronounced it as something near "Yerp") "every year and I'll tell you why." He paused and smiled again. "Yes, sir, every year and I'll tell you why. Because . . ." he banged his fist on the table "I believe in free and open prostitution (he pronounced it something like "proz-did-yew-shun") and that's what they have here. Free. And. Open. Proz-did-yew-shun!" He smiled his inward smile again, seemingly focused on his visions and not on the dingy ferry bar wreathed in cigarette smoke and smelling of beer and fried food.

We slept intermittently in the bar, waking to the pitch and creaks of the boat and, finally, to the watery cold light of dawn seeping through the portholes. We went up to one of the decks from which we could see the dark shoreline and, dimly, a few unprepossessing buildings. This was it. This was Calais; from it the road and the railway ran south to Paris—the City of Light and romance—and south from Paris the lightly peopled vastness of *la France profonde* and, beyond that, the sparkle, sun, sand, and sex of the Riviera and the Mediterranean. I knew all that intellectually, but my heart was disappointed to find that the first glimpse of foreign land, of a sliver of the northeastern edge of the great Eurasian landmass, was so drab and uninspiring. Subsequent years of traveling extensively have convinced me that there are few places on earth that inspire on first approach and many that depress but I did not know that then. The great boat clanged and thumped as it docked, and the metal ramps that had risen before we left Dover banged down and the clanking and roaring, the din of metal on metal and stone, of gigantic chains unreeling, of engines slowing down, of men shouting, of whistles, bells, and nameless mechanical activity heralded the imminence of the time to disembark. We left the boat and walked along the concrete to the customs hall. The *douaniers* wore blue uniforms and blue kepis, the working men all wore their *bleus* with a Gallic swagger. A few suspicious, alert looking policemen (I assumed gendarmes, but they could have been from any arm of the complex French police forces) scanned the passengers lazily but made no moves. My passport was stamped (for the first time) and flicked back at me dismissively. The customs shed smelled of briny air, engine oil, and the smoke of *Gauloises disque blue* (or perhaps they were Gitanes?)—my first really *French* experience—and it was with anticipation that we waited on the platform for the train to trundle off the ferry. Within the hour, we were back in the compartment with Tom, Bob, and John and off south to Paris. The countryside of northeastern France is undistinguished physically, especially on a slightly damp, cool day, but the names of the places on the way summoned the ghosts of the First World War and echoed in our minds—from St. Omer to Béthune to Arras past signs to Amiens and Cambrai, to crossing the Somme into Picardy, in which the roses still bloom. It was disconcerting to see these bland fields and huddled, quiet towns while remembering that they were the scene of unspeakable carnage and bloody folly only forty-two years before. The morning wore on and the names on the signs and stations were less familiar until finally we began to see suburban streets then tall city housing, vast cemeteries, the twists of the Seine, main roads, and all the other signs that we were on the Île de France and in the outskirts of the city. Tom, Bob, and John talked of their plans for Paris and hiring a car to drive to Moscow as the train rattled through concrete canyons and past tall blocks of flats. No one in my family even owned a car, though my mother talked nostalgically of driving during the war, and they might as well have been talking of chartering a rocket and riding to Venus. They had a hotel room booked; we, of course, had not. Eventually, the train arrived at the Gare du Nord in the 10th arrondissement and, amid the usual incomprehensible and clashing announcements, we took our bags and walked down the long platform to the concourse and out into the forecourt of the station on the rue de Dunkerque. It was a gray and slightly damp morning but as sparklingly foreign and French as our hearts might desire. There were wet cobblestones gleaming; policemen whistling and shouting; Peugeots, Citroëns, Renaults, and bicyclists careening everywhere; pavement cafes with red umbrellas over their tables; newspaper placards trumpeting stories about "KROUTCHEW" and "LUMUMBA"; art nouveau and art deco flourishes everywhere; posters advertising concerts, cigarettes, vermouth, singers, tinned goods, and the beaches of Normandy; and there was an overwhelming sense of foreignness and the possibility of adventure. We said good-bye for the time being to Tom, Bob, and John, crossed the rue de Dunkerque and looked back at the grand rose-gray stone facade of the station, the tricolor drooping in the still air above the highest of the heroic statues that adorn the roof and facade. It is still one of my favorite buildings—the gateway to another country and, it seemed at the time, another life.

We met Tom, Bob, and John a day later in their hotel room, noting at least one of their drip-dry suits hanging wetly from a doorjamb. On a later visit we entered the room in the aftermath of a fight over a dispute, about which museums to visit, between Tom and Bob that resulted in at least one split lip. We saw them, two of them for the last time, the day before they left for the drive east across the Iron Curtain to Moscow and a date with history. So there we were, knowing no one, with a few francs in our pockets, rudimentary French, the names of two contacts who, for all we knew, had neither knowledge of or interest in our existence, and no plans other than to change our lives.

I can recall the events of the next three months only in patches—often vividly illuminated patches, but patches nevertheless. We stayed in a small room in a hotel for the first weeks after our arrival; met the two people whose names had been given to me by my mother (they were friends of friends of friends, if that) and were treated to meals and advice by both; we secured menial employment in the OEEC headquarters; we ate in many cheap restaurants and cafes; we pawned some objects at a *mont de piété* near Montmartre; we walked along the broad banks of the Seine watching the lovers and the *bateaux mouches,* the painters and the tourists, the pensioners and the children; we drank a good deal of red wine; we individually had passages of arms with a few women, but had little to offer any of them; we went without food from one Friday lunchtime to the following Monday dinnertime and shared our last yellow Gauloise as we walked along the banks of the Seine on the Saturday of that weekend; we lodged with a family and improved our French; and we finally parted when I decided I had to go home in late September. Edith Piaf singing "*Milord*" and a band playing a bouncy song that sounded like "*Picarella de la luna*" were to be heard everywhere. To this day, just a bar or two of the Little Sparrow singing, "*Allez. . . . venez,. . . . Milord!*" can transport me to Paris in 1960. I wrote poems of a dreadful sort in hotels, in bars, and sitting outside churches and kept none of them; planned a novel that came to nothing; sought a better job that required better French than I possessed; and wrote to and received letters from Anne Gillett. I discovered that my bohemianism had its limits and I was not cut out for rackety, uncertain living (probably the most valuable lesson of my first foreign journey, but one that I resented and fought against).

Our trip to Paris was undertaken only two years after Charles de Gaulle had seized power in France and not much more than a year after the Fifth Republic was proclaimed with de Gaulle as its first president. There were palpable tensions in French political life between the left and right, the clericalists and the secularists, the students and the authorities, and, most important, over the still unresolved struggle for Algerian independence from

France. Everywhere in the streets of Paris there were armed policemen and soldiers, and there was nothing more foreign to a London eye than the sight of a smartly uniformed and booted officer gazing alertly from his reinforced surveillance post, automatic rifle over his shoulder, and with a look about him of willingness to use it. Stories of the bodies of Algerians being found in the Seine and registered as unsolved murders abounded, as did those the unsavory reputation of the *pieds noirs*—the unreconciled and seemingly irreconcilable French colonists who would continue to resist the independence fighters for two more years.

We began our visit by securing a cheap, small room on the Left Bank in the Hotel Panthéon, 19 place de Panthéon in the 5th arrondissement, in an eighteenth-century building in the heart of the Quartier Latin—old Paris—at the top of the hill of Ste. Geneviève. The hotel is opposite the Panthéon, the laicized church originally dedicated to Geneviève that contains monuments to, and is the resting place of, the great and the good of France—Voltaire, Hugo, the Curies, etc. It is very near the Sorbonne and the Jardin de Luxembourg and a short walk down the Boulevard St. Michel—the fabled *Boul' Mich* of young love and broken dreams—to the Ile de la Cité and the Cathedral of Notre Dame dominating the Seine riverscape. The little streets of the Quartier were the haunts of artists and revolutionaries, *apaches* and tarts, druggies, clowns and unicyclists, students, drunks, communists and anarchists, philosophers, *clochards,* writers, and musicians; old men in black berets who played chess at pavement tables; young women with scarlet lipstick and scarlet berets—people who I knew in my bones, if not yet in my mind, had freer spirits than mine would ever be. The streets of the Quartier were paintings of Utrillo made real, especially when the cobblestones were gleaming after rain on those late summer evenings.

The hotel is still there and now advertises itself as a place in which "stressed out businessmen will feel instantly soothed, hopeless romantics will be enchanted with the air conditioning in every room, you're sure to breathe easier and sleep better." There was not a hint of air conditioning in 1960 but, never having been experienced, it was not missed. Our room was dominated by a gigantic dark brown armoire with two tiny drawers. It had a washbasin, a tiny desk (at which I would write some of my execrable poetry) and chair, and a double bed, all diminished by and living in the shadow of the looming armoire. The bathroom was down the hall and had to be booked with the decidedly uncheery hotel clerk who sat glowering behind his desk in the tiny lobby day and night.

Parisian Metro Station

The clerk appeared to be on duty at all hours and was forever writing in various ledgers or penning complex receipts for every transaction with laborious care, looking up only when he had to and with ill grace. He had little patience with our imperfect French and was driven into a near rage when I, wishing to have a wastepaper basket in the room (to receive the crumpled remnants of my writing) and, having asked someone the French word for that useful article (it is *corbeille*) and misheard the answer, asked him three times for a *corbeau* (the French word for "crow"). His reaction to my repetition of what I thought was a reasonable request was to stand and dismiss me from his presence with an imperious wave of his right arm and a string of curses. One evening, I came in to the lobby and was arrested by another wave of his arm, open palm outwards. "Monsieur Gorman," he said, glaring at me, "*defense de craché dans la bassinet!*" Having said that, he lowered his head and resumed his writing. I remember reviewing my conduct quickly but, although some things that he might not like were he to learn of them came to mind, spitting in the washbasin was not among them. I had brushed my teeth there but was in the habit of sluicing water to remove the traces of toothpaste. Perhaps he had me figured as a potential basin spitter and this was a pre-emptive warning? I never knew.

THE MÉTRO

> *The apparition of these faces in the crowd*
> *Petals on a wet, black bough.*
> —Ezra Pound, "In a station of the Métro"

The sensory experience and the ambiance of the Paris Métro have remained with me for fifty years. Smells of French cigarettes, pungent garlicky food, and the stale, sourish, rushing subterranean air that assailed you from the point when you entered through the art nouveau green iron entrances designed by Hector Guimard, with MÉTROPOLITAIN in curving letters on the rounded white enamel under the canopy. After you had deposited your *jeton*—the metal token needed for access to the trains—steep stairs took you down to the semi-lit platforms and the evocative advertising posters, working men in blue denim with their lunch boxes, black-clad widows, working women with their ill-shaped packages and bulging shopping bags with baguettes protruding, the *Jamais plus d'un litre par jour* warnings and the posted law against public drunkenness (*Loi de repression de l'ivresse publique*); the notices that seats must be surrendered to the *mutilés de la guerre* (of which there were, sadly, still many in Paris in 1960); and the railway employees with their peculiarly French air of officiousness. The stations themselves were not unreasonably clean and, in many cases, showed their age, but they were magical places with magical names—way stations to yet more magical places, their names redolent of history, of battles, of commerce, of the éminences grises, saints, and soldiers of France. Who could resist a journey that takes you from Arts et Métiers to Porte des Lilas (lilacs) by way of Goncourt, Pyrénées, and the Place des Fêtes?

One of the names we had as contacts was that of a Jean W., the daughter of a French father and English mother who lived in Paris and worked for an international organization. We telephoned her and were very pleased to be invited to her flat in the rue St. Honoré in the 1st arrondissement—a short distance but a far cry from the Left Bank. This was the area of money, expensive shops, black-clad concierges behind shuttered windows, the Comédie Française and the Louvre, the garden of the Palais-Royale and the rue de Rivoli. We took the Métro one evening in July from the Cardinal Lemoine station in the rue Monge to the Louvre/Palais Royale station in the rue St. Honoré. After the usual difficulty, we managed to locate the building in which Jean W. lived, indicated by small cream numbers on a blue metal plate near an iron gate to a small, silent courtyard with a large stone urn in the center of the paving. We rang a bell and were admitted by the concierge who buzzed up and showed us the staircase to Jean's flat. It was very bourgeois and comfortable with cream, fawn, and rose colored furniture and what appeared to be Persian carpets. I had dreamed that Jean would be an elegant, worldly, Parisienne of a certain age eager to teach a younger man the arts of life and love—as with most young dreams, one that had only the most tenuous connection to reality. Jean was a very pleasant, nice looking, somewhat reserved woman who clearly regarded us as tall children. She was, as I now realize, generous with her time and in making a good meal for these perfect strangers who must have been of very little interest to her. The gramophone was playing Sidney Bechet—I remember "Stormy weather" and "Madame Bécassine"—and, as I write, I can hear that dulcet swing as if it were playing in the next room. I am not sure I had ever had a meal with a starter before and certainly I had never heard of, let alone eaten, Parma ham with cantaloupe melon. It was delicious but not sustaining (we were young and missing regular meals) and I was relieved to see the arrival of some chicken in a creamy sauce with potatoes and vegetables followed by a cakey dessert. This elegant food, the like of which I had never experienced, was accompanied by slightly chilled red wine—so I learned many things that evening even if it were not the sentimental education of my dreams. Jean cleared the table and, after having given us each a *fine*—another first—sat us down for a combination lecture and chat. It seems that she felt herself, in some vague way, *in loco parentis* or perhaps was simply a kindly soul who felt sorry for us. Amid all the information about what to see and what to avoid (we did little of either) was an opportunity for us to earn money. At that time, it was impossible for British citizens to work for French companies legally, but employment by international organizations was possible. Thus it was that, two days later, we found ourselves on our way to the western edge of Paris and the headquarters of the Organisation for European Economic Cooperation (OEEC), a complex of buildings at 2 rue Andre Pascal in the *très snob* 16th arrondissement near the Bois du Boulogne. (The OEEC was transmuted in 1961 to the Organisation for Economic Cooperation and Development—the OECD—with a wider membership.) The main building is the Chateau de la Muette, which stands on the site of an older chateau of the kings of France that was used variously as a hunting lodge and a place to entertain mistresses. The present chateau was built in the 1920s by a Rothschild. We took the Métro to the La Muette station on the rue de Passy and walked from there to an interview in one of the annex buildings by a very bored Belgian who explained briefly what the OEEC was and did, which had only a peripheral relationship to the task we were being hired to do—collating copies of the vast numbers of papers in English and French (the OEEC's official languages) that were the main product of the organization.

The journey from the Left Bank to la Muette soon became familiar, as did the 6 a.m. routine of café au lait and a buttered tartine while standing in one of the working class cafes near the Métro station and trying to read that morning's newspaper surrounded by men drinking their morning Beaujolais (at that time, there was said to be more Beaujolais drunk in Paris each year than the annual production of the region), Armagnac, or Calvados. Our fellow workers were a disparate lot, in age, origins, and every other way. We had many opportunities to talk to them while we sat at huge circular slowly revolving tables as leaf by leaf stacks of double-sided printed pages went by. These were reports on steel production in Europe in 1958, the prospects for jute imports in the next three years, studies of the German consumer, Portuguese exports, and the like. Our task was to take a leaf from each pile in order and to stack the completed reports in neat piles ready for stapling and onward transmission to an expectant world. We were equipped with little rubber thimbles that facilitated the retrieval of each leaf. It was easy work, if a little soporific, but we put in long hours.

The pages were printed from type set by hand by a large, friendly German-Swiss compositor called Herman Gilli, who wore a wide smile and his hair *en brosse*. He was married to a Frenchwoman and commuted from their house in Chantilly, thirty-five miles north of Paris. He took the time to explain the details and mechanics of the now forgotten art of hand setting—the placing of pieces of type into a "stick" from their cases and justifying (spacing) the lines before putting them, several lines at a time, into "galleys" from which proofs can be pulled. He did this with a speed and deftness born of a life of practice. Herman and his wife and children lived on the family farm, operated by her father. After a week or two he invited us to have Sunday lunch with the family—a gracious and welcome gesture. After lunch, the father took us for a walk around the small farm. At one point he stopped by a field near a wood, pointed in a north easterly direction and said, "The Germans" (he called them *les Boches*) "came from over there in 1940." He pointed a little bit more northerly and said, "And from over there in 1914." He wheeled almost due east and pointed, saying, "And from over there in 1870." He had witnessed the latest two, and his father had witnessed the first, he explained. He looked not sad, but reflective, as if he were wondering from which direction they would come next time.

There were a few young men working on the production of OEEC documents of whom I remember a sad-eyed Algerian who was fond of reciting an English poem he had memorized: "*I remember, I remember, the 'ouse where I was born /And the little window where the sun / Came pipping every morn*"; a flaxen-haired Russian who said his father was a nobleman displaced by the Bolsheviks; and an Alsatian called Schneider (the only pleasant person I have met by that name) who wore an astounding sky blue jacket that appeared to be triple breasted and was replete with many shiny brass buttons. Though I had never seen the like, he proudly called it *un blazer anglais.* I was most impressed by a grave, baggy-eyed, black-mustached Spaniard in his late 40s called Velasquez who worked in the printing area. He had been in France since 1938, having been driven out by what he referred to as *cochons fascistes* ("fascist pigs") and worse. He had been a Loyalist and fought against the Franco forces. I asked him once about the wider war and the German occupation of Paris and all he could say was that it was "difficult"—surely a massive understatement. Though he called himself a working man and wore *bleus,* he spoke French and English as well as his native tongue, and knew a lot about the history of Europe. He had tears in his eyes when he talked of his family and of his country, still in the grip of fascism, fifteen years after that evil had been defeated elsewhere in Europe. He grew angry when he spoke of the "neutrality" of France and the United Kingdom during the Spanish Civil War—a neutrality that amounted to siding with Franco. He spoke longingly of wanting to return to Spain but swore he would never do so as long as "that bastard" was alive. The Caudillo was to live for another fifteen years, and I have often wondered if that was too late for Señor Velasquez—communist and patriot. Another paper collator was a woman in her 60s, at least, with dyed black hair, rouged cheeks, and scarlet lipstick, not always applied as judiciously as it might have been. She had large, dark-pupilled eyes ringed with ebony makeup; those eyes were shiny as she told of being driven from her family home in Romania by "the communists," of how they came across the lawns shooting as they ran, and of her sorrow for the life that she had known that was no more. She almost whispered when she told us that she was a countess and disclosed that she had never been treated by the French with the deference due to her station. The tides of the wars of the twentieth century had washed these people up on the barren shores of the OEEC. It was a privilege to meet them.

Those three months in Paris did not change my life but they did teach me some things about myself and did make me think about a world beyond North London in which there were wonders, tragedies, and far more things than I had even dreamed of. I remember being in a vast crowd near the Champs Élysées on the 14th of July watching a great fireworks display to French oohs and aahs and the belting out of the Marseillaise—the most stirring and bloody of all national anthems—as a pyrotechnic work of art depicting General de Gaulle hung in the night sky and then dissipated in a shower of sparks and explosions. I remember being lonelier than I had ever been in my life, consoled only by the letters I received from Anne Gillett, full of news of Hampstead Library and books read and responses to my increasingly romantic missives. I remember writing into the night, half-drunk on the thin red Nicolas wine bought for very little in liter bottles with plastic stoppers. I remember dinners out in the apartments of kindly but formal people who seemed half-shocked, half-amused at our rackety lives. I also remember the few weeks we lodged with a couple with younger children in a Paris suburb at a reduced rent because we held English conversations with the children. I remember going to see films in dilapidated cinemas in the Left Bank, French films at which the inability to understand at least half the dialogue was more than mitigated by the beauty of the images and, most memorably, a showing of *Baby doll* subtitled in French. At one point Karl Malden's Archie Lee Meighen calls upstairs to his child bride (Carroll Baker) "Git your cotton-pickin' tail down here, you hear!" which the subtitle rendered as "*Allez-y.*"

To my shame, I never visited the great libraries of Paris during those months, but I did visit a municipal library in the 14th arrondissement, near the Avenue du Maine. It had massive closed double doors with a small grille in the center of each. There was no indication that I could see that the library was open but the right door opened when I pulled. Once inside the overwhelming impression was of silence and crepuscular darkness, ill-lit shelves bearing ranks of books in identical bindings, low tables and chairs of dark wood and a high desk in the same style. The walls were decorated with official notices in tiny type that detailed this and that law and warned of the penalties pertaining thereto. It was as far from the slightly dingy friendliness of Cotleigh Road, Kilburn, as a place could be and I felt a sharp pang of . . . what? A kind of bibliographic homesickness, a longing for the familiar and the safe mixed with a sense of not belonging that nothing else in Paris had elicited. A grim-faced mustached man in a tight collar, seated behind the desk, handed me a form, but I left without filling it in, knowing that is was not the place for me.

In the end, I realized that my dreams of being a starving writer in Paris would only be partly achieved —I was in Paris and I had been starving after all—and that I needed a life with more structure and in more familiar surroundings. So it was that I left Paris on the train in late September with a small amount of money in my pocket after paying the fare home, with no ideas about what I would do when I was back in England, with no prospects, with more burned bridges than a young person should have, and no compass. Mac, much better at forming social relationships than I and with far better French, stayed behind and lived and worked in Paris for three more months before returning in early 1961. Our friendship was renewed and remains in one form or another until today.

I remember that day in September 1960 vividly and the coldish rain-washed London that greeted me. The first thing I noticed was the difference in the light—so much cooler and paler than the intense light of Paris. By arrangement I met Anne Gillett at the station. We went to the hugely popular Picasso exhibition at the Tate Gallery after walking hand in hand from Westminster underground station, past the Houses of Parliament, down Millbank to Victoria Tower Gardens, and Lambeth Bridge to the queues, crowds, and massive stairs leading to the great gallery. It was, I believe, the first comprehensive exhibition in Britain of Picasso's art; it was certainly the first time I had ever been to such an event or, I believe, an art gallery. The next day found me deflated and planless in Hendon. My mother was pregnant with her last child—Paul—and my other siblings were 13, 11, 9, and 7. My parents greeted my return with a marked lack of enthusiasm, not least because of the need to make room for me in a house full of family and the lodgers. Anne and I were now officially going out together but that was the only spar to cling to in a sea of formlessness.

For reasons that now elude me, I had decided that I could not go back to work in Hampstead. Since I had left there on cordial terms with everyone, I can only conclude that it was some kind of foolish pride (is there any other kind?) that would not admit that my trip to Paris had been, on some counts, a failure. I had not, however, ruled out the idea of working in libraries. When I was working at Hampstead, I had taken classes at North-Western Polytechnic for the Library Association's First Professional Examination— the FPE (a precondition for entry to library school then). The class was taught by a genial man called Fred Bungay, then working as a librarian for the borough of Hendon (he later became a full-time library school lecturer). I did not take the examination then but was interested to see his name on an advertisement for a junior assistant position in the Childs Hill branch of Hendon Public Libraries. I telephoned Fred at the number given and discussed the position. It is a sign of how free and easy things were then that the conversation concluded with him offering me the job and, fatefully, as it turns out, making an appointment for me to start work in the next week. It was fateful, if farcical, because I did not turn up on the day and at the time arranged. This is inexplicable to me and would be inexcusable if I had ever had an excuse. The fact is that I did not go, was embarrassed beyond measure by the reproachful telephone call I received from Fred the next day, and decided that libraries were out for me. This pointless, foolish episode led me down a diversionary path that could well have ruined my life.

I had to have a job—my parents were explicit in telling me that I was not welcome if unemployed. There was nothing that I wanted to do and nothing for which I had any talent as far as I knew. After talking things over with Anne, I decided that I would seek employment in the commercial world and lay the foundations for a financially successful life. This plan was absurd in both its conception and execution. I was and am completely unsuited for work in the private sector, had neither the aptitude nor temperament to succeed therein, and had no idea how to go about forging such a career. This was proven amply (I now see) by what I did next. I saw an advertisement in the local paper for a position in the local branch of the Cooperative Permanent Building Society—the kind of low-level, white-collar job that was deemed to be ideal for those who had fallen at the O-level hurdle. In those far-off days and in that far-off place, banking and financial institutions such as building societies were very different from their counterparts today. Banks accepted money from their depositors and lent that money to people judged to have the means and potential to repay it. Building societies took deposits from their members—they were, in theory, owned by their members—and lent money for the purchase of houses to those with the ability to repay mortgages over many years. No one, in Hendon at least, had ever heard of derivatives, 100 percent mortgages, sophisticated financial instruments, subprime lending, or any the ruinous folderols and their consequences, such as foreclosures, that have, at the time I write, brought the Western world to its economic knees.

Hendon Central is an area defined by the intersection of the Watford Way (a section of an ancient road now unrecognizable as such and known as the A1) and Queens Road to the east and Vivian Avenue to the west. There was a planted roundabout in the center. The northeast corner of that intersection consists of a concave 1920s structure housing Hendon Central tube station and, in the 1950s, the Fiesta coffee bar. The southeast corner contained the Hendon Gaumont cinema, also dating from the 1920s. The northwest was an undistinguished assemblage of 1930s blocks of flats and shops. The southwest corner was a matching concave structure of shops and banks below and flats above. This was where the Hendon branch of the Cooperative Permanent was housed and to which I went for an interview with the manager, Mr. Jacobs, in October 1960. Alas, the interview went well and I was sent to their London headquarters in Holborn for appraisal and to take a test. Since I was determined to make my way in the financial world, I put my best foot forward and sought to impress with dress and demeanor—the very model of a quiet clerk—and did my best at the written test. The latter proved to be not unlike the Eleven Plus—a combination of "intelligence," verbal, and arithmetical tests—and, thus something for which I had been trained. I was called back a few days later for an interview in Holborn with the London area manager. He was very enthusiastic, told me that I had scored higher on the test than anyone in his memory and that I showed a lot of promise, and offered me the position with intimations of future training and unspecified higher things to follow. This confirmed my opinions that all such tests were bunk and, alas, that, given an opportunity, I could flannel my way through anything. I was greeted very warmly by Mr. Jacobs and my fellow employees at the branch on my first day of work the week after. The work was tedious but easy for me. It consisted largely in taking in deposits from and paying out withdrawals to the building society's local members, and recording the deposits and withdrawals in their passbooks; of accounting for those deposits and withdrawals down to the last penny; of opening new accounts and issuing the passbooks that came with them; and of receiving and keeping records of monthly mortgage payments and keeping records. Quite frequently, the interest rates on mortgages would go up or down and all the staff would work after public hours, in those precomputer days, on making the necessary changes so that all was ready for the next working day. I would also take bags of money to the National Westminster bank office that was separated from the building society by the local branch of the newsagent W. H. Smith. The pleasant bachelor bank clerk's invariable greeting was "How are things in Glockamorra?"

The assistant branch manager was a prematurely balding man in his 30s with a worried air. He was a bachelor and had two ambitions—to succeed

Mr. Jacobs as manager and to be married. He was also fond of beer, as was one of my two fellow clerks. The other played in a Salvation Army Silver Band and had married into the Army so was, perforce, a teetotaler. It seems that it was the music that drew him to that religious sect, not piety, since he complained about the narrow views and social attitudes of his coreligionists. The Sally Army was strong in Hendon for some reason and their navy uniforms and jolly music frequently enlivened Hendon's mean streets. He lived with his wife, who in no way resembled Jean Simmons in *Guys and dolls,* in a street that ran parallel to Sunny Gardens Road. At that time, all the houses had names as well as numbers, mostly of the tweely genteel type such as Dunroamin, Bideawee, or The Cottage, the names being displayed in pokerwork on carved and painted wooden plaques. His was called Yer Tiz, which I took to be Hebrew and, therefore, puzzling, but was, he explained, a jocular Mummerset rendering of "here it is." The staff was completed by a female secretary who took dictation from Mr. Jacobs and had a sort of chilly flirtatiousness that bespoke her status as the fiancée of an estate agent's clerk as loudly as the silver and diamond ring displayed above her cherry red pointed fingernails as she typed at great speed.

I worked in the Cooperative Permanent from October 1960 until May 1962, eighteen increasingly unhappy and fractured months. I was living three inconsistent and mostly incoherent lives. The first was that of my work in that restrained and conservative environment with people to whom I was a stranger and a puzzle. I ate sandwiches (cheese and pickle or corned beef) brought from a nearby sandwich shop in the Watford Way every day for lunch in the staff room behind the public room reading my way through novels, blue Pelican nonfiction books, and books of poetry. I showed up on time, took my breaks promptly and for only the allotted time, and left on the dot of 5 p.m., unless there had been a mortgage rate change and we all had to stay behind. I wore my dark suit, white shirt, and tie every day (sports jackets were permitted only on Saturday mornings and open collars were viewed much as we might think of open flies today) and went on the courses the building society demanded of me. The latter included a three-day affair held in the Bonnington Hotel in Southampton Row attended by promising Cooperative Permanent clerks from all over the country. The tedium of this event and its dinners was relieved only by my encountering a sardonic Welshman whose negative attitudes matched mine (he was very sarcastic about Kingsley Amis, one of his tutors at Cardiff University), as did his willingness to sneak out to a nearby pub for a few pints of beer one evening. I did as good a job as I could of dealing with the public—one of the main parts of my job—but found them much more demanding and inclined to be rude than the patrons of Hampstead's public libraries. To be honest, I think my attitude, given my utter unsuitability for the job, was a contributing factor. I well remember a rat-faced man shouting at me about his balance and, after he had been shown to be wrong, turning at the door and yelling "Remember, mate, the bonus is on you!"

My second life was lived mostly in the pubs and coffee bars of Hampstead, and often with my friends John Garforth and Mac (after he returned from Paris in early 1961), talking of politics, the cinema, books, and all the other topics that made up the parallel universe unknown to the Cooperative Permanent and its denizens. These were often drunken, disreputable evenings that did not always end with me going to the home from which I was increasingly estranged and occasionally resulted in my appearance at the building society (always on time) in yesterday's clothes and with a hangover. I had also become interested in two strands of radical politics—anarchism and the Campaign for Nuclear Disarmament (CND). I was very attracted to the ideas of philosophical anarchism typified by Kropotkin (not to be confused with the violent anarchism, verging on nihilism, of which Blanqui and Bakunin were the inspiration) and in particular his ideas on cooperation as an alternative to social Darwinism.

My third life, and my happiest, was with Anne Gillett. Early on, she was living in Mill Hill with her father, Herbert, a chief architect with the London County Council, her mother, Marjorie (née Cracknell), and her only sibling, her younger sister, Joan. In 1961, they moved to a house in Chorleywood, a town about twenty miles northwest of the center of London in a valley on the border of Buckinghamshire and Hertfordshire. We were becoming more and more romantically entangled and our times together, constrained by our meager finances, consisted of visits to public art galleries, walks in London parks, trips to the public galleries of the House of Commons, and other free entertainments.

Above all, we went to the cinema together—to one cinema in particular, the Everyman cinema in Holly Bush Vale, just west of Hampstead tube station and not far north of St. Mary's school that I had attended in the late 1940s. The Everyman was converted to a cinema (from a live theater that had itself taken over from a nineteenth-century drill hall) in the 1930s and, at the time of which I am writing, was a shrine for those who loved serious films. It was there that I saw films by Bergman, Fellini, Resnais, Antonioni, Truffaut, Godard, and all the other auteurs with whom I fell deeply and permanently in love. It was then a somewhat dingy, if enchanted, spot. The fun began with the queue—there was always a queue snaking down the narrow Holly Bush Vale to Fitzjohns Avenue. It was a small cinema. Buskers—including one called "the Earl of Mustard" who dressed in knee breeches and a powdered wig—entertained for small change; the poet Danny Abse sold copies of his books to the crowd; and the poet and editor Jon Silkin sold copies of his magazine *Stand*.

Once admitted to the sepia gloom, with the projector whirring and the dust motes dancing in the funnel of light above our heads, we would settle to watch these great works of art, almost all with subtitles. This being Hampstead, it was not uncommon for people to laugh at comic utterances in Swedish before the English subtitles appeared on the screen. Bergman's films being what they are, there were not a great many occasions on which to display this particular branch of filmsmanship. The Everyman is now a "luxury cinema experience in the heart of Hampstead Village" inviting one to "indulge on a sofa in our sumptuous screening lounge with waiter service and fine wines." It also shows first-run Hollywood films, which were not at all the fare in the early 1960s. I doubt the wonder of the glory days is still present.

The Everyman—combined with regular reading of *The observer, The Sunday times* (long before when it fell into the clutches of Rupert Murdoch), *The new statesman,* and other magazines—created in me a feeling that I was aware of the main political and cultural currents in Britain in the few years before all was changed utterly by the end of the Chatterley ban and the Beatles' first LP.

My three lives continued into 1961 with increasing disconnection between them. The dreary routines of the building society chafed more and more, my alienation from my fellow workers increased as they grew more suspicious of me—that suspicion being increased by the facts that I was known to read poetry and have left-wing views in an environment in which conventional Tory views not only reigned but were regarded as normal. My farouche night life contrasted with the time I spent with Anne and her family, now removed to their house at the top of a steep hill in Shire Lane (so called because it was the ancient boundary between two counties—Hertfordshire and Buckinghamshire) in Chorleywood in Metroland, the leafy suburbs strung along the Metropolitan Line and celebrated in the poems and other writings of John Betjeman. Things finally began to come to a head when, in the late spring of 1961, I proposed to, and was accepted by, Anne Gillett on the top deck of a Green Line bus traveling from Wendover to Chorleywood. I bought her an opal engagement ring with an unusual setting from a jeweler's in St. John's Wood High Street that she wears to this day—in defiance of the supposed fragility of that lovely stone.

I was turning 20, with no money, no qualifications, no plans, and few prospects. It is a sign of the kindness and strength of character of Anne's father, Herbert Gornall Gillett, then in the last years of his lengthy tenure as an architect with the London County Council, that he accepted our coming marriage without any expressed reservations and welcomed me into their family, despite the many and manifest inadequacies of my background and circumstances as a suitable husband. We planned to be married in a year, and I began to think about returning to libraries and buckling down to the task of becoming qualified and making a career for myself. This decision was not made easily and followed a couple of aborted attempts to create other careers. My enquiries of various publishers were met with justified rejection, though I still wonder how my life in publishing would have gone. I have no such feelings about accountancy, and my heart was not in the farce of subscribing to a correspondence course in accountancy from the beginning. I had no idea what I could do and be but was convinced—again justifiably—that accountancy was not my métier. Though I paid the £19 (almost a month's salary) for the course in advance, I never even looked at the wretched dreary typewritten pages after the first soul-crushing installment. The fact was that librarianship was the only profession in which I stood a chance of success, entry into that profession for a person who had left school at 16 was possible then, and my heart was in it as in no other line of work. The only other possibility was to revert to my 16-year-old state and work for years on gaining entry to university followed by years of study—all with no clear idea of what I would do when I possessed a degree. Since I wanted to get married and to get on with life, that path was unattractive.

Libraries it was, then, and though I carried on my three lives for a year after that decision, my course was set. I spent more time with Anne and her family, less time carousing in Hampstead, and the minimum necessary time in the Cooperative Permanent and with my family. I set myself the task of reading all of Anthony Trollope's novels and the sole happy memory of the Cooperative Permanent was sitting in their otherwise empty staff room at dinner hours and during breaks deep in a political ("Palliser") novel, one of the Barsetshire stories, the wonders of *The way we live now,* or the esoteric pleasures of the likes of *Miss Mackenzie, The Kellys and the O'Kellys,* or *Ralph the heir* (all then out-of-print books freely and easily available through the efficient interlibrary lending service, especially the Joint Fiction Reserve system of the London public libraries). When young, I read more quickly and more sustainedly than now and read at least one book a week, often more. The rift between me and Mr. Jacobs and the rest of the staff became complete. My no doubt sullen and antisocial demeanor toward them had a lot to do with it—at least as much as their hostility to me. They did club together to buy us a wedding present (which is more than I would have done for them)—a clouded glass jug and water glasses set of a "Scandinavian" design—but, when I left in May 1962, it was, I am sure, as agreeable a parting for them as it was for me. Not for the last time, I left a job with no fanfare and without a backward glance but never afterwards with such a sense of liberation. The rest is libraries . . .

A REMARKABLE WOMAN

When my family lived in The Grove, Golders Green, in the 1940s I acquired a stack of copies of Reader's Digest, and read them in sequence. The magazine was stapled, not perfect bound. These copies were published in 1947 and 1948, printed on glossy paper, and spoke of things about which I knew nothing. It was full of uplifting stories about people of whom I had never heard, usually of a Republican and evangelical stamp (it seems that someone called Peter Marshall loomed large in that world), information about American life that was, in equal parts, exotic and scarcely believable, jokes that I usually failed to get because of the unfamiliar slang, and a feature called "The most unforgettable person I've met." The latter was written by "ordinary people" and featured an array of crusty country doctors, judges, and the like, war heroes, blind pianists, nurses, politicians, Christian athletes, etc. These panegyrics fascinated me despite my ignorance of the people profiled and the world in which they lived. A 9-year-old in Golders Green in the late '40s knew less than nothing about doctors in Vermont—or about Vermont, come to that.

If I were forced to write for that feature, it would have to be about my mother, Alicia Felicia Gorman, née Barrett (1918–1998). She had an indomitable will, a wicked wit, a ferocious, ungovernable temper, and a bottomless capacity to charm, dominate, and avenge. She was handicapped by her cleft palate and by her lifelong penuriousness. She had six children but was not a natural mother or even someone who particularly liked children. She was a pious Catholic, a daily Mass-goer in later life, but scorned many of the strictures of her church and knew priests too well to have reverence for them as a class. She was monumentally insecure and violent in her response to slights great and small—a great bearer of grudges and grievances. She was also embarrassingly generous and a great party-giver whose only fault in that respect was that she never wanted her parties to end and, therefore, all such occasions ended in tears (to use one of her favorite phrases). One of the strangest features of her life was her lengthy involvement with the affairs of the Hospital of Saints John & Elizabeth—a Catholic hospital owned by the Knights of Malta and run by the Sisters of Mercy, a nursing order with a large convent adjacent to the main hospital. This despite her social standing, lack of money, and living far from the leafy splendors of St. John's Wood, once the home of artists and the mistresses of the elite but transformed into one of the chic areas of London. She became a member of the Ladies Association of the hospital—a group of well-off and well-connected Catholic ladies who held fêtes and the like to raise money for the hospital, was elected to the Board of the Association, worked tirelessly as their honorary (i.e., unpaid) secretary, became friends with many of the nuns (forming intense relationships and becoming privy to the secrets of the community), and generally created a place for herself in a milieu that was the preserve of the kind of people she wanted to emulate, but came to dominate and, in some cases, despise. She worked hard on behalf of the association (far harder than any of her wealthy fellow board members) and was rewarded by being part of all the intrigues of two overlapping worlds (the hospital and the association). She made friends and enemies among the doctors, the nuns, the senior nurses, and the mostly rich, upper-class women of the association. She gave parties to which many of these women and their males were invited. Surprisingly large numbers of them attended, despite the fact that many of them had only dimly heard of Hendon, they rolled up from Kensington, Chelsea, and St. John's Wood, no doubt puzzled by their surroundings and the mixed bag of locals that my mother had invited in her best grande dame manner. Thus it was that Lady This or That found herself conversing with the local greengrocer and Sir Somebody shared cheap sherry with a drunken Irish couple from further down Sunny Gardens Road.

My mother's association with the hospital went on for many years, as did the feuding and personal rows that gave her so much pleasure. Many of the connections she made lasted until the end of her life and some of the surviving ladies, nurses, nuns, and doctors attended her funeral mass in the Church of Our Lady, Lisson Grove, St. John's Wood, in December 1998. Here are my remarks, delivered with some difficulty and through tears during that funeral mass:

ALICIA F. GORMAN
NOVEMBER 6, 1918–DECEMBER 6, 1998

In my heart, I thought she would go on forever.

I have been thinking of my mother almost continuously since I heard of her death—a death that came as a powerful shock, despite her age and recent health. There was a life force in her that was stronger than any I have ever known, and I thought it would sustain her indefinitely. Perhaps the fact that that she had been mellowing in recent years should have been a warning. I have lived for more than 57 years in the light and shadow of her powerful personality and do not honestly know what my future will be like in her absence.

What are the words that her memory summons? The first that comes to mind is *generosity*. I do not just mean the generosity with things that made it perilous to admire anything of hers out loud. I mean a generosity of mind and spirit that made her, exasperating as she could often be, more of a presence than anyone else and better than most. The next word that comes to mind is *witty*. She was devastatingly, casually funny in a sardonic, accurate way that could, if channeled correctly, have made her a great playwright or novelist of manners. Then I think of *faith*. She was a true believer, a cradle Catholic who welcomed the eternal peace and eternal light promised to her by her religion. She was, however, a sophisticated person who knew and understood the perils, sins, and errors of the world and saw no problem in reconciling this earthly life and the life she believed was to come.

I remember my mother in many ways. My earliest memories are of a young woman, younger than my daughters are today, who was full of fun in what was for her a "good war." The rest of her life was often hard for her and for those around her but always lit by the frequent good times she enjoyed and created for everyone who knew her. She was a funny, difficult, gifted, opinionated, religious woman of enormous charm who made friends and enemies in a profusion that still astonishes. I have often wondered what would have happened had she been born male and received the education then given to boys and men. She was a devastating, if less than scrupulous, debater and, had that been backed up by a first-rate education, one wonders how far she could have gone in politics or any other sphere.

I miss her terribly and always will.

December 11, 1998

7

Marriage and Library School, 1962–1966

Anne and I were married in the Catholic Church of Our Lady Help of Christians in Rickmansworth, Hertfordshire, on March 6, 1962. Rickmansworth, known as "Ricky" to those who live in and around it, is an old town with historic streets and interesting buildings that has been completely ruined by vehicular traffic, its proximity to a major train line into London and, in recent years, a major motorway. Then and now, you could see relics of the old town muffled, but not completely obscured, by scruffy shops and the fume of car exhaust. It was chosen because of its proximity to Chorleywood and for no less utilitarian reason. The event was cloaked in the acrimony that my mother brought to all family occasions. At that time, you had to obtain parental permission to marry before your 21st birthday. My mother withheld that permission so I chose to be married on my 21st birthday. She was still threatening not to attend an hour before they had to leave for Rickmansworth. I spent the night before the wedding drinking with the two German lodgers with whom I shared a bedroom—an unconventional but not wholly unsatisfying stag night. On the morning of the wedding, I put on a white shirt, my best navy suit, and a dark blue silk tie from Jaeger in Regent Street and set off down the road to catch the number 113 bus to Finchley Road Station. I met my best man—Mac—there and we took the Metropolitan line train to Ricky. Anne is not a Catholic but was brave enough to undergo a few sessions of "instruction" with a priest in Hendon. They terminated when he informed her that the Catholic Church was the fastest-growing church of all and she replied that was not surprising given their medieval attitude to birth control. I am a baptized Catholic but had long since ceased to believe, so the Catholic marriage—an abbreviated affair prescribed when one of the parties is not even nominally a Catholic—was a matter of tribal loyalty and a vain attempt to please my mother.

It was a small wedding presided over by Father Richard Clarke, S.J., for whom I had been an altar boy at Mass in the chapel of the Hospital of SS. John & Elizabeth every Sunday for a number of years in the 1950s. Anne's parents were there, as was her sister Joan. My mother came, reluctantly, with my five siblings (then aged 15, 13, 11, 9, and 1 1/4) and my father, soldierly and neat in his dark suit and polished shoes. My mother's participation in the ceremony was, at best, grudging. Anne's best friend, the lovely Jo Mochrie (who had worked with her in Hampstead) was her matron of honor. Jo's handsome husband, Blair, my silent, unbending grandmother, and my best man were the other guests. Anne wore a cream and white silk dress with matching jacket, both made of braided silk ribbons, a round straw hat, and white silk shoes and carried a bunch of freesias. I thought she looked quite lovely and the photographs bear that out. I look thin and absurdly young in those same pictures, unsmiling and with the inevitable cigarette. After the wedding and the signing of parish and government ledgers, we boarded cars to go from Ricky to Amersham Old Town and the Red Lion Inn. The Red Lion, now closed, was named, as were the hundreds of other pubs of that name in England, after the blazon of John of Gaunt, son of King Edward III, and stood in the High Street of the old market town, near the still standing corn exchange. It was an old coaching inn with a courtyard and the mullioned windows. We took lunch there and then went back to the Gilletts' house in Chorleywood for pictures and tea. I remember very little of that day but recall a moment in the car heading for Amersham when we came over the crest of a hill to look down on the wide sunlit valley beneath—a quintessentially Chiltern view—and was overcome by a feeling of momentousness and promise, the promise of a new life and a new way of living. That evening we celebrated by having dinner in the West End before going to see *Last year at Marienbad* with Mac and Anne's sister Joan. Our wedding night was spent in our flat in Wembley.

One of my mother's friends who was an estate agent had found the "flat" (in actuality the top floor of a terraced house in St. Johns Road, which ran between the High Road and King Edward VII Park). Wembley was, if anything, a suburb even more depressingly gray than Hendon and the circumstances of living in a two-story, one-bathroom house with our noisy Irish landlady, her silent Londoner husband (whose main occupation, when not working, seemed to be sorting the tools, nails, screws, and the like in his collection of toolboxes), and their small son were less than ideal. However it was cheap and we both enjoyed the independence and the opportunity to be together so much that the disadvantages paled in comparison. The latter included sharing a bathroom with the family downstairs, especially as the landlady had a conniption fit when she found that we were taking more than one bath a week each. Our honeymoon (the rest of the week off) was spent in the conventional manner interrupted by trips to Hampstead for meals, shopping, and visits to the cinema. I felt a freedom that made the dreariness of my work and the dullness of Wembley fall away into insignificance. Life seemed full of possibilities, and both Anne and I were happy.

Anne was, by then, the librarian in charge of Kilburn Library, so I was able to visit my old haunts frequently. Wembley had many grim cavernous pubs and was entirely free of decent restaurants in the early 1960s. When there was a football (soccer) match at the nearby Wembley Stadium, we shopped early and retreated to our flat for the day to escape the hordes of drunken Scots, Mancunians, lowlife Londoners, and the like who roamed Wembley's barren streets in search of drink and nonexistent big-city delights and eventually, giving up their previous searches, of a good punch-up. All we ever did in Wembley was go to the cinema in the High Road (we went to see the comic genius Tony Hancock in *Punch and Judy man* to celebrate our first wedding anniversary); otherwise we took the tube to Finchley Road and on to the delights of Hampstead and West Hampstead. Anne worked evening and weekend hours so I, plugging on in the last months of 9-to-5 work in the building society, was often at a loose end. We decided, shortly after our marriage, that I would leave the Cooperative Permanent and pursue a library job with the object of going to library school and obtaining my qualifications. I had first to find a job, since we needed two incomes. It took me only two months to find a position in Ealing Public Library in west London, to hand in my resignation (gratefully proffered and received), and to leave Hendon Central forever in May 1962.

Ealing, then known as the "Queen of the Suburbs," was the home of the famous film factory Ealing Studios (the progenitors of the Ealing comedies of the 1940s and 1950s), which was in the same neighborhood as the central library. The latter was in a handsome house standing in a 28-acre estate known originally as Pitzhanger Manor. It was built by the eminent architect Sir John Soane and completed in 1804. It was acquired by what was then the Ealing District Council and used as their central library from 1901 until 1984. It is now Ealing's museum and an art gallery. At the time I worked there it stood in Walpole Park, not far from Ealing Broadway. The librarian who hired me was a tall, hunched, dark man called Norman Binns, the author of a standard book on the nearly forgotten art of historical bibliography and an avid philatelist. Though I only discovered this after I had left the Library, Norman Binns had other lives as a book collector—not surprising in one of his professional interests—and as a professional magician on stage and television under the name of Anthony Norman, which was and is surprising. His deputy, an affable man called T. J. Rix, seemed to be the main manager of library services for the borough. It was the first time that I was conscious of the very common library administration pattern of a chief who did most of the work relating to the larger agency of which the libraries are a part (in this case, the councilors and senior managers of the borough) and to the wider profession—Mr. Binns was very active in the [British] Library Association—and a deputy who actually ran the show. From my lowly vantage point, it seemed an efficient and harmonious relationship, one that I noted but had very little to do with my daily life.

Ealing Central Library was broad sunlight after the crepuscular dusk of the building society branch. I was working in a beautiful building set in an extensive park, albeit for a pittance (£350 a year, as I recall), I was working with congenial, interesting people, and, above all, I had an aim in mind—that of going to library school as soon as I could. I was 21, newly married and independent, and, for the first time in my life, had a sense of purpose. The 83 bus from Wembley to Ealing was the conveyance that took me to and from a happy home to a congenial workplace—all the more agreeable for being part of a path ahead. I remember seeing, twice each working day on the way to and from Ealing, a factory in Alperton that was built in the Arts and Crafts style and had the words "Life without industry is guilt. Industry without art is brutality" in golden Gothic characters on an arch over the main doors. Ruskin's words still resonate down the years. I also remember being on the top deck of the 83 (you could smoke on the top deck) and hearing two Irish laborers talking of the sorrow and the shame of some event and the effect on "the poor little kiddies." It was the evening of November 22, 1963.

I worked principally for the wry and witty Mr. "Bill" Fodder, who took pains to conceal from most that his actual given name was Horace, the head of the lending library, a man from whom I learned a lot about reference work, cataloguing, and library policies without him ever being didactic or patronizing. He later taught cataloguing and classification at Ealing library school and was described as "not over ambitious for himself . . . [but] ambitious . . . for the well-being and success of the cohorts of students he taught over the years." A quiet young man called Melville was the only other qualified librarian in the lending library, which was run, in effect, by a rather frightening senior staff member—a single lady in her 50s who enforced an inflexible dress code, rules about neatness in shelving, and other irksome regulations that, nevertheless, resulted in that being one of the most orderly and efficient libraries in which I have ever worked.

The women on the staff, who were numerous, young, and mostly pretty, had to wear regulation pale blue nylon work coats that had to at least reach the knee, could wear only the palest of lipstick and no eye makeup, and were forbidden colored stockings. A particularly attractive young woman had the temerity to appear for duty in dark green stockings and was immediately sent home to change them for regulation nylons; another took her blue work coat home and raised the hem to the height of her invariably short—for the time—skirts; within five minutes of appearing in this forbidden garment, she was supplied with scissors, needles, and thread and sent to the staff room to re-hem it to knee length. There were only two other young men. Though we had to wear jackets and ties and though dark-colored shirts were subject to a reproving, pursed-lip look, we were far less trammeled than the women in that unenlightened age. The preponderance of females, even camouflaged in pale blue nylon work coats, made the library an appealing workplace for me, especially as a contrast with the beery masculinity of the building society. I was entranced by some of the young women with whom I worked. One, a sparky Geordie with big blue eyes, had a hobby of creating romantic entanglements with Israeli airline pilots. According to her roommate, another woman library worker, the pilots were all short, dark, and intense with "eight hands, all up her skirt." Another tall, dark-haired woman resembled Jane Russell, facially and because of her buxom build, and was a particular favorite of older male library patrons, especially an infatuated elderly Irishman called Mooney who visited the library every day and always inquired after her with the utmost solicitude if it were her day off. A scholarly man who worked elsewhere in the library always timed his tea breaks to coincide with hers when, his round metal tea infuser bobbing in his cup, he tried—usually in vain—to converse on topics of mutual interest. I told him he should ask her out, but he never dared. None of these people, and none of those with whom I had worked in Hampstead, "looked like a librarian." I have never understood the force of that cliché. After many years of knowing attractive stylish librarians and library workers of both sexes, why the stereotype is fixed in the popular imagination is a mystery to me, and why so many librarians fixate upon it is equally baffling.

The Cuban missile crisis in 1962 brought the reality of the nuclear threat home and reinforced my evolving beliefs, generally in pacifism, and specifically in the idea of getting rid of Britain's nuclear "deterrent." I remember returning from the library in October 1962 and walking down dark, damp St. John's Road thinking that the world could well come to an end in the nuclear war that would result when the Soviet ships tried to break through the American naval blockade of Cuba, listening to the radio waiting for news bulletins (no all-news services then), reading Bertrand Russell, and feeling completely helpless in the face of catastrophe. I remember thinking how glad I was that we had no children—the only consolation in the face of an overmastering fear.

It is a matter of mystification and sadness to me that the means of wiping humanity out are still held by the great nations and, even more so, the futile vastly expensive stupidity of the United Kingdom maintaining its own tiny stash of these bestial weapons long after the fraud of their deterrent function has been exposed by the end of the Cold War. I flirted with anarchism and with radical socialism but ended up as an uninvolved democratic socialist and someone who never has and never will vote for anything but the Labour Party, despite the shocking betrayal of its ideals by the Blairist "Third Way" reformers. To me, Margaret Thatcher was the enemy without and Tony Blair the enemy within the family. I never expected anything good from the former, but the latter was far more of a wounding disappointment to me and a whole generation of Labour supporters. But Thatcher and Blair were far in the future, and the personal and political crisis of the late 1960s—though gradually building (as it had been all my life)—had not yet come upon me fully.

There were two things to be accomplished before I could go to library school. The first was to obtain two Advanced (A level) school certificates, since my measly four Ordinary (O level) certificates were not sufficient to render me eligible to take the First Professional Examination (FPE) of the Library Association, the necessary ticket for admittance. I had decided to go to the library school in Ealing Technical College (as it then was). The only alternative in London was the larger school at the North Western Polytechnic in Kentish Town, the school my wife had attended. However, I liked Ealing and was guaranteed a professional job in Ealing's library upon graduation. I did A levels in history (Victorian and on) and English literature (modern—i.e., Dr. Johnson and on) in 1963 after attending night classes at Ealing Technical College for the former and reading for the latter. I received respectable if not brilliant marks, took a short refresher course in the FPE, and passed that examination with high marks in early 1964. I was admitted to the library school in Ealing, took two years' leave of absence from the library, and attended library school from autumn 1964 to the end of the spring term in 1966.

Those two intervening years were full of incident, mostly forgotten, of the odd lost evening away from both Wembley and Ealing, of learning, sometimes too late and sometimes unsuccessfully, to be a husband and a grown-up, of living with political and personal passions and their consequent ups and downs, of long evenings spent with John Garforth and his new wife, Susanna, and our friends Phil Johnson-Laird and his librarian wife Maureen (Mo) née Sullivan in endless discussions of politics, cinema, literature, and popular culture washed down by cheap red wine.

LUCCA

> *Andando noi vedemmo in piccolo cerchio*
> *Torregiar Lucca a guisa di boschetto.*
> *(The poet describes coming to the circular walled city and seeing its "forest of towers.")*
> —Fazio degli Uberti, *Dittamondo*

It was during my time in Ealing Public Library that Anne met a new colleague in Hampstead—a librarian called Geoffrey Phelan, one of the most complex characters I have ever known. He was a man of all-consuming interests to which he devoted himself and in pursuit of which he strove for excellence. He spoke Italian fluently, having learned it when in Malta doing his National Service in the RAF, from Dom Mintoff, that island's future prime minister. He was an accomplished classical guitarist and an extremely good chess player. He was devoted to Italian motorcars—especially Lancias. His wife, Anna (née Cortopassi), was from Lucca in Tuscany. She was a beautiful, calm person with dark eyes and hair and a broad intelligent brow who looked upon her restless, fidgety, driven husband with indulgence. They were then living in his parents' house in Acton—a west London suburb even meaner than Hendon. His mother and father were xenophobic and resentful of their lovely daughter-in-law. On one occasion, when Geoff fell ill, his mother said "No wonder, what with those worms *she* feeds him!"

Spaghetti was, to them, an exotic and dangerous food. Anna longed for Italy in the cold, damp streets of Acton, and Geoff was increasingly tired of libraries and of London. In 1963, I left England for the second time in my life, when Anne and I traveled with the Phelans to Lucca in one of his beloved Lancias by way of the ferry to France and on to Bern and then Brig (we stayed there overnight) in Switzerland. My first sight of Switzerland left me less than impressed, and sleeping in a hotel with the wall of the Alps looming blackly was more frightening than inspiring. The next day took us through passes and tunnels to Domodossola and my first sight of Italy. On to Milano and then Piacenza (where memories of Arabella seized my heart) and Fidenza, down the terrifying *autostrada* to the Ligurian Sea, then by way of Carrara and Viareggio inland to the old Renaissance walled city of Lucca on the River Serchio in the plain of the province of Lucca, which we entered through one of the four great gates into this, the largest intact walled city in Italy. It was, and remains, unlike anywhere I have ever been. Everywhere you look from the wide walls you see, virtually unchanged, the background of many Renaissance paintings. It was a scenic view crying out for a sad-eyed Madonna and Child in the foreground. Anna's mother, with whom we stayed, lived in a flat in a house built into the side of, and on the ruins of the seats of, a Roman amphitheater. Her kitchen counters and sinks were made entirely of Carrara marble. She would roll her homemade pasta on the cool, smooth marble in a kitchen full of the garlicky smell of a herb-infused tomato sauce in an iron pot. The street on which she lived—off the via Fillungo—was so narrow that one could almost reach out and touch the flowers on the iron balcony of the apartment opposite. Vespas and tiny Fiats buzzed everywhere in the narrow streets and the wide piazzas. Then there was the Bar Disimo, with its dark wood, beveled mirrors, glass shells of mysterious beverages and violently colored syrups in tall bottles, long bar, and slender flared glasses of Prosecco or dry vermouth over ice in the dark long room offering solace and refuge from the blinding light in the street outside. Nello, who ran the bar, was a friend of Geoff's, a kindly provider of drinks and conversation in that place that was said to be the favorite bar of Giacomo Puccini (one of three famous Lucchese composers—the others being Catalini and Boccherini). One afternoon, Nello invited the four of us to have lunch with him at his house. It was a square typically Tuscan house with small windows, cool interiors, and massive dark furniture. We were introduced to Nello's wife, who greeted us warmly, served us with *aperitivi,* and went off into the kitchen. When she came back, half an hour or so later, she was carrying dishes from which she served us, then she left the room. As Nello passed the wine around, we noticed there was no place set for her. We returned to the Cortopassi house after the meal for a siesta, while Nello took his before returning to reopen the Bar Disimo at 5:30. The Piazza S. Frediano, which housed a communal tap from which we drew our potable water every day, was nearby to the northwest. The Guinigi Tower, famous for the full-sized holm oak trees that grew on its top was to the southeast of the amphitheater, which housed Lucca's open-air market. We visited Florence, Siena, Assisi, the nearby Bagni di Lucca, and, most often, the sandy beaches beyond the aromatic pine woods of Viareggio with our sunscreen and picnics of olives, cheese, bread, and wine, but mostly my heart and fond memories return to Lucca—my Italy with its narrow cobbled streets, sunlit piazzas, restaurants on the walls, its aromas, the tastes of pizzas straight from wood-burning furnaces, vegetables cooked in olive oil and garlic, and subtle cheeses, and the beauty of churches, statues, devotional paintings, memorials, and women on bicycles. Lucca in its unspoiled Renaissance setting spoke to all my untutored senses in a way no other place ever has or ever will.

....

The most interesting person who worked in Ealing Library when I was there was Dr. J. A. Toufar, the head of the reference library, which included Ealing's rare book collection and local history materials. He was a well-built, dark-haired, imposing man who wore berets and long dark overcoats, sported a goatee beard in the days when such betokened a European intellectual and not a conjurer or lager sodden yob, and spoke excellent English with what I learned was a Czech accent. He was a learned bibliophile who had connections with the Czechoslovak government in exile. It was said that he had a position in the last Czechoslovak government of Edvard Beneš before it was overthrown by Gottwald and the Communists in 1948. He had a great tolerance for anyone who came to his library with what he deemed to be a sincere interest in its holdings, and I well remember several instances in which he patiently explained something about early printed books to me without ever being patronizing or dwelling on my palpable ignorance of all such matters, which was such that I had never heard then of such things as incunabula, or the short-title catalogues of early books.

Those two years went by very pleasantly. Sometime in 1964, Anne and I moved from St. John's Road, Wembley, to the far more prepossessing environs of St. John's Wood. We exchanged the Spartan rooms and shared bathroom in Wembley for a small apartment in the much grander estate of a 1920s block called Grove End Gardens that fronted on to Grove End Road, directly opposite the Hospital of SS. John & Elizabeth, and at the rear to Abbey Road, almost directly opposite the famous Abbey Road recording studios. If you leave Grove End Gardens by the Abbey Road entrance and look to your left you will see the zebra crossing of which the famous photograph of the Beatles that adorns the sleeve of the *Abbey Road* album was taken. Shortly after we moved there, I left the flat to walk to Lords cricket ground (the home of English cricket and the proximity of which was far more important to me than that of the recording studio) and saw walking toward me the unmistakable figure and face of the great violinist Yehudi Menuhin. He was clad in a long, expensive-looking tweed overcoat of antique design and a black slouch hat. It was that kind of area. Opposite Grove End Gardens and next to the hospital stood the house and gardens of the famous Victorian painter Sir Lawrence Alma-Tadema. One could still see the "Greek" columns, arches, walls, and arbors that formed the background of his paintings of fondly imagined classical beauties in or out of their flowing, pastel-colored, diaphanous clothing.

Then, the library schools in Britain (as did many in the Commonwealth and the few remnants of Empire) had a curriculum that was prescribed by the [British] Library Association. The course leading to qualification consisted of two years, the first consisting of four mandatory subjects—bibliography and book selection; library organization and administration; English literature; and cataloguing and classification. In the second year the student could choose subjects providing more advanced study in an area of her or his choice. Given the solid grounding of the first year—the fact that all who proceeded to the second year had demonstrated knowledge of the same comprehensive subjects to the same national standard—the student was in a good position, with advice, to choose an area of specialization, or a series of linked subjects, suitable for work in a particular kind of library in an informed and productive manner, quite unlike the higgledy-piggledy selection of courses that prevails now.

I was able to attend library school because, at that time, there was no tuition fee, and grants to cover living expenses were available to all who qualified for admittance to a recognized program. My grant—£300 a year (about £4,300 or $7,000 in today's money)—was far from princely, but it and Anne's salary made my library education possible. I suppose these arrangements might be scorned as "socialized education" today in a world in which the individual ability to pay affects all aspects of life—medical, legal, educational, social, political, and even access to knowledge and information—but, leaving aside the jargon, that system was an efficient provider of a supply of demonstrably qualified and educated librarians to the nation's libraries, something that cannot be said of LIS schools in either the United Kingdom or the United States today. The latter, infested as they are by "information scientists" and other academic refugees, have what might be characterized charitably as an uneven approach to librarianship and produce a demonstrably uneven cadre of graduates—many of whom are ignorant, through no fault of their own, of some of the fundamental values, tenets, policies, and procedures of our profession.

In those distant days, British public libraries were not only a national treasure—a major component of the social and educational life of their communities, offering a range of reading and reader services that would be almost inconceivable today, and known, justifiably, as the "universities of the poor"—but also the major source of library educators. What resulted was not vocational education but a process of learning from people who were innovators and observers of innovation, because it was in the public libraries that the most exciting developments in British librarianship took place—in cataloguing, reference service, collection development and management, children's services, and the application of technology. Thus it was that the education I received was rooted in library reality, even in its most theoretical courses, marrying theory and practice in a way that made the former relevant and the latter interesting, and providing a solid platform for a career in any type of library. The curriculum was developed by national consensus within the Library Association and taught by people who knew both the realities of library life and the possible ways in which those services might develop.

There were many good teachers in the Ealing library school in the 1960s, but only two of them changed my life. I had gone to library school with the vague idea of returning to Ealing Public Library and working as a reference librarian with Dr. Toufar. That all changed because first Alan Thomas and then Eric Stone (both former public librarians) opened my eyes to the intellectual delights of cataloguing and classification and, in doing so, determined the course of my life. I became obsessed with the subjects and with the Great Names associated with them—Cutter, Dewey, Brown, Bliss, Ranganathan—and, because my teachers were up on what were then the latest developments, Lubetzky. This was a revelation to me and, for the first and last time in my life, I felt that I had been born to study and practice a particular discipline within librarianship.

Descriptive cataloguing is the practice of describing library materials of all kinds and of assigning formalized tags based on names and titles. Subject cataloguing consists of, first, applying labels based on the names of subjects ("subject headings") and, second, assigning classification numbers to the items and to the descriptions created as part of descriptive cataloguing. Both of these activities are, broadly speaking, to enable the retrieval of individual items, or the surrogates for those items (catalogue records) and the grouping of items and their surrogates that share a common characteristic (by the same author, manifestations of the same work, or on the same subject). These are, viewed broadly, very simple matters; but given the almost infinite numbers of texts in all languages, collections of images, etc., in a multitude of formats, that make up the records of humanity, and given the countless millions of authors and other creators of those texts, etc., the millions of works they represent, and the millions of subjects upon which humans have written, it can readily be seen that vast, complex retrieval systems (including library catalogues) are needed to enable access to the human record. At the time of which I am writing, people, including some of genius, had been applying themselves to the theory and practice of those retrieval systems and to the creation of codes of practice (cataloguing codes, classification schemes, and lists and thesauri of subject headings) for more than a century—with the aim of standardizing practice to allow maximum retrieval of relevant items and to facilitate cooperation between libraries to benefit the users of those libraries. The latter was hampered by the available technology—card and book catalogues and typewriters—with their inherent problems in lack of currency and inflexibility. The problems that interested me most and that I saw as the most pressing were those caused by standards (national and international) and, in particular, the codes of cataloguing, which were outdated and theoretically unsound in many respects, and existed in British and North American variants even within English-speaking countries—not to mention the widely divergent codes of other major languages. It was this that was to consume the next twenty years of my professional life, though I did not know that when in Alan Thomas's first-year cataloguing class. I was also very interested in the theory of classification and was to pursue that in Eric Stone's second-year classes. I enjoyed the other classes, was intrigued by the dim hints of technological change to come in libraries and society, and generally blossomed—realizing what I had probably known all along:

that libraries were my métier and my life's work. The perennial concerns of so many librarians—Is librarianship a profession? Have librarians a bad "image"? Are we still relevant?—that were subjects of discussion even then, hardly ever crossed my mind and have exercised it very little since.

During those two years, I went to the library school in Ealing every working day, studying in the library when not in class or in discussion with one of the teachers, though I did often take time out to play tennis in a nearby park with one or more of my female fellow students or, on fine days, to take the bus from the stop outside the college to Kew Gardens, which were then the best value (admission 3 pence) in London and a wonderful place to sit on a bench to read. I remember reading Licklider's futuristic ideas about technology and libraries and the philosophical polymath Bar-Hillel's essays on information and language, but I remember precious few other books on aspects of librarianship other than cataloguing and classification, of which I read everything I could find. One course I greatly enjoyed, despite my manual ineptitude, was that on bookbinding taught by a retired fine binder. Not only did we learn about gatherings, signatures, quartos, duodecimos, folios, half leather and perfect bindings, and all the other arcana of the art and trade, but we also bound a book of blank pages and rebound a book. I still have them, the former in blue three-quarter leather with plain linen covered boards, the second (a Victorian edition of *Plutarch's Lives* withdrawn from "New End Library") in brown half leather with marbled paper-covered boards. I was proud of having skived the leather for both books myself—the work of many hours. One can only imagine the scorn with which a contemporary failed economist turned LIS educator would greet the idea of such a course, but it taught me the vital role of good binding in the preservation of books and, hence, the onward transmission of the texts of the human record, and the dangers of bad binding and bad conservation techniques, not to mention putting in me in touch with a tradition that has underpinned learning and scholarship for centuries.

My fellow students were mostly young women (some very pretty, if not as dramatically so as the students in the art school in the same building) but there was a sprinkling of men, including two young men from Nigeria (who wore brightly colored towels as scarves in an unusual sartorial touch), another from Cyprus (a Greek Cypriot who later became his country's national librarian), and an orange-robed, shaven-headed, middle-aged Buddhist monk from what was then Ceylon. I remember his name as Sumangala, but I don't know whether that is his personal or family name. He spoke English in a very deep, heavily accented voice, but very rarely and then only a few words. He did not take any notes in any of the classes. I could not tell if he did not understand what was being said or if he was committing the teachers' words to an unusually capacious memory. Beyond a courteous inclining of his head, he seemed oblivious to the other students.

At the end of the first year, I and fellow students throughout the country and the Commonwealth took the Library Association's first year examinations. These were invigilated written examinations taken by everyone at the same time on the same days. When the results came out, it transpired that I had the best marks of anyone taking the examination that year and, hence, was awarded the annual Cawthorne Prize given by the Library Association. This honor was named after Albert Cawthorne, a man of whom I knew nothing then and know little more now apart from the fact that he was the librarian of the Stepney, East London, public library in the 1920s and that he was a Freemason. It was the first prize I had won since the *Boy's book of saints* was awarded to me for coming top in religious instruction (in itself a singular event) in my last year at St. Alban's and was a far more satisfying achievement, as there were hundreds, if not thousands, of others taking the examinations.

I had a good summer following that first year, doing a project in a company library in the City of London organizing their meager collections of books and reports, playing tennis, and going on a two-week holiday in the southwest of Ireland with my parents and some of my siblings (including the 5-year-old Paul who, it transpired, had arrived in the house my parents were renting in Waterville, County Kerry, with no clothes except those he stood up in and a striped football shirt). This was a notable trip in many ways. It included my first flight—on a BEA plane from Luton Airport (which at that time seemed to consist of two runways and two shedlike structures) to Dublin. I was petrified with fear. I had regular nightmares about plane crashes since I was a small child witnessing that military plane spiraling out of the blue sky with its deadly trail of thick black smoke following it down, and as an older child seeing the death of John Derry. A few drinks got me on the aircraft then, my heart pounding and my hands gripping the armrests, ashen with fear and in the grip of acute claustrophobia. The propellers speeded up and the plane rattled down the runway and bucketed up into the heavy cloud cover until it burst through into a world I had never seen, cerulean above the gray army blanket of clouds. The fear remained but its most obvious manifestations abated as we droned on. The cloud cover never broke during that flight and the captain spoke to us only once, when he said, "We are now passing over Lichfield, home of Dr. Johnson." The clouds over Lichfield did not differ from those over the rest of the Midlands or those that covered the Irish Sea and the east of Ireland on that day. We were met in Dublin Airport by a Kerryman who had signed up to drive us to the holiday house. He had spent several years working in Nottingham and was full of praise for that city, waxing most eloquent when we were driving through the green beauty of the Ring of Kerry on our way to Waterville, West Kerry. We stayed in a house on the Cahirciveen Road on Ballinskelligs Bay. I spent hours in those two weeks drinking Guinness with my father in small dark pubs full of men in blurred tweeds. One elderly man told us about working with "Mr. Marconi" when the wireless pioneer was setting up his trans-Atlantic connection in County Wexford more than sixty years earlier. Another sat silently in the corner nursing his pints all evening. My father asked who he was and was told he was "The American." It turned out that he was someone who had left the area more than forty years ago to work in America, who had saved enough to return to his childhood home when he retired and lived alone in a small stone cottage in a field, walking into town to drink his silent pints every evening. We visited Kerry, went to a racecourse near Killorglin, and, most memorably, had a seaweed bath in Ballybunion. Huge sheets of bladder wrack (*Fucus vesiculosus*) were placed in the bottom of immense enamel bathtubs with rust stains down the side with the taps. They were covered in a foot or more of very hot water into which I lowered myself in a gingerly manner (there were separate bath sheds for men and women) and lay for half an hour. The idea was to emerge from the shed and run across the shingle into the cold Atlantic. I declined this part but can say that my skin had never felt better before nor has since.

My second year in library school was consumed by the study of cataloguing, classification, and indexing in both practice and theory. I took every such course I could and can say that I read everything written on the topic in English that was then available. I formulated theories of my own about faceted classification and indexing practice, and developed a scheme for the revision of the cataloguing rules that would align American and British practice and, in its simplest form, could form the basis of a truly international code. No one, other than Alan Thomas and Eric Stone, showed any interest in my reformulation of Ranganathan's "principle of inversion," and no one at all showed any interest is my ideas on using classification indexes to provide complex indexes of serial literature—but, as fate would have it, revision of the cataloguing rules would be the basis of my professional life for the next decades. When I was a second year student, I became friendly with Diana Williams—the tall and very beautiful daughter of the actor Peter

Williams—who had been a junior assistant in Hampstead PL and was then a first-year library student. Diana was a practitioner of yoga and a vegan at a time when neither were common; this and her great beauty made her distinctive, as did her gift for writing. Her parody of Lewis Carroll on cataloguing and classification published in the *Assistant librarian* when she was a first year library student was deservedly reprinted in Norman Stevens' excellent compendium of the best of library humor. Later she married my brother David and left librarianship.

I sat my final examinations in May 1966 and received excellent marks. This made me eligible to become an Associate of the Library Association (an ALA), which I duly did, being admitted to the Register in May 1967 after the required year of approved professional work. I left Ealing Library School having received the gift that all good professional education should bestow—a life- and career-changing experience. I had gone there with the vague idea of being a reference librarian in public libraries (Ealing at first). I left there determined to pursue cataloguing and, with luck, the making of cataloguing codes. The hinge of fate that enabled me to pursue the latter came, as so much in my life, more or less by accident when I was presented with a unique opportunity.

8

BNB, Children, Cataloguing, and a Crisis, 1966–1969

In June of 1966, I sat at the table in the bow window of our small living room in Grove End Gardens looking with decreasing expectations and enthusiasm through the job announcements in a pile of library and other journals. I did not want to leave London (among other things Anne was pregnant with our first child and this seemed no time to move to a place in which we knew no one), was more depressed than inspired by the numerous advertisements for special librarians in firms and research centers (knowing that their cataloguing and indexing would be unchallenging at best and deadly dull at worst) and the positions in public libraries (I could always go back to Ealing if that were what I wanted). My mood changed when I saw an announcement of a one-year joint appointment by the British National Bibliography (BNB) and the library school at North Western Polytechnic. The primary job to investigate the application of the new Anglo-American cataloguing rules, which were to be published in 1967 and implemented in 1968. The appointee would also be required to teach a course on cataloguing in the library school. I wrote and posted an application that afternoon. I have no idea how many people applied for that position—it may well have been only one, since, even then, the details of cataloguing were a minority interest to library school graduates—but I was asked to show up for an interview at North Western Polytechnic, which was then in Kentish Town (on the corner of Kentish Town Road and Kelly Street). The NWP's large building is now given over to commercial use, and the magnificent library is now a branch of the chain Pizza Express. So many places in which I have worked are either libraries no longer, or have been demolished. Is it karma or just the sullen, inexorable tread of time?

In those unsophisticated times, an applicant for professional library positions showed up for a relatively brief interview with a panel, was told to wait outside with the other applicants, and was told whether he or she had the job shortly after the interview. I do not know how it is in Britain now but, since my native country adopts American food, processes, habits, and culture with an enthusiasm that has an inverse relationship to their worth or utility, I imagine the dreary and extended panoply of search committees, extended telephone and face-to-face interviews with all and sundry, etc., now occurs there when choosing people for jobs. In this instance, the panel consisted of Edward Dudley, a library school teacher called Brian Redfern, and BNB's Joel Downing. Dudley showed no sign of having met me before; Redfern, whose genial, burly exterior hid, as I was to discover, a genial, kindly interior, had very few questions; and Downing, who was to loom large in my working life for the next ten years and beyond, was full of questions and explanations of the job. There were no other applicants present. To my surprise, I was not asked to withdraw while they deliberated, and sat there while they had a very brief whispered exchange. Dudley offered me the job. It was uncharted waters for all of us, and all I knew for sure was that I was to show up at BNB's office in two weeks' time. It was a one-year contract but, for some reason, I felt that I would be able to work for BNB after that year if things went well. I was determined that they would.

THE BRITISH NATIONAL BIBLIOGRAPHY (BNB)

Britain was late coming to the idea of a national library and to the idea of a national cataloguing agency. The National Libraries of Wales (established in 1907) and Scotland (constituted in 1925, and based on the Advocates' Library of Edinburgh, itself founded in the seventeenth century) were going strong and the British Museum library departments, chiefly that of Printed Books (which collectively were often called, wrongly, the "British Museum Library"), were said by many to be the de facto national library, but, even among these national and quasinational institutions collectively, there was no idea of a national library service providing, among other services, catalogue records to Britain's libraries and an authoritative listing of current British publications. Perhaps the latter was felt to be, somehow, a "foreign" idea and, therefore and for that reason, not acceptable in Britain. The Library of Congress (also a de facto national library) had begun its catalogue card service at the time when the nineteenth century gave way to the twentieth and countries all over the world (not including the United States) had national bibliographies, listing all the publications of the country. This was long before 1950, when A. J. "Jack" Wells and four colleagues began the British National Bibliography. The twin purposes of a national bibliography are to provide an authoritative record of the nation's publications and to be a source of standard cataloguing data for the nation's libraries. In order to be effective a national bibliography must have ready and timely access to all the nation's publications from publishers large and small. The only way in which this was possible in Britain was to use the legal deposit laws which, at the time, required every publishing house to deposit one copy of each of its publications with the British Museum Department of Printed Books (and at five other institutions, one of which, in a typically British twist, was in another country—the Republic of Ireland) within a year of the date of first publication. The drawback, as far as Wells was concerned, was that those publications, once deposited, were forbidden by law from ever leaving the museum's premises in Bloomsbury. This meant that, if BNB were to have convenient access to all new publications, they would have to be housed in the museum. The British Museum is bounded by Montague Place to the northwest, Montague Street to the northeast, Great Russell Street to the southeast, and Bedford Square and Bloomsbury Street to the southwest. Bedford Square, once a tranquil spot in Bloomsbury made up on all four sides by Georgian terraces, is now, as in 1950, reduced by WWII bombing and made noisome by traffic. Thus it was that the founding members of BNB set up shop at number 6 Bedford Square, a five-story Georgian terraced house owned by, and abutting, the museum. They were A. J. Wells, Joel Downing, Bob Gayler, Eric Finerty, and Eric Coates (the latter no relation of the popular light-music composer). It is said that they were shown into the handsome high-ceilinged room on the ground floor of number 6 and were pleased to think that this was their workplace, only to be disappointed when they were given access to five desks in a capacious bay window area, with British Museum staff occupying the greater part of the room. However it may be, they had access to all newly published books, which were brought over daily from the adjacent Department of Printed Books Acquisition section and, since both buildings were owned by the museum, the books could not be said to have contravened the law by leaving the museum. From the outset all the newly published books were catalogued fully, using a variant of the 1908 Anglo-American cataloguing rules (AA1908), classified according to the latest (at that time the fifteenth) edition of the Dewey decimal classification, and provided with a detailed and highly effective subject index using a system called chain indexing, developed from the ideas of S. R. Ranganathan, of whom Jack Wells and the others were devoted disciples. From the beginning, the cataloguing was complete and efficient, managing to keep up with new British publications with a lag time of weeks (contrasting with the months and, in some cases, years-old cataloguing backlog in the museum itself). It is a telling sign of the insularity of the museum that the books, once catalogued by BNB, were trundled back those few yards into the museum to be added to the shelves upon shelves of books awaiting "official cataloguing" by the museum's cataloguers (according to the rules drawn up by Sir Anthony Panizzi in 1841 and revised little since then). The BNB records of new publications, arranged by the Dewey classification, were published weekly and cumulated monthly, quarterly, annually, and, eventually, every three years.

At the time when I first worked for BNB in 1966, number 6 Bedford Square (apart from the flat on the top floor, which was occupied by Bentley Bridgewater, the Secretary of the British Museum and a single gentleman with a wide acquaintance) was entirely occupied by BNB. (It is now occupied by, among others, the New York University in London.) Four of the five founding BNBers were still there (Eric Coates having left early on to edit the British Museum Catalogue of Music). Jack Wells was the lord of all he surveyed, a man like so many who are great innovators, supremely focused on that innovation and confident of its excellence and unimprovability. He could be pompous in manner but was an instinctive democrat who treated everyone equally and was as likely to be found in the basement explaining some new machinery to the caretaker as he was trying to gain some favor from one of the grandees of the museum. Joel Downing was his anxious deputy, a kindly, deeply sentimental, nervous man from the Potteries who thrived on crises real, imagined, and self-created, and in the absence of a crisis chewed his moustache in boredom. Bob Gayler was the head of cataloguing, and Eric Finerty in charge of subject cataloguing and indexing. Eric was courteous but very reserved in manner. He had been a conscientious objector in the Second World War on, I believe, religious grounds, and had spent those years working on farms. Other prominent staff members were Richard Coward, a brainy Sandhurst graduate and Wells favorite; Derek Austin, later a pioneer in classification and subject heading research; and Miss Mac, a middle-aged woman with a sardonic tongue given to outbursts of temper, the former being vastly more entertaining than the latter. On my first day, I met Richard "Dicky" Bird, an enthusiast who, many years later, left librarianship to take up a successful dual career as a book indexer and writer of gardening books. He is about my age and became my best friend at BNB. I wrote my first article with him—it was on government standards and published in *Catalogue & index*. Another cataloguer, named Brian Holt, was an officer in the Territorial Army—a weekend warrior, as my father would have described him without affection—and was my peer in age and (lack of) seniority. Brian was moonily in love with Eunice, a woman in Wells's office whom he later married. He was an unusual man with a rigid approach to life and work, but by no means the most unusual in BNB's ranks.

No one had any idea of how I should work, since BNB had never had a research assistant or knew what exactly such a person should do. The problem was clear—a new code of cataloguing practice was to be published and implemented in the following year, and BNB needed to know what the scale of the changes would be, how much re-education of its cataloguers would be necessary, and what the effect would be on the large numbers of libraries who subscribed to BNB's cataloguing service. I will deal with the question of cataloguing codes more broadly in chapter 12 and will just mention here that the code used in British libraries in the 1960s was published in 1908 (an American code published in 1949 was not adopted in Britain). Since the world of publishing had changed greatly in the previous sixty years, the 1908 rules were inadequate for BNB's purposes from its inception and, as a consequence, numerous exceptions and additions had been made. Unfortunately for me, those extensive variations had not been committed to paper and existed in their purest form only in the mind of Bob Gayler. Since I had to compare their current cataloguing practice with the drafts of the proposed 1968 code (still incomplete), my task was to report on the differences between two documents, one of which was an outdated standard with an extensive gloss that did not exist on paper and the other only in draft form, and that only partial. I decided to interview Bob Gayler at great length and in detail and then commit his unique cataloguing knowledge to paper. Gayler was a jolly man who had been marked by a prolonged period of incarceration as a POW behind German lines in WWII. He was preoccupied by his hypertension and was a great gossip who larded our interviews with many indiscreet stories about the other BNB personnel. He was generous with his time and knowledge and I worked for the best part of two months on a first draft of what amounted to the BNB code of cataloguing practice. I also taught an introductory class on cataloguing at the Polytechnic twice a week. I found it enjoyable and got on well with the students, most of whom were either my age or a little younger. That class in 1966 was the first in what turned out to be more than forty years of part-time teaching. I cannot recall the names of any of the students and imagine that those who went on to careers in libraries are now long retired. I also liked meeting the full-time teachers, getting to know Brian Redfern a little and talking to Harry Taylor and Tom Morgan, both of whom taught cataloguing in the school, as did the glamorous Jack "Dark Satanic" Mills, the author of an influential book on classification. Mills was of medium height, his black straight hair swept back in Brylcreemed perfection, and exuded a raffish charm. He was reputed to begin his lectures while still many yards from the classroom door, and to enter the class in full spate and midsentence. The female students were all, as far as I could tell, greatly smitten. Mills also said that, if the laws of Britain were adequately catalogued and indexed, 90 percent of the nation's lawyers would be out of business—something that could only happen if they were also rendered into clear comprehensible English, but he had a point. Antony Croghan, a red-haired, irascible eccentric of Irish extraction had begun teaching in the library school the previous year and argued enjoyably (for him, less for me) about all cataloguing matters. He later tried to revive the nineteenth-century tradition of single-author cataloguing codes and classification systems in a series of self-published books—a quixotic but gallant endeavor.

I was immersed in cataloguing matters and, in that if no other area, had a measure of self-confidence that carried me through both my research and teaching duties. The months went by; I produced what amounted to a BNB cataloguing code—a written statement of all I had learned from Bob Gayler and the other cataloguers of the variations from, and extensions of, the 1908 code. That done, I started to compare that cataloguing practice with the drafts of the British text (there were major differences between that text and the American text) of the new, and as yet unfinished, cataloguing rules. This was difficult, painstaking work that involved a considerable amount of attention to detail, but had the advantage of making me thoroughly conversant with every aspect of the new rules. Its immediate product was a report, initially for internal use and later published, that would serve as a blueprint for BNB as it switched to the new code. The report covered only the headings (access points) that would need to be changed because BNB had taken a position that it would adopt the new descriptive rules (affecting the transcription of titles, names of publishers, etc.), despite the fact that the British text of those rules had not then been completed, but on the very reasonable grounds that, sight unseen, they could not be worse than the current rules. In addition to my study and teaching, I was deputed to help Mary Piggott, then a teacher in the University College library school (she taught there from 1947 to 1974), in her work on the new descriptive rules, my first taste of what turned out to be a quarter of a century's work on the Anglo-American cataloguing rules (see chapter 12). Miss Piggott was a formidable woman with an elliptically ill temper that I found quite intimidating. She wore the muted garb of an interwar bluestocking, and her dark and steel gray hair was arranged in a sort of straggling, tumbling bun secured by long pins. She had an intimidating habit of making points by stabbing the relevant papers with savage, bony fingers. From our first meeting in her paper-littered office in a building in Malet Place, it was clear that she regarded me with a wariness bordering on dislike, but I gained some measure of her favor by bringing a little order to the chaos of snipped and pasted rules, comments on rules, and manuscript notes ("cutting and pasting" in the precomputer era was not metaphorical but involved scissors and glue). I could still see clearly that she thought me not up to snuff, but she seemed to appreciate the work I put into organizing and, even, after a while, welcomed some of my suggestions for changes of wording. I found that work very congenial, since I was helping to organize the ideas of others, though I chafed at my inability to change the rules for the better or even to make wording suggestions beyond the correction of bad grammar, spelling, and punctuation.

My first daughter, Emma Celeste, was born in the Hospital of SS. John & Elizabeth on November 27, 1966. The hospital was run by nuns (Sisters of Mercy) and starched senior nurses, both had mid-twentieth-century views on the role of men in childbirth (essentially confined to the begetting of children) and I was not allowed to be present for the birth. I suppose I should be ashamed that I was secretly relieved. I have never been one for medical matters. I was allowed a brief visit hours after the birth and was happy to find Anne well and radiant with motherhood, holding a baby with wide blue eyes who was as firm, round, and smooth as a pebble. All seemed to be more than well as I went into the St. John's Wood night intending to cross the road and go back to our flat but suddenly being seized with the idea of walking while I tried to absorb the novelty of fatherhood. I was 25, a father for the first time, with work that was rewarding (except in the pecuniary sense); life seemed full of possibilities. Being a father was daunting and I had no good model for how to do it, but I had great and well-justified faith in Anne's capacity to lead the way and to be everything a parent should be. I walked around St. John's Wood in the twilight and into the evening. As I made my way home Stephen Spender, who lived in a house in Loudoun Road, just around the corner from Grove End Gardens, was standing, tall, white-maned, serious, and silent at the gatepost of his house. We greeted each other with offhand courtesy. It seemed a good omen.

I had been a consistently heavy smoker since I was 16 and working and able to afford my own cigarettes. Some of my first monthly paycheck (amounting to a little over £19) went to a packet of oval Russian cigarettes in maize paper. Poverty in Paris had converted me to French cigarettes—Gitanes or *Gaulloises disques bleu*—and the film *A bout de souffle* made the conversion permanent. It was the addiction to the pungent cigarettes, driven by penury and affectation, that, I am convinced, saved my life. A few days after Emma's birth, she and Anne came back to the flat, which consisted of, essentially, two rooms. After a first night of sleeplessness caused by Emma's incessant snuffling, gurgling, crying, and various other forms of self-expression, we decided that she would have to sleep in the living room. The drawback was that the air and the curtains and soft furnishings of the room reeked of cigarette smoke—a highly unsuitable atmosphere for a newborn baby. So, in a display of willpower that still astonishes me, given its uniqueness in my life, I decided then and there to give up smoking forever. I have not smoked a cigarette since December 5, 1966, despite being up to thirty to forty cigarettes a day before that date. It was not easy and I craved cigarettes for a year or more, especially during the events I am about to describe, but the fact that, when I was with smokers (who were everywhere in those unenlightened times), I almost invariably encountered only the sickly sweetish smell of the Virginia tobacco found in English cigarettes, which made it easier to resist those cravings. I consumed peppermints (Mint Imperials) by the handful, drank more beer and wine than before, and, inevitably, put on weight, but I did not die of tobacco as a number of people I knew well did in the coming years. When I see a still of Belmondo in *A bout de souffle* or Bogey and Bacall in *To have and have not,* I recognize the power of the image of smoking, but now am repelled by the practice.

It was not long after the happy November evening of Emma's birth that the great crisis of my life began. As such things do, there were small, unnoticed beginnings that even now do not form a coherent narrative in my mind. I sometimes think it began with my constant dreams of that plane spiraling out of the skies over the Cotswolds during the war; sometimes I wonder if it all dated back to the arrival of my father back from the war—an arrival that changed my life jarringly and for the worse; and perhaps there is something defective in my psychology, some deeply buried tensions that cause the tectonic plates of my deep unconscious to slam into each other with a devastating effect on my conscious life. I had decided years before that I was a pacifist and, as with many of my generation, was deeply opposed to nuclear weapons. I had joined the Peace Pledge Union and the Campaign for Nuclear Disarmament, participated in two of the Aldermaston marches and other nuclear protests, and, though I was in no sense a political activist, counted myself as a unilateral disarmer and supporter of peace causes. I read *Peace news* regularly, but, one day, early in 1966 decided that I could do so no longer—not because I disagreed with its editorial position but because I could not bear to read about the possibilities and consequences of war. I felt that I had looked into the abyss too often and could do so no longer. Sometime around then I went to see Peter Watkins's film about a nuclear attack on Britain—*The war game*—with Phil Johnson-Laird. Less than ten minutes into the film, I started shaking and, a few minutes later, told Phil that I had to leave. He, a level-headed, kind man and though a film fanatic, agreed to leave with me and conversed calmly as we walked down the street until the shaking stopped. I should have seen both of these events as warning signs, but I am sure that, even if I had, it was too late. As I neared the end of writing my report on BNB and the new code, I began to have what I now know to be panic attacks, became weighed down with feelings of existential dread, and was subject to a form of agoraphobia. I was walking one sunny afternoon in the spring of 1967 in Regents Park and found myself in the middle of a large expanse of grass—an expanse that seemed to stretch on forever and then to tilt and right itself and tilt again. I was convinced that the commercial planes in the sky that afternoon were bombers or would soon come crashing down on the helpless Londoners beneath. I was having difficulty breathing, thought that I was oppressed with some nameless illness, and started to run. By the time I reached the Inner Circle road, I was drenched in sweat, gasping for air, and desperate to be still and at home. I brushed aside two people who, seeing my distress, offered to help, and somehow managed to get to and on the bus to St. John's Wood. I have always taken an interest in national and world news and, after that event, focused incessantly (this was long before 24-hour news channels) on everything I could read or hear about the Middle East. I became convinced that the war I knew was coming would result in a nuclear confrontation and the annihilation of the world and everything on it. I was obsessed with the reports from Israel of an American reporter called Michael Elkins on the BBC and, when the so-called Six-Day War came in June of 1967, it was his harsh, grating, and authoritative tones that were the soundtrack of my terror. It was not that I thought nuclear war was coming—I *knew* it was. I turned in my report to BNB and bought railway tickets to the furthest place from London that I could think of—Aberystwyth, in the west of Wales. Anne was understanding in the face of my panicked irrationality and packed our bags, including the paraphernalia of 7-month-old Emma for us to take the train west, to change in Birmingham and on to Shrewsbury and, in another train, across the Welsh border through the tranquil Welsh countryside to Aberystwyth. Each train was smaller than its predecessor and the surreal events were rendered, somehow, more surreal, when we found ourselves in a carriage with the novelist Margaret Drabble, immersed in her reading and wearing a shiny brown leather hat with a wide brim. It was a very strange week. The Israelis swept all before them, there was much talk of nuclear alerts, and the world seemed out of kilter. We ate in fish and chip shops and walked along the shoreline. I attended a Methodist (*Yr Eglwys Fethodistaidd*) church service in the hopes of . . . what? I said I wanted to go because I wanted to hear a Welsh choir singing. The congregation did sing beautifully when the time came for the hymns, but they and the dark simple church with its black beams, clear windows, and whitewashed walls did not bring peace, nor did the long sermon in Welsh, delivered with great *hwyl* but, since the only words that I understood were "Martin Luther" (with the *r* in both names being rolled with ineffable passion) and "John Wesley," it was a sonic aesthetic experience and no more. One sunny afternoon we took a picnic to a hill overlooking the sea, spread a checked tablecloth and put out the sandwiches, prepared to luxuriate in the green silence and the sight of waves. I felt less tense and frightened than at any time since we left London. Seemingly out of nowhere and with no warning, three fighter aircraft, black and menacing as daggers, screamed across the sky out over the bay at great speed making a terrifying noise, circled and came back in at an even lower altitude. They repeated this maneuver four times. I was pressed flat against the grass, shaking with terror, and in fear for both my life and reason.

After a week, we returned to London. My fear of imminent war abated, though I still had nightmares, often about war, every night. Worse, the symptoms of the crisis—fear of crowds, enclosure, sudden panic attacks, high anxiety to the point of not being able to function, a constant dread that people would know what was going on—stayed with me to a greater or lesser extent for the next twenty-five years. The most serious effect on my life was that I developed acute stage fright, at a time when I was beginning to be called upon to address groups within BNB, in library schools, and at conferences. I sought help from professionals to no avail. I told as few people as possible what was going on and managed to hide my problems from most. Those problems were the mental backdrop of my life for many years and, consciously and unconsciously, colored much of my working, personal, and emotional life.

Before we left for Aberystwyth, I made the mistake of confiding in one of BNB's senior staff. On my return, I was accosted by an unpleasant young man who worked as his assistant and made the recipient of some sneering jokes in front of others. Since I knew the assistant's main hobby was going through papers on the desks of his fellow employees after they had gone home for the night, I tried to heed my mother's constant advice to "consider the source," but felt wounded and embarrassed and became even more secretive than before. Emotional illnesses are real illnesses and, logically, no more to be embarrassed about than, say, a broken leg or flu, but that is not how the sufferer sees things. Looking back now, it is evident that I was suffering from a variety of anxiety disorders rooted in some psychic lack or injury; that, had I sought and found adequate counseling and treatment, things would have been a lot easier for me and others; and that, no matter how well I can cope with those disorders, they are still lurking. One can only hope they continue to lurk mostly unmanifested until the end of my days. I may mention this topic in passing occasionally later in this book but only when it affects the events or the people I am describing.

I had finished the report on the adoption by BNB of the new cataloguing rules and, shortly after my return from Wales, was offered and accepted immediately the permanent position of Author Cataloguing Reviser, reporting to Bob Gayler, and, essentially, given the task of implementing the recommendations of my report. I organized and spoke to a number of meetings of BNB's cataloguers about the new cataloguing rules. These meetings were held in our new quarters in Rathbone Street in the area of North Soho (north of Oxford Street) known as Fitzrovia, after the Fitzroy Tavern in Charlotte Street, a favorite haunt of Dylan Thomas and the other postwar bohemians. Though I did not know it at the time, in the 1880s and 90s, long before it was the bohemia of austerity London, the area was a hotbed of anarchists, home of exiles like Louise Michel, the "Red Virgin of Montmartre" of the Paris Commune, and of John Neve and other anarchist luminaries, of Russian spies and agents provocateurs, the stuff of Joseph Conrad's *Secret agent*. I do not know if we were ejected from 6 Bedford Square by the museum or if, as I think more likely, Jack Wells wanted a larger theater for his dreams of the future. The regulations of copyright deposit had been changed to allow the copyright deposit books to be delivered to the new BNB headquarters before they went to the museum. Wells was afire with technological ideas. I, though mainly preoccupied with the details of cataloguing rules, became interested in his, and Richard Coward's, ideas about the use of computers to, in the first instance, print bibliographies and catalogue cards far quicker and more efficiently and, later, to replace cards in a new era of computerized catalogues and all their untold possibilities.

Dicky Bird's enthusiasms were numerous, intense, and wide-ranging but his genuine desire to communicate and share his pleasures kept him from being tedious. One enthusiasm was for the opera and, on one occasion, he cajoled me into accompanying him to see one, my first. I think it was *A masked ball (Un ballo in maschera)*. I am afraid I was deeply bored and grateful the opera was over before pub-closing time. Another of his enthusiasms was for plays. Dicky had discovered a theater just off Shaftesbury Avenue (a ten-minute walk across Soho from the new BNB building) that put on one-act plays every Friday lunchtime. He organized a group (including his future wife—pretty, dark Hilary Farmer) to attend these performances at which we saw a number of such plays by, among others, Anouilh, Durrenmatt, Ionesco, and N. F. Simpson. The cost of admission included a box with sandwiches—cucumber, salami, ham, or chicken, and the like—all garnished with sprigs of parsley, which, unlike all the others, I ate. I cannot remember the titles or details of any of the numerous plays we saw on Fridays or the name of the theater, though I can visualize its interior clearly, but, even to this day, the taste of raw parsley evokes the streets of Soho and Dicky's good-natured thespian enthusiasm.

It was about this time when a young—and younger-looking—woman called Cynthia Paterson began to work for BNB. She was ethereally pretty, very Sixties in her "look" and clothing, and, in that quintessentially Sixties way, a former art student. I was smitten immediately. She liked my navy and white floral-patterned Liberty's shirt and matching tie and the fact that, when Otis Redding died, I was the only person at BNB who knew who he was. She loved my family and my daughters loved her. Though I have not seen her for years, she will always be a fond friend.

I published an article in the *Library Association record* (then edited by

Edward Dudley) on the first AACR and a flowchart of the rules. I also attended, and participated in, a national conference on the rules held in the University of Nottingham in March 1968. I met all of the cataloguing luminaries in British librarianship there and was gratified to be treated as an equal, as brash as I undoubtedly was, by almost all of them. I am struck, looking at the proceedings of the conference, by how often I intervened in the discussions and how often I, less than two years out of library school and 27 years old, was deferred to by my elders and betters. I suppose it was because I had studied the rules more carefully and closely than most, having been paid to do so for a year, but it was also due to my successful impersonation of someone with unshakeable self-confidence.

Jack Wells was given to grand gestures. He lived—with his first wife and, it was rumored, unhappily—in a flat on the east side of Bedford Square. He loved having visitors, especially those from other countries and, among those, especially Americans, and did his very best to impress them. I was a not entirely willing attendee at the some of the dinners in restaurants he gave for foreign dignitaries, all with a great show of knowing the waiters ("Is François here this evening?" "François, sir?" being a typical exchange), ordering his favorite meal (not on the menu—"Have you any of your excellent veal, Marcel?" "Veal, m'sieur?" and so on), ordering expensive wine and sloshing it around in the tasting glass ("Hmmmn, yes, I think so")—and all manner of fussing and the behavior that the lower middle classes from which I came hated more than anything else—"showing off." All this was a shame because he was a brilliant man in so many ways and impressive except when he went out of his way to impress.

On one occasion in 1968, we had a visit from three Library of Congress interns who were doing a tour of British libraries. Jack Wells decided to put on a catered lunch for them in his flat, a lunch to which Dicky Bird and I ("Two of our promising young men," said Wells, conjuring up hordes of such on the BNB strength) were invited. One of the visitors was a woman called Wilma Morris, from Wisconsin, whom I enjoyed meeting but have not seen since; another was Art Plotnik, who became a good friend in subsequent years; and the third was a familiar-looking man called John (I did not catch his last name at first). When all the preliminaries—"I always order from X. I find they do a decent little lunch" and "Do try this wine, it's highly recommended"—were over, we began to eat. As we talked of this and that, I could not refrain from looking at John, becoming ever more certain that we had met before. Suddenly, it dawned on me. I leaned across the table and said "You are John (of John, Bob, and Tom) and you took the night train to Paris on June 30th, 1960!" He was that very John. The odd thing is that he had no idea of becoming a librarian when, as a student, he traveled to Europe in 1960 and, I believe, took up librarianship after working in a military library when conscripted. When we had recovered from the improbability of this coincidence, he (John Y. Cole) told me of the rest of their trip and seeing the Powers trial in Moscow in particular. In subsequent years, he took a permanent position with the Library of Congress, he works there to this day, and is now a very distinguished librarian, the director of the Center for the Book established by former Librarian of Congress Daniel Boorstin, and the author or editor of a number of scholarly books.

In March of 1968, we moved from the splendors of St. John's Wood to Bloomsbury Court, a newly constructed cooperative housing project in Moss Lane, Pinner, on the northwest edges of greater London. (Before the early 1970s, the farther-flung areas of Middlesex were in separate boroughs outside the municipal definition of London, which was the area covered by the London County Council.) Pinner is an ancient village that has been swallowed by the urbanization that came into flood in the 1920s with the speculative building along the Metropolitan Line of the London Underground—the area of the fabled Metroland—a land of the imagination celebrated in the poems of the beloved John Betjeman.

> Early Electric! Sit you down and see,
> 'Mid this fine woodwork and a smell of dinner,
> A stained-glass windmill and a pot of tea,
> And sepia views of leafy lanes in PINNER—
> Then visualize, far down the shining lines,
> Your parents' homestead set in murmuring pines.
> —"The Metropolitan Railway"

Pinner's old High Street follows the route up a hill that it has followed for more than a millennium. It leads to the Parish Church with the Norman tower that was said to have been visited by Thomas á Beckett in 1170 on his peregrination to Canterbury, in which he was murdered by King Henry's minions. It is the site of the annual Pinner Fair, held on the Wednesday after the Spring Bank Holiday, and founded by Royal Charter of King Edward III in 1336. There is a jumble of old-nineteenth- and twentieth-century buildings on each side of the street—for example, on the left side a half-timbered pub (The Victory), built in 1580, jostles two Georgian houses that now have shops on the street level and flats above, and they in turn have more modern companions. This ancient street is surrounded by acres of speculative buildings, mostly semidetached and detached houses built in the 1920s and 1930s but including some grander dwellings dating back to Victorian times and older former farm houses. Bloomsbury Court and adjacent Chiswick Court consisted of clusters of then newly built two-story buildings of plain design each containing four flats, two up, two down, each with the same floor plan. The living rooms on the ground floors had sliding glass doors opening on a communal lawn and the expanse of green of Pinner Park and Hall's Farm beyond. The latter was, at that time, still a working dairy farm and our daily deliveries of milk came from the cows we could see in the fields past the communal lawn. Shortly after we moved there, we were looking out from our unlit living room one night and saw, by the light of the moon, a vixen and four fox cubs in line, no doubt moving over the old fox trails on the farmland upon which the apartment blocks were built. We saw them several times in the next weeks and then no more.

Anne's sister, Joan, and her husband, Peter Butcher, lived with their young son, Paul, in a flat in the same building as us. A little later, my Hampstead friend John Garforth and his lovely young second wife, Susanna, moved into a flat in the adjoining Chiswick Court. Anne and Joan were very close but I had an uneasy relationship with Peter Butcher. He too was a librarian and, at the time when they moved to Pinner, worked at Marylebone Public Library (in which he and Joan had met) and, later and briefly for BNB. The unease was due, in large part, to him sharing a flat, before he and Joan were married in April 1964, in Balcombe Street in Marylebone (he and Joan both worked in Marylebone Library) with the first person I had ever met who was an avowed fascist. This man, who later became a fairly well-known librarian, was the son of a writer and polemicist whose claim to fame was his renunciation of Communism in order to become a far-right Catholic, the subject of a fleetingly famous autobiography. Because this person was present at a number of social occasions that his friends attended, I met a number of people that I would rather not have met. I particularly remember one describing his "joy" at seeing Leni Riefenstahl's *Triumph of the will* as his voice rose and his eyes glistened. Peter was not a fascist, but the company he kept was, to say the least, disconcerting.

It was sometime about then that I met John Linford, a peripatetic librarian who had worked for BNB before my time but had left to teach in library schools in Malaya (before the creation of Malaysia), Ghana, and Trinidad, all of which followed the Library Association curriculum. On his return from Trinidad, he was hired by Jack Wells as a consultant on the MARC project and later as an employee. John was a magnetic and exotic personality with a complex personal life, extremely intelligent and winning, with a dark complexion, curly black hair and beard, and a farouche way of dressing. He was fond of a drink and we rapidly fell into the habit of lengthy pub lunches and, every so often, carousing in the evenings. He had the verbal tic of inserting "sort of" at random and often into his speech. I once heard him give a lecture during which he, speaking to a group of European librarians, referred to the "British National sort of Bibliography." He was given to brilliant inspirations, especially in the field of automation. I do not think he had any particular training in that field but his agile mind, in those very early days of computerization, was capable of creating solutions before most of us had fully formulated the problems. Though I was wrapped up in the task of implementing the new cataloguing rules, I was intrigued by the possibilities that were opening up and upon which Richard Coward and John Linford were working. These included discussions with the Library of Congress on reconciling cataloguing practices and, in particular, using the new MARC format for exchanging cataloguing data. John and I wrote the first British MARC format manual in 1970, I believe the first anywhere outside the USA. I cannot remember when I first met Henriette Avram—the godmother of MARC—but think it was when she visited BNB in 1968, an unforgettable, alien presence who later became one of the people I most admired in the field.

I was at the early stages of John Linford's progressive party for his 40th birthday in the late 1960s. These early stages took place in three Fitzrovia pubs and then in a Charlotte Street restaurant to which the party adjourned. I left the restaurant and have no idea to where the party went after that. Legend has it that at some advanced hour of the evening, John found himself alone with one of his numerous lady friends and took a room for the party of two for the night in a small hotel with rooms over a newsagent's in Store Street opposite the headquarters of the Library Association in Ridgmount Street. John told us all, with glee in his eyes, how he and his lady friend lay on their bed the next morning in their bohemian aerie watching the staff of the LA going to their offices and mundane tasks.

Though I was working hard during long hours and had some of the responsibilities of a family man, I was also having a species of delayed adolescence in the louche atmosphere of Fitzrovia and Soho with my friends and colleagues. Drinks after work often turned into prolonged evenings, which were followed by remorse and hurrying home after work for a day or two, and then a fall from grace, after which the cycle began again. I was still suffering the consequences of my psychological crisis, and alcohol and good company were as good a way of getting through bad times as I knew. We would end up eating and drinking Retsina in a Greek restaurant in Charlotte Street called the Anemos, which, because the waiters always seemed to be quarreling with each other (there was one scene in which one waiter ran from the restaurant pursued by another brandishing a cleaver), we called "The Animosity," or traveling from the Fitzroy to the Black Horse or the Marquis of Granby, or leaving one of them to cross Oxford Street in to Soho to eat pizza or spaghetti and drink carafes of wines of dodgy provenance but low prices. This way of life was the cause of the beginnings of strains in my marriage. Anne, a much more mature and balanced person than me, was left to maintain our home and look after Emma, then a toddler, and, later, the baby Alice without the kind of assistance that more enlightened husbands supplied, even then.

I first met Anthony Thompson in 1968, in BNB's offices at 6 Bedford Square in London. He was then the secretary general of the International Federation of Library Associations (IFLA), a tall man with a small, neat head and the kind of upper-class English accent that seems to have died with David Niven, whom he resembled in features, accent, and courtly manners. Herman Liebaers, a former president of IFLA, described him as "a highly educated gentleman-librarian who lives surrounded by beautiful and important books." Mr. Thompson was there to offer me a project, funded by UNESCO and administered by IFLA, to compare descriptive data from a variety of national bibliographic services and, if possible, to prepare a synthesis of these cataloguing practices embodying all the elements that were common to the services in the order of the majority. I was offered 100 pounds sterling (approximately $300 then) for this work. I accepted the commission, driven by both professional interest and impecuniosity. I chose eight national bibliographic services in languages that use the Roman alphabet. LC cards and BNB entries were obvious choices. In addition, I recall using the Swedish, West German, Hungarian, and Argentinean national bibliographies (the latter in the vain hope I could correspond with Jorge Luis Borges—then the national librarian of Argentina). I cannot remember the other two. (For details of the report I wrote and its subsequent history, see chapter 12.)

Gathering data for the IFLA/UNESCO report involved the study and careful comparison of thousands of bibliographic records. In addition to doing that work outside regular working hours, I had both a demanding job working with Bob Gayler and the other cataloguers on the descriptive cataloguing effort that, along with the classification and other subject efforts led by Eric Finerty, was at the heart of BNB's work, two hours total travel to and from Pinner each day, and an interior life in which I was struggling, with mixed success, to deal with the fallout from my crisis of 1967 and subsequently. I fell into a pattern of working and playing too hard for weeks and then having a sort of collapse, the worst manifestations of which made it difficult for me to leave my house for fear of anxiety attacks. One of the hardest things to deal with when it comes to anxiety and other life-hampering psychological ailments is that as a sufferer you feel a deep sense of shame, a desire above all others to conceal the effects from other people. This irrational shame plays a part in reluctance to seek assistance or even discuss the problems with those close to you. In my case, the instinctive wish to seek solitude when ailing and a deep-seated secretiveness born of my unhappy childhood mixed with shame in a devil's brew of silence and bluffing my way through awkward situations.

One welcome interlude was a second holiday in Ireland with my family. This time we went on the ferry from Holyhead to Dun Laoghaire and from there by car to Waterville, County Kerry, in which my parents had rented a house.

I finished the UNESCO/IFLA report and presented it to Anthony Thompson and to Dorothy Anderson, a New Zealander who was then working with A. H. Chaplin, a very senior person in the British Museum, on establishing a presence within IFLA dealing with cataloguing standards, a presence that later became the IFLA UBC (Universal Bibliographic Control) office, of which she was appointed head. Her office at that time was in 6 Bedford Square, in which BNB had been housed previously.

I will deal with the ISBD more fully in chapter 12, but will mention here that my report found a considerable degree of uniformity in the descriptive part of the records for the eight countries and that the major difficulty in using the records from countries with unfamiliar languages (such as Hungarian) was that, though the elements were presented in a nearly standard manner, the lack of standard punctuation made them difficult to decipher. Therefore, my report proposed that the few variations in description be resolved to provide an international standard for the order of the elements and that the elements be presented with standard punctuation that allowed the user to understand records even in languages with which the user was not familiar. My report was circulated widely to cataloguing experts in IFLA and was generally well received (though subject to a withering criticism on all counts by a lady called Lucille Morsch, who I was told at the time was a stalwart of the old guard in the Library of Congress).

Somewhere in Kerry, Ireland, July 1969. Left to right: Joanna, MG, Anne, Alicia (mother), Emma, Philip (father), Philippa, Paul.

Here is a paragraph from the Hungarian library educator Domanovsky's digest of comments on my paper:

> In judging both the extent of Mr. Gorman's success in attaining his end and the method employed by him, unanimity is replaced by a wide range of divergent opinions. At one end, Mr. Sebestyén declares Mr. Gorman's survey excellent, his recommendations realistic, and that the DE2 represents a considerable progress toward standardization. According to Miss Verona, the survey is "excellent and very systematic," so that no comments on the form and lay-out of the material seem to be necessary." Mr. Maltese considers the document a good basis for discussion, the method adopted realistic, and the limitation of the enquiry to national bibliographies very sensible. Mr. Šír thinks the arrangement of the study very good. At the other end, Miss Morsch considers DE2 a "superficial and careless piece of work," and does not approve of the method chosen.

My document survived Ms. Morsch's bilious commentary and I was greatly encouraged by kind words from the Hungarian expert (and national librarian) Professor Geza Sebestyén and the Italian expert Diego Maltese, among others, and by statements from others that my proposal was generally acceptable in their countries. I made a number of small modifications and was pleased to hear that my report was accepted as one of the two "documents for examination" of a conference called the International Meeting of Cataloguing Experts (IMCE) to be held immediately before the annual IFLA conference in Copenhagen in August 1969. I remember being on the train to Pinner the evening after I had heard that news and thinking about the strange turns that life takes. I had, in three years, gone from being in library school to being not only an official "international expert" in my field but also the author of one of two discussion documents for the whole international conference (the other being revision of the Paris Principles that had given international ratification to Lubetzky's ideas in 1961). Though I had worked hard on the report and had shown some initiative in its proposals, I realized that so much of what had happened was due to being in the right place at the right time. The chairman of the IMCE was to be Arthur Hugh Chaplin, who was said to have a close friendship (how close was a matter of lively speculation) with Dorothy Anderson, who had been instrumental in hiring me for the UNESCO/IFLA project, and I am sure that either Jack Wells or Joel Downing had suggested I might be the person to do it. Despite my gratification over these events, I was completely aware of the tenuousness of events and how things could have turned out very differently. Had it not been for that report, I might not have been invited to join the British Cataloguing Rules Committee (later the British Library/Library Association Committee on Revision of AACR) and might never have gone from there to be, at first, the British editor of AACR2. Had I never met Anthony Thompson, my professional life would have been very different and the events that were set in train at that meeting—that, among other things, took me to the U.S.A. and changed everything—might never have occurred.

I left for Denmark three days before the IMCE was due to start. My aerophobia caused me to travel by train from gloomy Liverpool Street station in east London to the gull-haunted Essex port of Harwich and from there by ferry across the gray, choppy North Sea to the east Danish port of Esbjerg, a journey that took twenty-four hours. I had a tiny sleeper cabin and spent the journey in the cabin, in the bar and restaurant, and on deck reading and looking out on the expanse of sea and thinking of the maritime history that had linked Scandinavia and Britain across these waters for more than a millennium. The few things I knew of Denmark before my trip were connected with Hamlet, dairy produce, Hans Christian Andersen, and the Danes' heroic pacifist reaction to the German occupation in World War II. That evening, in the ferry's restaurant, I saw a vision of loveliness—a dark-haired, very beautiful woman in light-colored, flowing clothes. I was entranced, as were the two men in expensive suits accompanying her and, I would surmise, all the men in the restaurant. It was, I learned from the waiter, Anna Karina, the Danish actress who had been married to Jean-Luc Godard and who graced his films (*Pierrot la fou* and *Alphaville* among others) and those directed by Roger Vadim, Agnès Varda, George Stevens, and others. The IMCE was already a bibliographic fairy tale to me; the sight of the lustrous Anna took me to other, more beautiful realms. We disembarked in the port of Esbjerg and, after going through the impeccably polite Danish customs formalities, I boarded a train that took me across the center of Jutland (Jylland), through orderly fields and small towns by bridge to cross the island of Fünen (Fyn), and through H. C. Andersen's Odense to Nyborg to board another ferry to the coast of the island of Zealand (Sjælland) and the final train into Copenhagen, situated on the east coast of Zealand and on the island of Amager in Denmark's far east. This was my fourth foreign country (after France, Italy, and Ireland). What struck me was that it was so like England, with the essential and important difference that it was a more orderly, almost idealized, version. From the trains I saw red cows, as if in a fairy tale come to life, thatched red-painted barns like illustrations in a child's story book, and most surprising of all, farm workers in the fields wearing clean white jackets; all this in a gentle, verdant landscape like that of my childhood viewed through the lens of some magical sprucing device. Copenhagen was, after one had traversed the scruffy preliminaries that seem to attend train stations all over the world, a clean, well-lighted revelation with more bicycles than cars, people of all ages clad in unostentatiously stylish clothes, tall, well-designed apartment buildings, green trams and trolley cars, comfortable warm cafes next to bakeries, and the wondrous yet somehow modest Tivoli Gardens. I lost my then susceptible heart to Denmark within hours of alighting from the train. My warm feelings were strengthened by a number of visits over the years and, especially, by having made a number of Danish friends. Copenhagen is a member of a trinity (the others are Paris and Lucca) of cities with which I fell into an early love that still lingers.

    I was housed, as were some of the other conference participants, in a modest hotel near the Royal Library School (Danmarks Biblioteksskole), in which the meetings took place. Each morning for three days we—thirty-eight people representing thirty-two countries—went to a large classroom in the school's building off a side street called Birketinget. After we were greeted by the distinguished and neatly bearded rector of the library school and

IFLA treasurer, Preben Kierkegaard, the meetings were opened and chaired by Hugh Chaplin. The official languages of the IMCE were English and French, both of which Chaplin spoke fluently but very, very slowly. A tall man with old-fashioned airs, he would uncoil himself from his chair, rise, look out across the room in silence until all talking had ceased, then begin "Good ... morning ... Bon ... jour ... " his invariable preliminary, which seemed to take five minutes to deliver. His following remarks (sequentially delivered in English and French) seemingly had the same time-stretching quality. Though I remember the room well, I cannot recall any details of the discussions. The first three sessions of the first day (August 22) were taken up with the Paris Principles (Lubetzky, their main begetter, was not among the delegates) and plans to provide an annotated version of them, an effort that the conference decided would be led by the formidable Eva Verona, the Yugoslavian cataloguing expert. The third and fourth sessions of that day and the first session of the following day were devoted to my "document for examination" and reviewed that draft at great length before deciding to refer the matter to a working group. The remaining sessions of the second and an abbreviated third day considered a number of topics and papers to, as far as I could see, very little purpose beyond fostering international amity and cooperative spirit or, less charitably viewed, to fill the time allotted.

Mme Verona was one of the luminaries attending. I also remember meeting Leonard Jolley, the Australian delegate and the husband of the novelist Elizabeth Jolley; the Italian Diego Maltese, who wore thick dark glasses and, because he had no peripheral vision, was escorted everywhere by a graceful, dark, young Italian lady; Henriette Avram from the Library Congress and her assistant Lucia Rather; Guust van Wesemael, the Dutch librarian who was ubiquitous in IFLA for many years; and the imperious French delegates, Mme Suzanne Honoré and M Roger Pierrot of the Bibliothèque nationale. I especially remember the delegate from the German Democratic Republic, Heinz Höhne, a ramrod-straight, dark-suited man who, upon being introduced to me, clicked his heels as he shook my hand and said, not unkindly but obviously disappointed, "Herr Gorman, I thought you were a much older man," in a German accent *(I sought you ver a merch eolder men)* that, together with the heel-clicking, had a powerful effect on this war baby. Two Danish librarians—Eigil Balling and Birgit Larsen—were observers and subsequently became good friends.

After the second day's proceedings were over, I went out on the town with Kay Guiles, one of Henriette Avram's loyal lieutenants, a young Nebraskan with a passion for tennis and cataloguing; and Ros Kerr, then working in the library of Queen's University, Belfast, a young woman who was there to translate (she was fluent in German and French as well as her native Northern Irish English). We stepped out, taking in bars, *smørrebrød* restaurants, the Tivoli Gardens, and a night club. The long and alcoholic evening ended in the small hours of Sunday morning. I had a serious hangover the next morning and, having prepared myself for the day with care and difficulty, went down to the breakfast room of the hotel, to find myself sharing the lobby with a number of Japanese men, all of whom were as tall as or taller than my six feet. For a moment, I though the beer and *snaps* (schnapps) of the previous evening had taken their toll, but was relieved to learn that they were a visiting Japanese basketball team. Luckily, I had no part to take in the morning-only final session, but two delegates who had taken no visible part in the conference made their first and final contributions, which were quite long and delivered in their languages, of which they were the only speakers present. This gave the world the skewed unreality familiar to the hung-over. I returned to England the next day. The North Sea was choppy and the ferry bucketed its way under gray skies to the grayness of Harwich, from which the train took me over flat East Anglian fields to London.

My second daughter Alice Clara was born on October 3, 1969, at St. Andrew's Hospital in Dollis Hill. This was a Catholic hospital, administered by the Sisters of Mercy, the same order of nuns who then administered the Hospital of SS. John & Elizabeth. As with Emma's birth, the nun-nurses took a very dim view of the presence of men in maternity wards, allowing husbands to visit only when the children had been delivered and safely swaddled in the then obligatory cream-colored knitted shawls. My first impression of my new daughter was that she was exactly the hue and tint of a magnolia petal and, in the exuberance of the moment, suggested that she be called "Magnolia." This profoundly non-Catholic name shocked the nuns and, anyway, was vetoed immediately and wisely by Anne. The baby was duly named Alice, after my grandmother, my mother (obliquely), and the heroine of Lewis Carroll's book; and Clara, after a beloved great-aunt of Anne's. Despite my many prolonged and grievous shortcomings as a father, my daughters have, in so many ways, been the light and pride of my life.

9

BNB, the British Library, 1970–1974

From 1969 on, my working life entailed frequent traveling, within the United Kingdom and in Europe. I attended meetings in Paris and other European cities of the task force established in Copenhagen, and attended the annual IFLA conferences. I participated in the EUDISED project in its early days when it was largely a Francophone enterprise, and that work took me and John Linford to meetings in Grenoble, Geneva, The Hague, Brussels, and Paris. I was called upon to speak in meetings held by the Library Association's Cataloguing and Indexing Group. Travel took me away from home and my family and tipped my life even more out of balance than it was before. My professional life expanded greatly in the years after the IMCE. I was appointed to the Library Association's cataloguing committee and became editor of *Catalogue & index,* the journal of the Cataloguing & Indexing Group of the LA, in addition to my work on BNB's cataloguing and as secretary of the Standard Bibliographic Description Working Group set up by the Copenhagen conference. The cataloguing committee included Peter Lewis, then at the Board of Trade Library and later a colleague in the making of AACR2 (see chapter 12); the charming Northern Irishman Patrick Quigg, then at Queens University, Belfast, and later librarian at the University of Cork; the voluble, opinionated Alan Jeffries; the Liverpudlian Eric Hunter; Tony Curwen of the College of Librarianship Wales; Mary Piggott; and Joel Downing, my boss at BNB. They were all leaders in the Cataloguing & Indexing Group and leading lights among the very active British cataloguing fraternity.

I still have vivid memories of my travels in that period, though it is hard for me to place the trips in chronological order. I remember sitting in a bar in Estoril, near Lisbon, with Henriette Avram, her assistant Lucia Rather, and Sumner Spalding, the editor of the first AACR and a courteous and scholarly gentleman, drinking white port and eating homemade potato chips and, later, visiting a modern art museum with whitewashed walls with Sumner on the last day of that meeting while we waited to go to the airport for an evening plane to London, me with barely suppressed nerves and him with complete equanimity. That meeting considered drafts of the ISBD for monographs, then a late stage. I remember going with Ros Kerr to a restaurant high in the hills above Grenoble for Sunday lunch in a white airy, sunlit room. We watched the large French families gathered around long tables, the generations interacting with ease and grace in a way I had never seen before. That was during an IFLA meeting. I had not done my homework on the local weather and was unprepared for the heat of a Grenoble August. I went to a clothing store and bought two pairs of light cotton trousers and three white T-shirts to wear for the whole conference, abandoning jackets and ties for the first time in my working life. I visited Copenhagen for the second time and have happy memories of the warmth of my reception by Eigil Balling and Birgit Larsen (whom I had met in 1969) and other Danish librarians. Birgit had a small house in the country, in Næsby in West Zealand. It was a simple cottage set in the neat, magical, gently hilly countryside. It was painted red (a "*lille røde hus*" in the Danish that looked so simple on the page and was impossible for me to pronounce) and had a thatched roof. Her nearest neighbors were artists, and I still have a woodcut of the local fields in winter (*Sne i Næsby,* "Snow in Næsby"). I also met Danish colleagues from the Royal Library (including Karen Lunde Christensen, Inger Warmind, and Mogens Wedemeyer). Though I had meetings in the Royal Library and visited the Bibliotekscentralen (in which Birgit and Eigil worked), the purpose of my visit was to speak at a conference in Elsinore (Helsingør). The castle there is where *Hamlet* is set (and the place in which the marvelous Russian film of *Hamlet* starring the splendid actor Innokenty Smoktunovsky was filmed). It was an experience to remember, speaking in a large conference room with windows looking out on to Elsinore Castle and the Swedish shore across the Øresund with the blue Kattegat to the north. I think it was that visit in which I first went to Louisiana, the stunning museum of modern art in Humlebæk, a village in northern Zealand, with its panoramic view of the Øresund. That visit inspired me to start writing poetry again after a hiatus of years following the private humiliation of my Paris writings. I have vivid memories of the train journey home, which took a southern route through the tranquil fields of Schleswig-Holstein, the subject of a mid-nineteenth-century dispute of which Lord Palmerston is alleged to have said, "The Schleswig-Holstein question is so complicated that only three men in Europe have ever understood it. One was Prince Albert, who is dead. The second was a German professor who became mad. I am the third and I have forgotten all about it" and which, nevertheless, resulted in the defeat of Denmark in the Danish-Prussian war. At some point, the train crossed from Denmark into Germany. The affable Danish customs officer, with whom I had been discussing the BBC's Dave Allen television show after I had shown him my passport, left the train at the border crossing. Moments later the door of my compartment opened. It was a German border official in a cap with an almost vertical peak that covered his eyebrows. He looked around the tiny sleeper without saying a word, then snapped his fingers and said, "Passport!" When I handed mine to him, he scrutinized it suspiciously, looked me up and down, stamped a page with an air of infinite distrust, turned on his heels, and left. It was this that led me to write an unpublished paper called "Travel narrows the mind," the burden of which is that unless one is very careful travel reinforces rather than dispels stereotypes.

JOURNEYING BOY

When I think of that man, an imperfectly recalled stranger now, who traveled to all the places described here and to Geneva, Paris, Madrid, The Hague, Amsterdam, Prague, and Brussels in those years, I wonder who he was. I know what he has become, but I do not know what, apart from the obvious and predictable, was on his mind in his late twenties and early thirties. A father and a son with still-living parents and five brothers and sisters, was he as oblivious of the future as I seem to remember? Six feet tall, still slender, with a mass of dark brown hair, he seems to have skimmed over the swamp of insecurity and anxiety that lay beneath his progress through the worlds in which he lived. He read his way across Europe and at home in the suburban silence, happier in the past than in the present—that present that is now a distant past to so many. In remembering those trips and my life in London, it is as if I am writing in a dark house of many rooms lit only by sudden bursts of lighting that illuminate the flickering figures and freeze them briefly for examination and chronicling. The rest is a matter of darkness and partially grasped, untrustworthy memories. I see him in a bar in The Hague, reading a book that he has taken from his black leather briefcase, and drinking beer. Where was he staying, who was he traveling with, and for which purpose? I see him the next day in a paneled conference room in a university library, doodling on ruled paper, and wishing for the evening to come. I see him coming home to Pinner and welcome banners his small daughters have made, glad beyond measure to see them, but yearning for the next time he could journey and shake off his uneasy life in Britain.

....

I remember a trip by ferry and train from London to Helsinki that took me east from Copenhagen (a trip I had taken before) across the sea to Sweden and across the green flatness of southern Sweden to Stockholm. I was surprised to see respectably dressed businessmen drinking large steins of amber beer with their 7:30 a.m. breakfasts in the cavernous café in Stockholm's station and agreeably surprised, after thinking "when in Stockholm . . ." to discover how tasty scrambled eggs and toast can be if washed down with enough Swedish beer. The ferry from Stockholm crosses the southern end of the Gulf of Bothnia and swings around the Åland islands on its way to Turku in Finland—a spectacular sight. I missed some of the scenery on the trip by spending an hour and a half in the piney sauna on the huge ferryboat. It was curiously relaxing to be that hot in the steam, sitting on a pine bench wearing only a towel, feeling the gentle rocking of the ferry, and hearing lazy conversations in Swedish, a language whose cadences were familiar from so many Bergman films, and Finnish, of which I knew and know nothing. When the train from Turku drew into the station in Helsinki, it seemed as though I had left Europe. Scandinavian architecture and well-lit familiarity gave way to Eastern architecture and looming massiveness. This was at the height of the Cold War, and the sense of Finland suspended between the East and the West, partaking of both and different from both, was embodied in the look of their capital city. I walked for almost all afternoon around the center of Helsinki in the watery northern sunshine and scarcely ever saw a word that meant anything at all to me on the shop and road signs. This was my experience in another other capital of a country with a Finno-Ugric language—Budapest.

Of all the train trips I took in those years, the journey along the route of the Orient Express to Budapest was the most memorable. I boarded the eastbound train in Dunkirk; from there it went through northern France and on to the Rhine and down to Switzerland following the great river and its melodramatic scenery and Ruritanian castles. After changing trains following a five-hour layover in Vienna, we set off in the late afternoon for the Hungarian border. I was questioned by the Hungarian border guards and was glad that I had thought to bring my letter of invitation to show them. Once the train left the border, the countryside looked older and less well maintained, and the farmhouses and buildings antique. I was the only guest in the early part of the evening in the cavernous dining room of my Budapest hotel. A weary waiter handed me a menu, which I was relieved to see was in German as well as impenetrable Hungarian. The waiter and I shared menu German so I was able to order food and a carafe of red Hungarian wine, which I enjoyed despite it managing to be both fruity and thin. (It was listed as *Ungarische Rotwein* only, so I had no idea what I was drinking other than as to its color.) Four musicians in what I thought to be Romany costumes were playing in the far corner of the restaurant. Halfway through my meal I looked up from my book to see, with horror, that the quartet was making its way across the room to my table. When they arrived, the leader, a violinist, said something to me in what I took to be Hungarian, smiled, lifted his violin as they began to pay a wild, melancholy, Gypsyish tune, followed by another in the same strain. When that was finished, I said "*Danke, danke*" and grinned at them idiotically. I offered some forint notes. They took them and walked away, still playing. Fortunately, two other tables were now occupied and I was able to leave, never knowing whether I had given them the equivalent of pennies or a princely sum. Things looked up the next morning. My guide to the National Library was a charming woman called Ilona Kovacs, and I met Dr. Géza Sebestyén, the national librarian, who had been so helpful with my IFLA report. Ilona Kovacs took me to the historic town of Esztergom, with its ancient basilica and high, fortified walls, on the day after my talks in Budapest; there I bought some brightly painted plates with old Magyar floral patterns. On my return, these artifacts from the eastern extremity of historic Europe hung in our Pinner kitchen on the western. I returned to Budapest for an IFLA meeting in 1972 and marveled again at that scarred rebuilt city that had suffered horribly in World War II at the hands of the invading Germans and the "liberating" Russians and from the fraternal attentions of the Warsaw Pact in 1956. The few buildings that had survived the Hungarians' tribulations were still pocked with the effects of mortar, shell, and small-arms fire.

THE BRITISH LIBRARY

Britain, a country rich in libraries and with a rich library history but so long a country without a national library and an organized national library service, acquired both in 1973 with the establishing of the British Library. Its formation was foreshadowed in the late 1960s by two important reports that are known by the names of their chairmen—the Parry report and the Dainton report. The former called upon the British Museum to assume more responsibilities (including a national interlibrary lending system, the provision of foreign publications in conjunction with major university libraries, and the creation of a national reference service). It recognized that this assumption of new duties, and incorporation of services being given elsewhere, would require substantial additional funding and a new "British Museum Library" building (a project that had been in the works for many years but was bedeviled by local and national politics and stymied by lack of funding). The Dainton report took these concepts further and called for the creation of a National Libraries Authority, charged with managing the British Museum's library departments (including the National Reference Library of Science and Invention—NRLSI—which absorbed the old Patent Office Library in 1962 and was administered by the British Museum); the National Central Library [NCL], which was, essentially, the national coordinator of interlibrary lending; the National Lending Library for Science and Technology [NLLST], a vast collection of books and documents located in Boston Spa, Yorkshire; and the British National Bibliography. The Dainton plan was a gathering together of the components necessary to carry out the services envisaged in the Parry report, but with the difference that it recommended a new national library not an aggregation of powers into the British Museum Library. The Dainton recommendations, but not the wording used to designate the services, were approved by the government of the day and incorporated into a white paper (a statement of government policy) published in 1971. The British Library Organizing Committee was set up in that year, the British Library Act was passed and became law in 1972, and the British Library (BL) came into being on July 1 of the following year. The first director-general of the BL was Harry Hookway, a senior civil servant who was not a librarian, the first of many errors. The BL had three major divisions, each also headed by a director-general: reference, lending, and bibliographic services (Jack Wells was the latter's first director-general), and was housed in a variety of buildings great and small in London and in Yorkshire.

....

The four or five years leading up to its incorporation into the BL were times of major change for BNB. There was the change wrought by the introduction of MARC and the production of BNB on microfiche produced from computer records (the online provision of catalogue records was some years in the future) and there was the looming and disruptive change, the more disruptive for being largely unknown, that would come about with the increasingly inevitable national library. That time encompassed the brief heyday of ultrafiche—a technology that led the fervid to believe that we would soon be walking around with the contents of the Library of Congress in a briefcase—an odd anticipation of Google's hubristic schemes forty and more years later. At some point in 1971, I was asked to join a small group headed by Richard Coward, to be called the British Library Planning Secretariat. My task was to look into the cataloguing practices of the various parts of what would become the BL with a view to rationalizing those practices. I left BNB on secondment to the Department of Education and Science as a species of temporary civil servant but I was, as it turned out, neither to return to BNB nor to earn my living cataloguing—one of the few things in life at which I was really skilled. It is perfectly possible that I was, as the vast majority of people are, an example of the Peter principle in action, but this new, unfamiliar, baffling, wider world was interesting if not ultimately satisfying. We set up shop in offices on the 6th floor of a large Victorian office building between Scotland Yard and Whitehall Place, next to the huge Norman Shaw Gothic former headquarters of the Metropolitan Police, and near the Houses of Parliament and Westminster Abbey. It was the first time during which I had worked in an environment in which the tasks to be done were not clearly defined and there were no regular hours. We were a group of only six people, each with an area both ill delineated and with few links to the others. My work was planned in consultation with Richard Coward and was carried out largely via conversations with cataloguers in the British Museum and the NRLSI on how we could harmonize their and BNB's cataloguing practices. The vast collections of the National Lending Library in Boston Spa were not catalogued but arranged by author and title in the pious hope that those data given on the spines of the books were, first, the forms by which they were sought, and, second, agreed with the data given on the title leaf. The perceived beauty of the NLL system, designed by Brian Urquhart, its founding director, was that it could be administered by clerical staff and run with assembly-line routines.

I attended many meetings in the museum, the National Central Library, and the NRLSI; the latter was then housed in a building in Bayswater that used to be Whiteley's (Britain's first department store) and had the chilly, somewhat faded grandeur appropriate to its former role. Two memories of those meetings abide. The first is when I asked the person in charge of cataloguing in the British Museum's Department of Printed Books, R. S. Pine-Coffin, if the cataloguing staff of the museum could consider adopting the new cataloguing rules (an international standard) when the British Library came into being and was told that he did not care which code was used "if we have to give up proper cataloguing." By the latter he meant the idiosyncratic, largely unrecorded practices built on the rules set out more than a hundred years before by Panizzi, and last revised in 1936. Mr. Pine-Coffin was a gentleman with perfect manners, a scholar, and a member of an old and grand family but, like the vast majority of his colleagues, not a trained librarian. One of the things that had ossified the practices and attitudes of the museum's library departments (printed books, maps, manuscripts, music, and Oriental books and manuscripts) was the institution's habit of hiring staff, very often from the universities of either Oxford or Cambridge, who had excellent academic qualifications but absolutely no knowledge of librarianship and no grasp of the service ethic of that profession. Therefore, new staff brought intelligence and learning to the institution but very little original thinking about library services and collections. Each generation learned from its predecessors and was taught, inter alia, that what they were learning constituted the "proper" way to do things. This, combined with feeling several cuts above the common herd by reason of academic achievement and indisputably high levels of scholarship, manifested itself in, from my point of view, a disdain for bibliographic standards or indeed any cataloguing other than that done in the museum. This attitude, I was to discover, was not unique to the British Museum but it did not make my task easier, nor did another meeting this time with Julian Roberts, then in the antiquarian books section of the Department of Printed Books. Julian, another scholar and gentleman, had showed me the cataloguing process for early books and the shelves full of uncatalogued acquisitions. Since I was doing a survey of all the cataloguing operations and, among other things, was listing the size of cataloguing backlogs, I asked him to estimate theirs.

He told me that it was about five years' worth of acquisitions. When I asked him if they had plans to reduce the cataloguing arrears, he replied, "Dear boy, if a book were published in 1621, what does it matter if it is catalogued this year or next?" I had no suitable response.

There was an awful tragedy in my family at this time. My sister-in-law Joan, Anne's only sibling and the mother of our nephew Paul Butcher, had contracted a liver disease under unknown circumstances while on holiday in Austria with her parents in the early 1960s (before she married). This illness transformed her, in very few years, from a vital, healthy-looking, very attractive young woman to someone who endured many extended hospital treatments from which she emerged looking bent and older than her years. She died in May 1970, aged 29, leaving her son, who was then not quite 5 years old. Not long afterwards Peter married an American who had worked for BNB; she continued to work there after he had left BNB to work for City University. He contracted a third marriage years later, had more children, and died of smoking-related illnesses in his early 50s.

In 1971, the Planning Secretariat was moved to offices in Africa House in Kingsway, Holborn, just west of Lincoln's Inn Fields. This vast, ornate Victorian building had marble stairs on either side of an open elevator with exterior and interior sliding grille doors. There were a multitude of carvings of allegorical figures and beasts (elephants, lions, and the like)—the embodiment of the high Victorian idea of the "Dark Continent" of their imaginings—on the classical pediment above the main entrance. I worked most closely with my BNB colleague and friend Andrew Phillips, a Welshman with high intelligence and a dry wit, and with Richard Coward and John Linford. We each had high-ceilinged, chilly offices with large desks—all, as I recall, covered in memorandums, drafts, and manuscripts that were, at least in my case, spectacularly untidy and inefficient document-retrieval systems. I think we were all inventing our jobs, allowed to speculate and to write innovative proposals for how cataloguing might be handled in the national library that was aborning. My memories of my working days at that time are of long meetings in various parts of London, of frequent travel, of the morning tea and bread roll taken in a little café in Little Turnstile Lane, just around the corner from Africa House, of lunches in the Princess Louise—a beautiful but slightly dowdy Victorian pub in High Holborn, now spoiled by an ill-advised refurbishment—washed down with schooners of Amontillado from the cask, in the Spaghetti House in Sicilian Avenue, or in the Bung Hole, a dark bar in High Holborn frequented by lawyers from Lincoln's Inn. Some of those lunches were prolonged and unusually vinous, which led Andrew to suggest that our Civil Service files were stamped NGITA, standing for "No good in the afternoon." Despite that, each of us accomplished a lot, and the deficiencies in the technical processing arrangements of the British Library, when it came into being, were not due to the plans we came up with but the difficulty of integrating them into the complexity of amalgamated large institutions, each with their own history, allegiances, and inward-looking staff, compounded by bureaucratic inertia and the inherent and obstinate irrationality of even the newest large institution.

GUIDO MORRIS

Guido Morris (né Douglas Morris), 1910–1980, was a supremely gifted typographer, part of the Arts and Crafts movement of artists in various media that flourished in Cornwall in the decade before and after World War II, and a notoriously erratic person who led a louche and ultimately sad life. His work reached its peak in his Latin Press, which he founded in St. Ives after the war and that flourished artistically and languished financially until it folded in 1953. He was so much in debt after years of combining jobbing printing with fine printing that he had to surrender his press to his principal creditor—a printer called Worden's—who sold it to Kim Taylor for the Ark Press that he established in 1954. Though well known in his circle and highly regarded as a fine printer, he never again had the means to work at his art and craft as he would have wished. He worked for years as a guard on London Underground trains (on the District Line). Anthony Baker published an article on Morris in 1969 that caught the attention of a BL colleague of mine called Steve Holland, who had made it his job to seek out the faintly remembered and underregarded book artists of the time. (He had met and befriended the elderly and ill David Jones, the poet, painter, typographer, and author of "In parenthesis"—a remarkable long poem that almost no one now remembers but was called "a work of genius" by, among others, T. S. Eliot on its publication in 1937.) Steve, who was close to my friend and colleague Ken Price, sought and found Guido Morris, then a frail and impoverished 62, in the tunnels under London and brought him to a pub in Holborn that was a frequent lunch place for Ken, me, and my brother David, who was then working in Holborn Library. Guido was in dire need of money. I am a little hazy on the details but somehow, using the money that we clubbed together to pay, Steve managed to gain access to a tabletop handpress for Guido. We also commissioned small printing jobs from him under his new imprint—Officina Mauritiana. My order, paid for in advance, was for one hundred bookplates to be designed and printed by him under his new imprint. The book plates are simple, use the Bodoni typeface Guido loved, and read "E LIBRIS / Michael Gorman / Apud Guidonem Mauritium / Impressa"—he prided himself on his Latin and claimed that the much more common *Ex Libris* on bookplates was a vulgar error. We also subscribed to two small pamphlets that he produced—only one of which I still possess, a poem by his fellow outcast and disappointed artist, the man who called himself Baron Corvo. After a while we did not see Guido, though I believe Steve would run into him occasionally.

....

In early 1972, we moved from Bloomsbury Court not much more than a mile away to a onetime workman's cottage in Waxwell Close, a semicircle of identical, (barely) semidetached, pitched-roof cottages with a semicircular copse within a broad gravel path. It was our first mortgage. The house cost £11,000 (approximately £180,000 or $290,000 in today's money). I was more than surprised to find that it sold for £450,000 in 2007, presumably to someone who now regrets the purchase bitterly. It had two stories and a small front garden bisected by a path of crazy paving. There was a minuscule front room, a marginally larger sitting room, a kitchen, and a tiny hall on the first floor, three bedrooms (tiny, small, and of medium size) and a bathroom on the second. One saving grace was the back garden in which Anne grew flowers in a patch beyond the lawn and before the garden ended at the River (more properly, rivulet or brook) Pinn. The Close lay across the old Waxwell Lane from a large house with an old-fashioned English garden behind low stone walls. That house, Waxwell Farm Cottage, was inhabited by Mrs. Olwen Bridgeman, whose late husband Reginald, the grandson of the 3rd Earl of Bradford, was a diplomat and left-wing politician. She was born Olwen Jones, the daughter of a pharmacist in Wembley, a worthy position in life but far removed from her husband's ancient family and noble affiliations. Reginald Bridgeman's advanced views had led to him building the Waxwell Close cottages for farmworkers and, though the houses had been sold and most of the farms of Pinner were a distant memory, his relict still retained something of the chatelaine about her when she "popped in" to inquire as to the welfare of those who, in some nebulous way, she saw as dependents of the Bridgeman family and recipients of their largesse. She was kindly, if a touch condescending, and took pleasure in seeing the children, of whom there were a number in the Close. Mrs. Bridgeman died in 1985, at the age of 82, and tasteful low blocks of flats now occupy the site of Waxwell Farm Cottage, thus obliterating even the nominal memory of what was, in Betjeman's words, a "parish of enormous hay fields."

It was about this time that I began to teach a part-time course on cataloguing at the library school that was then part of West London College, near Barons Court and Hammersmith tube stations and not far from the Olympia conference and event center. The library program was run by Albert Standley, a kindly man with a mane of light brown, patently artificial hair. I taught an evening class twice a week for three terms, which involved leaving my work about half an hour earlier than usual, traveling by tube to Barons Court, having a hasty sandwich and beer in a cavernous gloomy pub near the college, which was situated in Gliddon Road, and getting to the class in time for the 6:30 p.m. class. The students were studying for the Library Association's first-year examinations, so the syllabus was both set and something with which I was very familiar. Though the fees paid were small, they represented a welcome addition to my still quite low salary and provided me with useful teaching experience and a measure of self-confidence in my teaching ability. Other negatives were the long days that teaching involved and, in the last term in which I taught there, a recurrence of attacks of stage fright and, on really bad days, panic attacks that on two occasions prevented me from reaching the classroom at all. I was not there for the last class of my last teaching assignment at West London College and sent the end of course grades in by post.

My brother David and his wife, the former Diana Williams (see chapter 7) separated in 1972 and a short while afterwards he came to live with us in Waxwell Close. This was, as are all such arrangements, the source of both pleasure and friction. David resumed his bachelor ways and pursued his interests with a number of his lady friends, mostly consecutively. He was also a keen footballer and cricketer. For a while, I would meet him after we had both finished work (he had a succession of temporary positions) and go to the Oddfellows Pub on the corner of Waxwell Lane and Bridge Street to drink beer and play darts before dinner. His stay with us lasted for more than a year and ended in strained relationships, as is the way. He divorced Diana (or Diana divorced him), and he married a woman called Jenny who was not the Jenny who was the proximate cause of him parting from Diana.

The period between 1972 and 1974 was, I now realize, a kind of interlude in my life, a time in which I worked hard but did little more than try to get by each day dealing with my mental turmoil and trying to hide it from all except a few friends. During that time, the British Library was established, BNB ceased to be an organization and became a publication of the Bibliographic Services Division of the BL, the work of the Planning Secretariat came to an end, and I was, after a perfunctory interview, appointed as head of the newly established Bibliographic Standards Office of the BL with the remit of working on the ISBDs, the various EUDISED projects, and the coming revision of the Anglo-American cataloguing rules. I traveled to many places, worked initially with Andrew Phillips before he went off to grander things with the Reference Services Division, carried on a complex, fitful social life, played a minimal part, alas, in my daughters' upbringing, though I have loved them fiercely all their lives, and, if truth were told, which I seldom did to myself, I became bored with my life. I was, I suppose, in waiting for something big to happen, as two things did.

My restlessness and desire to escape had led to me, in 1970, sending off for the application forms for a librarian position in Red Deer, Alberta, a place I had never heard of before its name in a job advertisement caught my eye but that I assumed was very different from anything I had known. I told Jack Wells of my intentions and he persuaded me not to go through with the application. Another step not taken that could have changed our lives forever. This was before the days of the Planning Secretariat and for a while I lost the desire to move.

In early 1974, a bolt from the blue in the form of a letter from Herbert Goldhor, director of the library school at the University of Illinois, Urbana, provided a safer way to do something different without necessarily changing the course of my life. It offered me a temporary teaching position, from August 1974 to May 1975, to substitute for a teacher of cataloguing who was taking a sabbatical. I knew less than nothing of Champaign or Urbana, universities, Dr. Goldhor, American library schools, the life of American faculty members, and many other things that might have informed my choice. I knew, but not precisely, where Illinois was and had extensive knowledge of literary and cinematic America—knowledge that proved to be, and to put it mildly, inapplicable. I later learned, not always with pleasure, that *A kiss before dying* (the Robert Wagner vehicle) was no guide to campus life, that none of Nelson Algren's *Man with the golden arm,* Farrell's Studs Lonigan novels, or Mike Royko's biography of the first Mayor Daley gave the whole picture of life in Illinois, and that speaking English did not always mean one could communicate with Americans smoothly and efficiently. As I was to discover, to misquote L. P. Hartley, America is another country; they do things differently there. It was easy to obtain a year's leave of absence without pay, it seemed that it would be an interesting experience for my daughters, early enough in their lives (they were short of their 8th and 5th birthdays on the day we left) not to be a major disruption, my wife went along with the idea, and it was, above all for me, a change, a temporary escape from the pressures of a life that was, on occasion, insupportable to the point of being impossible to live.

The other big thing that happened was that planning for the revision and harmonization of the 1968 cataloguing rules began in earnest. The Library Association's cataloguing committee (with representation from the British Library) decided that, unlike in the previous decade, there should be a British coeditor to work with the American editor. Though this was not yet agreed, Peter Lewis, then working at the University of Sussex, was to be sent as a delegate to the organizing meeting, and it was decided that that I should accompany him as the British editor-designate. That meeting was held in Chicago, at the headquarters of ALA, in March 1974. The attendees included representatives of the three "Anglo-American" countries—the U.K., U.S.A., and Canada—and the American editor-designate, Paul Winkler. It did not include me. The decisions taken by this organizing meeting are described in chapter 12 of this book. I was due to attend that meeting after my first trans-Atlantic flight and duly purchased a ticket, spent two days packing for this unfamiliar adventure, and was driven to Heathrow on the appointed day, in her Austin Mini, by my friend Cynthia Paterson. We parked that car and she came with me to the departure gate. My aerophobic terror had been mounting for more than two days and, as I left Cynthia and walked toward the ticket collector, I felt the floor beneath me tip and sway, lurched and would have fallen to the ground if not steadied by a man in a gray overcoat in the shuffling line. I felt that I had to sit down, found a chair, put my hand to my face, and found it bathed in sweat on that cold March day. I looked up and saw Peter Lewis smiling and waving to me on the other side of the departure gate and realized with dreadful clarity that I was incapable of joining him, despite the fact that it seemed the opportunity of a lifetime was drifting away from me and despite the swamp of humiliation in which I was about to be submerged. I waved back at Peter, called out "I can't," stood up and turned away. Cynthia accompanied me to a desk at which an airline employee, sympathetic to my evident distress, arranged for a refund of my ticket price. Cynthia then drove me home. Both Anne and she were more than kind, but I felt humiliated, inadequate, and sad, thinking that I had the chance to enter an important race and had fallen at the first hurdle. This was a shattering event. For several days during which I did not leave my house, I thought seriously about refusing the honor of the rules editorship, of writing to Dr. Goldhor declining his offer, of leaving the British Library, and of seeking a public library job in a provincial town (Winchester? Plymouth? Worcester?—but no further north than the latter). I envisaged a life in which I would cease to play a part in national and international librarianship and would travel, when I did, by train and ferry, if going to Europe or Ireland (I would not entertain the idea of traveling more extensively). I doubt I would have enjoyed such a life much but perhaps it would have been better for all of us. In any event, it remained another path untaken. When Peter returned from America, it was with an agreed plan for how the new rules were to be devised and coordinated (see chapter 12) and with the (somewhat surprising) news that they still wished me to be the British editor (now retitled "associate editor"). I learned later that another member of the cataloguing committee had, on learning of my failure to attend, put his name forward as a possible British editor. I have no idea why this kind offer was not accepted. Peter gave me a day or so to respond to the offer. I decided that, one way or another, I would accept the offer from the University of Illinois, get myself to the U.S. by plane, and play a full part in the creation of the new rules. I had five months to change, since I would have to be in Illinois in August of 1974, at least a week before the beginning of the new academic year. I wrote to Dr. Goldhor accepting his invitation, I accepted the position of associate editor of the new rules, and spent those months working on various projects for the BL and in connection with the first standard edition of the ISBD(M), which was published in mid-1974. I was also working on the preparations for the new rules and the momentous trip to America in August. The news in those months was consumed by the travails of President Nixon and the Watergate investigations. Nixon was even less popular in Britain than in the U.S. I harbored a particular animosity towards him because of the nuclear saber-rattling in which he and the evil Kissinger had indulged in 1973, so was not in the least unhappy to see him in distress. As things turned out, we arrived in America exactly a week after he resigned and found the papers full of the implications for policy, and the homely details of the domestic arrangements, of the presidency of the far more agreeable Gerald Ford. This time, Anne's parents took us to Heathrow. I desperately wanted to conceal my mounting fear and anxiety from my daughters, who were themselves nervously excited and clutching their Sacha dolls. Anne was aware of my state and managed to remain calm despite what must have been a nerve-racking experience for her too. I drank a glass of brandy before we said good-bye to Waxwell Close for, as we thought, the next nine months. My memories of the farewells at the airport and the formalities of tickets, checking luggage, etc., are sketchy at best but I remember with crystal clarity the moment when I followed Anne and my daughters over the line that separated the outside world from the enclosure of those irrevocably committed to a flight—the line that I had been unable to cross six months earlier. I remember the flight as bumpy, though it was probably very little different from the at least a hundred times I have crossed the Atlantic subsequently. I was in a haze of suppressed fear and nerves the entire time and remember looking out of the window only once—at the Greenlandic scenery far below, peaceful in the sunlight and shadows (we left at about 4 p.m. and arrived at about 6 p.m. so it was afternoon all the way). When we left the plane with thanks to the flight attendants whose faces I had studied for signs of panic for the entire flight and deep gratitude in my heart for my preservation, we had to walk across the tarmac to the terminal (these were the days before skyways). My solemn daughters clutched their dolls, I felt elated, Anne, smart in a linen Jaeger suit, tripped on something, fell, and grazed her knee. This was not a good omen. We were met in the terminal by the associate director of the library school, Bob Brown, and his wife, who had driven up from downstate Illinois to meet us. An act of kindness but no doubt a source of puzzlement to him, since he had probably never met adults who did not drive. Bob, an unquenchably genial and friendly man, was one of the largest men I have ever met, by which I mean he was tall and broad with large hands, a booming laugh, and a strong handshake. He and his wife lived in a small town near the university called Mahomet, and JD (of whom more later) said that, when he left for the day, it was the only known case of "the mountain going to Mahomet." His wife, it transpired, was a doll collector and she bonded with my daughters, examining their Sacha dolls and their clothing with great care. The Chicago freeways, the signs saying "MEMPHIS 400 miles," the strip malls seen from the freeway, and the houses and billboards giving way to the rural flatness of "downstate," were all as strange and alluring in their strangeness, not as if we were on the Silk Road to Samarkand or in the souks of Marrakech but because we were in a seemingly familiar world that had been expanded and skewed. We were dazed with the strangeness and the time difference as the darkness fell. A McDonald's in all its cruel brightness and primary plastic colors on the outskirts of Kankakee served as our oasis on the road south. I had never been in such a place and did not at all like what I saw. The girls were half-asleep and past hunger so we were soon back on the road.

We were to stay in a house, 501 Westlawn, that was rented to us by a faculty member called West who was on sabbatical in Europe—an arrangement that had been made by the library school. It was quite dark and late (about 4 a.m. in England and our heads) when we arrived at the house on a quiet, curving street of lawns, trees, and wide sidewalks—just like something out of a 1950s film about the complicated lives of American academics and their rebellious children. One last wonder for that day was the discovery that the supermarket on the other side of Mattis Avenue was still open at that late hour. This was at a time when, in England, the shops closed at 7 p.m. at the latest and there were few supermarkets anywhere (none in Pinner), still less anything of the size and variety of contents of this IGA store. I felt as if I were on another planet, one in which anything anyone would want was available for purchase at all hours of the day. The experience tipped over into complete oddity when I saw the store's security guard, an overweight man in his 50s with a pistol in a holster on his expansive hip. I was a child of war and the son of a career soldier and had never, up to that date, ever seen a pistol that was not on a cinema screen. Indeed they did do things differently here.

10

Illinois, 1974–1975

Champaign lies to the west of Urbana, the older town and the county seat of Champaign County. When the railroad came to the area it was kept to the west of Urbana for economic, geographic, and murkily political reasons. In due course, the settlement of West Urbana, which had grown largely around the Illinois Central station, became Champaign Township and then in 1860 the city of Champaign. At that time both cities had minuscule populations, mostly engaged in businesses dependent on agriculture and the railroad. Over the years, the cities have grown together, enclosing the "third city" of the University of Illinois. Though the cities have separate identities and, to some extent, separate characteristics, their separate municipal existences are a financial and governmental nonsense. When we arrived there on that late August evening in 1974, the cities had a combined population of less than 90,000 (the university had about 30,000 students, the vast majority of them resident in Champaign-Urbana in the main semesters), two mayors, two city halls, two public libraries, three police forces, etc.

We woke early the next morning in 501 Westlawn. We had lived all our lives in a temperate climate and my travels had exposed me only briefly to midcontinental weather. An August day on the prairie came as a shock, with its heat (in the mid-90s degrees Fahrenheit) by midday, powerful sun, glaring light, and high humidity, with the latter the least bearable, especially when we decided to walk to the supermarket to buy some food later in the morning. We had only to walk a few blocks from the house but we were unsuitably dressed for the heat, the pavements that we soon learned to call "sidewalks" were nonexistent in this part of town, the main road (Mattis Avenue) that we had to cross contained more lanes and more cars than we were used to, and the latter were on the "wrong" side of the road. We had never seen a stop/walk signal and had no notion of the function of the stop signs where we felt there should have been traffic lights. Just getting to the tarmac expanse of the "Country Fair Shopping Center" became another adventure. We passed no one on foot going, or returning. The icy cold of the IGA was a welcome respite from the outside but the cold neon expanse was cheerless and baffling. We wandered around the IGA's aisles wondering how we were going to cope with all these unfamiliar products in such profusion. We left the shop with three paper bags full of basic provisions and looked around in the glare of the sun at this alien world of contradictions and unknown habits. Nothing in all that I had read about America equipped me to deal with being in this place so far from home, a home that was, for the next nine months at least, barred to us. We found sanctuary in a pizza restaurant in the same shopping center, another new experience. Though we had eaten pizza in Lucca, this dark, high-ceilinged, largely empty place was something new. We asked for tea and received a large brown translucent plastic jug of ice and a beverage called Teem, a carbonated drink that was also new to us. At least it was ice cold. The pizzas were hot and cheap. We trudged back to the house carrying our brown bags. Our spirits lifted when we were invited to dinner with Herbert Goldhor that evening. He lived with his wife (a medical doctor) in a house built by an artificial lake and, though the size and what we saw as the opulence of middle-class houses made it even clearer that we were strangers in a strange land, his geniality and kindness to us made things look up.

In 1867, pursuant to the Land Grant Colleges Act signed by Abraham Lincoln, the state of Illinois established the Illinois Industrial University on many acres of scrip land in the center of Illinois. The university's first building was located on the fields between the courthouse in Urbana and the Illinois Central station in Champaign. The institution was renamed the University of Illinois in the 1880s and, in the 90 years between that renaming and 1974, had grown to be one of the most important research universities in the country and to possess, more important to me, the largest academic library in a state university in the U.S. (smaller only than those of Harvard and Yale) and, as it remains, the largest library in the world that is nowhere near a major city. Out there, in the middle of the corn and soy fields there stood and stands something akin to a library miracle which was the result of a deliberate policy undertaken and supported by governmental action over many decades. The policy on the size and scope of the library collection was first set out in 1912 by university president Edmund James, who told the trustees that the library should accumulate "at least a million of books as rapidly as possible" and that the state should "spend a million dollars to build a new building to house the collections." Successive presidents and strong university librarians, principally Phineas Windsor, Robert Downs, and Hugh Atkinson, ensured that growth for almost a century.

The main building of the U of I library stands astride the southern end of Wright Street, the boundary between Urbana and Champaign. When it was dedicated in 1926 it must have been surrounded by fields, especially on the western (Champaign) side. It is a huge squarish building with four floors and a basement to which have been added six book stacks (the latest in the 1980s). The library collections and staff were moved from Altgeld Hall, a Romanesque structure designed by two university professors and opened in 1897 as the University Library. It was taken over by the law school when the library moved out thirty years later and renamed in honor of the socialist John Peter Altgeld—"the forgotten eagle"—in 1941.

In 1974, what was then called the Graduate School of Library Science occupied offices and classrooms on the third and fourth floors of the main library. A wall on the third floor bore a bas-relief in bronze of Katharine Sharp, the founder of the school, accompanied by a plaque commemorating her achievements. The lady's nose was shiny unlike the rest of the portrait, the result of affectionate rubbing, mostly by students, over the years. Miss Sharp faced a classroom and, beyond her and some offices, lay a comprehensive library science library. I was soon to discover that the physical proximity of library and library school did not lead to close ties between the library and library school staff. Though I met the university librarian, a gentle, courteous man called Lucien White who held that position from 1971 to 1975, and his predecessor, the dominating Robert Bingham Downs (his tenure was 1943–1971), who spent much of each day in the library building, in which he retained an office, I met very few of the other staff, and I do not believe any of them taught library school classes then. It was my first glimpse of the gulf between librarians and library educators, which, visible even then, has widened catastrophically in the thirty-five years since. Fortunately, the vast majority of the library school faculty members in 1974 were librarians with strong library backgrounds, though in some cases, the librarianship they were teaching bore little relationship to the librarianship being practiced all around them.

It was simultaneously bracing and intimidating to be welcomed into an institution of which I knew nothing with duties that were a mystery to me, apart from the fact that I had to be in certain classrooms for certain hours each week once the semester had started. I knew that American universities were run on different lines to those in Britain, but the differences meant nothing to me as I had very little knowledge of the latter. What were syllabuses, lesson plans, multiple choice questions, pop quizzes, semester breaks, and semesters? What were my hours of work? To whom did I report? I knew almost everything there was to know about cataloguing and a lot about the public libraries of London (which might as well have been the public libraries of Inner Mongolia for all the relevance they had to my predicament). I was too proud to ask my new colleagues and, for their part, they assumed that I needed neither information nor assistance in understanding what were arcana to me and general knowledge to them. The person whom I was replacing temporarily while she was on sabbatical (what *was* a "sabbatical"?) was in her office and, I was to discover, was physically present in the library school for all that year. A brief conversation led me to believe that our views on cataloguing were very different and I could not look for help from her. One wall of her office was adorned with a piece of stitchery depicting a cat sitting on a log, a repellent visual pun. My office was the west end of a large room on the fourth floor of the library, separated from the east end by a tall barrier of bookcases. That office east of mine was occupied by the singular self of James L. Divilbiss (known to all as "JD"), an electrical engineer who had become an expert in library automation and systems, a wit, raconteur, and inspired teacher. He was not a librarian but I thought him more simpatico than many of my temporary colleagues who were. I attended his systems classes on many occasions and found them most enlightening. Another faculty member was Walter Allen, a cultivated man who owned a number of vehicles including a Rolls-Royce and a Volkswagen convertible. In the first week, he invited me to have lunch with him in the "carvery" of Jumer's Hotel in Urbana (a bizarre architectural mating of stockbroker's Tudor and a German hunting lodge). He had told me that they sold very good beef sandwiches. I ate meat in those days and had a clear idea of a beef sandwich—two or three thin slices of overcooked beef with mustard between two slices of buttered white bread, a staple of railway buffets. I was surprised to be presented with a plate piled high with thick slices of medium-rare beef with no visible bread and a large dollop of horseradish sauce. There was a piece of gravy-saturated bread hiding beneath the beef. Even the mundane sandwich was different in this newfound land. F. Wilfrid Lancaster, the only faculty member of whom I had heard previously, was born in the northeast of Britain but had worked for the U.S. Department of Defense and the National Institutes of Health as an information specialist and pioneer in information retrieval systems before taking up library education. Wilf and I became cagily friendly and we visited him and his American wife Cesaria (née Volpe) for dinner once or twice. JD was very friendly with a former faculty member, Fred Schlipf, a man of my age who had just become the head of Urbana Public Library. He was another wit—the co-inventor with JD of the First Church of Christ Podiatrist—and someone whom I have always enjoyed meeting over the years. The courtly Rolland Stevens taught reference classes and treated me with great kindness. He wore brightly colored clothes made of "knit" and accessorized them with, on occasion, white shoes and a white belt—an arrangement that I later learned was called a half-Cleveland (a white tie would have to have been added to create a full Cleveland). Rolland was the founding president of the Beta Phi Mu honor society for library science, which began in 1948 at the University of Illinois.

Clothes were a problem for me. The heat and stifling humidity made it impossible to wear three-quarters of the clothes I had brought from Britain. I had never been to work without a jacket and a tie and struggled to keep to that habit though I noted that many of the professors dressed less formally (and more sensibly). The lack of efficient air conditioning in the fifty-year-old library made matters worse. The classroom opposite Miss Sharp's nose had two fans that were seven feet tall and three feet in diameter; they could be adjusted to provide direct gales of warmish air but that was not much help. The weather, internally and externally, was a real problem for me that went far beyond discomfort. I had discovered, in the previous seven years, that heat and bright lights were efficient triggers of stage fright and, in worse cases, anxiety attacks. Thus it was that I stood in that room in late August 1974 looking at thirty or more young men and women of whom I knew nothing, feeling that I was on the edge of a precipice and wishing that I had not committed myself to teaching for a year. Compounding this near panic was the fact that I had three or four handwritten sheets containing notes on the topics I intended to cover but had no such list of topics to hand to the students, as they obviously expected. Alan Thomas, who had taught me cataloguing in his first year as a teacher, told me then that you always remember the first class you teach and that, in subsequent years, you see students as remanifestations of those in that first class. Though I did not become a full-time teacher, it is true that many of those students from 1974 remain clear in my memory—some because they later became friends and colleagues, some because they impressed themselves on me for a particular reason. The former is true of Bill Potter, who went on to work with me at the University of Illinois and in a number of ALA activities; he is now the head of the library at the University of Georgia. The latter is true of many, including Richard Terry, about whom I knew two things—that he had been in the Coast Guard and that he was from Fresno, California. I had never heard of Fresno and assumed, because of the Coast Guard connection, that it must be on the coast. I was not to be disabused of that idea until I was interviewed, fourteen years later, for what turned out to be my last job, in Fresno in the heart of California's Central Valley, known for good reason as "the other California." The students were very friendly to me and seemed, at worst, to be puzzled by my evident unfamiliarity with the policies and procedures of universities in general and graduate schools in particular. I was assigned a graduate assistant called Terry Sklar, a Francophile who, like most of the students in Urbana-Champaign, came from the Chicago area—Skokie in her case. She helped me to turn my outline notes into something resembling a syllabus and told me about what the students would expect in the way of quizzes (they struck me as more suitable for kindergarten so I eschewed them), assignments, papers, etc. In addition, I enlisted one of the students to take detailed notes on my class and share them with me each week. The student who volunteered to do this was Marilyn Norsted, who went on to have a successful career in the library of Virginia Tech in Blacksburg and, alas, died young. I still have her neatly written, comprehensive notes and used them to develop courses on cataloguing for a number of years.

I was determined to teach cataloguing as one of the fundamental bases of librarianship, not as a specialized skill of use only to a few. I wanted the students to understand that cataloguing was, as I put it later, "the way librarians think." I told the students in the first class that this was not a class on how to become a cataloguer but on how knowledge of the bibliographic architecture that enables the retrieval of carriers of knowledge and information is an essential part of being a librarian, no matter in which kind of library they worked or what their primary duty might be. My class focused on the principles and structure of cataloguing and how those structures are manifest in codes and classification schedules. This approach was light on the kind of practical cataloguing exercises that typify courses designed to train cataloguers. This "lack" was the proximate cause of a rift with the person I was replacing while she was taking a local sabbatical. It soon became evident that my approach was not only radically different but was, because of that difference, deemed to be inferior or even inappropriate. New as I was to this world, it was a pleasant thing to discover the force of the principle of academic freedom. It was hinted, by Dr. Goldhor among others, that I "might like to reconsider my approach," but when it became apparent to all that I was not about the reconsider, the topic was dropped. The animosity towards me on the part of the cataloguing teacher remained, as I was to discover later. Very few of the students in my class had any intention of working as cataloguers and it was salt in someone's wounds to discover that my classes were popular and that a number of students were pleased to take a course that had some intellectual content. It is impossible to teach a general cataloguing course without some consideration of cataloguing rules and classification schedules and their applications, but these should always be to illustrate the underlying structures and the principles they embody. In its way, this mini tempest in a tiny academic teapot was a manifestation of the constant tug between vocational training and academic education in library education that goes back to its very beginnings. My view was, and remains, that as long as library education takes place in the postgraduate setting, the tilt should be in the direction of intellectual content and not training. The latter is the responsibility, not always assumed, of the library school graduate's future employers.

As the weeks went by, I settled into a routine of spending my weekdays in the library science library, my office, the classrooms, and, on occasion, the campustown bars with groups of students and or library school teachers. I learned that American beer has its uses in very hot climates and that, if I did not think of it as beer, it provided an acceptable ice-cold refuge from the scorching sun and high humidity. I learned, sometimes to my cost, that alcoholic drinks in the U.S. were far cheaper and more plentiful than in the U.K. I bought a bicycle and used it to go to and from the university and came to like the unfamiliar rhythms of campus life and, even, as the heat and humidity of the summer gave way to the relative freshness of autumn, the generally dreadful climate of the prairie. Someone has observed that the number of towns in the Middle West with French names (Bourbonnais, Terre Haute, Des Moines, La Grange, etc.) is not matched by the number of inhabitants with French names. I am convinced that the early French traders, explorers, and settlers stayed long enough to name places and to discover that the climate did not suit them, and then moved on.

My daughters were enrolled at Westview School in Russell Street, only two or three blocks from where we were staying. Every morning they would take their packed lunches, join a growing and disorganized group of children, meet their friends, and walk to the school. They adapted quickly and, within a week, nearly 5-year-old Alice had a strong American accent and spent much of her waking hours with a gaggle of small girls rushing around the unfenced yards until bedtime. Emma, older and naturally more reserved, was more often in the house reading or spending time with the one or two girls with whom she had made friends. They both had some problems with American spellings (*honor, catalog,* etc.) and different American words for familiar objects (*elevators, sidewalks, automobiles,* etc.) but did very well at school and liked their teachers. A few ladies took pity on the carless English people and would take Anne to the supermarket and to other shops so she did not have to repeat the hot march down Sheridan Road to the IGA. One of those ladies was Kay Draper, the librarian of the library science library, with whom we became very friendly. Thus we settled into our family life in a strange land.

One student, a tall, friendly, bearded man had been in combat in Vietnam, an experience that he hated and that had left him with such disdain for the 37th president that, after he had completed his military service, he stayed in Europe and lived there and in North Africa. His exile ended with the resignation of Richard Nixon, fortuitously in time for him to begin library school two weeks later. I greatly enjoyed playing tennis with him in the courts just west of the library (even in the stifling heat) and found that, despite our different experiences in life, we had much in common. I made many other friends among the students; at 33 I was nearer in age to many of them than the rest of the library school teachers. Many of the female students were very attractive and open and friendly in a manner with which I was not familiar. This was both exhilarating and confusing. The social boundaries and rules for relationships between the sexes that I knew did not seem to apply and I did not know those that were in force.

I soon learned to avoid other English people. I rarely talked to Britons, either other visiting faculty members or expatriates, and when I did, the almost invariable topics of conversation were how awful modern Britain was and/or how awful the U.S. is. I was not interested in pursuing either topic. Other faculty members from various departments proved to be far more interesting. I met a Japanese theater professor, a German linguist, and several professors of English literature, including the fine poet Larry Lieberman, who taught English and whose wife worked in a local public library. I was at a dinner party on one occasion when an older female professor who was originally from Germany was bewailing the soullessness of the shopping malls then being constructed all over the U.S. She summed up our feelings about them when she complained that they had "forty places to buy shoes, and nowhere to buy an apple." Many faculty members lived in the area around Westlawn, and I went to a number of cocktail parties and found myself listening to conversations about agricultural topics that proved to be more understandable than I had feared, learning to steer clear of political topics with political science professors, and hearing more than I wanted to hear from monomaniacal researchers. This was a wholly new world and quite congenial up to a point but, as the weeks went by, I found myself more detached from all around me, not less.

"Campustown" ran along Green Street west of Wright Street for a few blocks and spilled a little into the side streets. I spent some time in Murphy's, a dark bar full of booths with scarred tables that was a favorite of graduate students—many of whom seemed to have held that status for a good number of years; in Eddie Chin's Chinese restaurant in S. 6th Street; and in Deluxe Lunch & Billiards, playing pool with Bill Potter, while eating their incomparable fish sandwiches on Friday lunchtimes. I acted as Bill's research assistant when he created a flowchart of a game of pool for JD's library systems class—the most enjoyable library research I have ever undertaken. There were a couple of other bars in Urbana, just east of the campus and next to each other in Goodwin Street, called Treno's and the Thunderbird, the latter named after the cinema in the same block. Wilf Lancaster held court upstairs in the Thunderbird every Friday afternoon, happily surrounded by students and dispensing plastic jugs of beer. Wilf, unlike some of his colleagues, always treated the students as equals and was invested in their success. The classes went well, I was enjoying my first taste of university life (encountered too late, though I did not know that at the time), cycling all over the campus, and studying what I later came to realize was only a small part of a vast, diverse country. I also had a foot in the life that I had left temporarily in that I was still working on drafts of AACR2 and papers for the Joint Steering Committee, preparing for what turned out to be seven JSC meetings between the beginning of 1975 and the end of 1976.

The first of these was in Chicago—it was the meeting at which I was formally appointed as joint editor and first met Paul Winkler, with whom I was to have a personally cordial but professionally clashing relationship over the next decade. Paul was a longtime Library of Congress employee (then the principal cataloger) and something of a protégé of Sumner Spalding, the editor of the first AACR and the supplanter of Seymour Lubetzky in that role. At that time, the Library of Congress was a retrogressive force in cataloguing, eager, willing, and able to defend all its entrenched practices and, through its dominant position in North America, to enforce its reactionary will. Sumner had managed to resist Lubetzky's more radical ideas and to produce the unhappy compromises of the 1968 code (most of which were only compromises in the sense that they preserved LC's existing practices), and Paul was keen on playing the same role. Thus it was that, from the beginning, there was a fault line in the JSC, since the intentions of the parties were radically different. LC wanted the new code to cause the minimum disruption to its cataloguing operations. Many American librarians not employed by LC, the British, and to a lesser extent, the Canadian participants wished for a new code that would lead to major changes in how cataloguing was to be done. Such changes would inevitably lead to substantial disruption in LC's (and others') cataloguing practices. The fuse that led to the War of AACR2 (see chapter 12) was lit when Paul was appointed as chief editor. Paul was a middle-aged single man with a passion for the music of Wagner (he took his annual holiday in Bayreuth for the festival) who was very conservative in dress and very quiet in his manner. Someone told me that he ate his dinner at the same table in the same restaurant at the same hour each evening but I do not know if that were true, though it was indubitably believable. I cannot remember when I first met John Byrum, then at Princeton's library and the chair of the ALA cataloguing committee, but, whenever it was, it was the beginning of an alliance concerning AACR2 and a friendship that has lasted more than thirty years. John later went to the Library of Congress and rose to be head of one of their major cataloguing divisions (the internal organization of the Library of Congress remains a mystery to me to this day). One evening during the JSC meeting in Chicago, I went out to dinner with Peter Lewis, who had been appointed chair of JSC. We were seated in a booth as the waiter approached our table and, as waiters did in those days, said "Hi, my name is Wayne, I'll be your waiter this evening." He had hardly finished this pro forma statement when Peter, taking it to be a courtesy, rose to his feet, an awkward thing to do when you are tall and in banquette seating, put out his hand and said, "Good evening, my name is Peter Lewis." The waiter sprang back, startled, as Peter resumed his seat, and began to rattle off that evening's specials at great speed, clearly anxious to be away.

Fall in downstate Illinois is brief and charming—a few weeks of leaves turning, humidity declining, and heat decreasing tempered by what is, at first, freshness but soon becomes a chill presage of the winter to come. There the sun is your friend in fall and not the glaring brutal enemy of summer. I went with Bill Potter to see the university's "Fightin' Illini" play football (the American variety, in which feet have very little to do with the ball) in their giant Memorial Stadium, haunted by memories of Red Grange—the Galloping Ghost. I have no interest in the football played in the rest of the world (the one in which the foot engages with the ball all the time) and could not follow what was happening in the field so far away, but was fascinated by the marching bands, cheerleaders, gymnasts, and other anthropological details of the halftime show. The most fascinating and repellent aspect was the cavortings of a student clad in faux Native American garments including a full feather headdress and calling himself "Chief Illiniwek." Since the Illini were the original inhabitants of the state that is named after them and the vast majority of them were wiped out in the wars of the eighteenth century (the few remaining being exiled to Oklahoma), this seemed tasteless at best. The Fighting Illini lost and there was bitter talk of the "Fumblin' Illini" in the crowds around us. Afterwards we went to the house of friends of Bill's and sat on their porch drinking beer, feeling happy, chatting idly, and watching the evening come to Champaign.

I knew nothing at all about Thanksgiving when the holiday came around in 1974. A neighbor, thinking erroneously that we would be lonely if left alone on that Thursday, kindly asked us to share Thanksgiving dinner with his and other families in the area. The long table in their dining room contained more food than I had ever seen assembled in a private house. We shifted nervously as the neighbor, who, it transpired, was a clergyman of some sort though he wore no clerical clothing, invoked the blessing of the Lord in an unfamiliar manner that verged on the embarrassing to our taste. The invitation was a kind gesture but we were too shy to ask about the holiday and its meaning and they assumed that we knew both. On top of this, much of the food was unfamiliar. Even the order in which it was to be eaten was a puzzle. I was asked if I would like some salad and was given a small plate of colored jelly with some vegetables in it. It was like being at an observance with zealous adherents of a faith that one neither shared nor understood. Emma, an animal lover and a vegetarian to this day, had decided early in life that she would not eat meat and was picking at some of the vegetable dishes when the clergyman offered her a plate containing slices of roast turkey. She sat tightly wound and white-faced and said, politely but decisively, "I don't eat dead birds." We made our excuses and left soon after.

The fall faded into winter and, after many cold days, the snow came. Despite the Hallmark view of Britain as a place of white Christmases and apple-cheeked carol singers, snow is rare in the south of England and, when it comes, is soon gone. The fact that, eleven years later, I recalled the snowfall of January 1963 that cloaked Chorleywood in whiteness for two days is a testament to its rarity. Snow on the prairie is an annual occurrence differing only in the depth of the drifts, how early or late it arrives, and how long it lingers. Since we had no car, we did not have to clear the drive but watched with fascination as the neighbors cleared theirs with noisy machines they pushed in front of them or tiny tractors on which they sat ungainly like guilty uncles enjoying the children's toys. The white fields stretched flatly outside the towns and snow was banked up at the side of the road in the towns and on the campus. Two things became apparent. We did not have the right outerwear for this weather and the glaring sunlight on the whiteness was threatening to my eyes and my equilibrium. We equipped ourselves with warm zipper jackets, woolly hats, warm underwear, boots, and sunglasses, and were able to brave the cold, the drifts, and the blinding glare with adequate success. My daughters enjoyed the opportunities for sledding, sliding, making snowmen, and the other snow activities rarely found then in the south of England.

I set a paper as the term assignment rather than holding a final examination—this too aroused the ire of the regular cataloguing teacher but I was, by this time, not interested in her opinion and therefore did not inquire as to how I had transgressed. The papers were mostly very good and showed some signs of reading beyond my recommendations. The only problem was that I had to assign letter grades, something that smacks of the lower levels of education to me and is, anyway, a farcical practice in a world in which the letters mean one thing to the school and quite another to the students. To the latter, a C grade is regarded as an arrant failure, whereas its formal meaning is average or adequate. As do most university teachers, I assigned an A to the good papers and an A+ to a few excellent papers and a B to the relatively few that were not good but showed some sign that the student had tried to engage with the topic. It saddens me that the letter-grade farce goes on still. My view of graduate education is that a course should offer the opportunity to acquire new knowledge through reading and discussion, and from a teacher who knows more than the students about the topic. Those who take advantage of these opportunities should be deemed to have passed and those who do not, should not. Higher education today is full of fashionable cant of which the idea of teacher and student "learning together" is one of the most egregious. Who in their right mind would pay to take a course on anything from someone who knows no more about the topic than the students?

We celebrated Christmas in the house on Westlawn and early in the new year moved to another sabbatical house, 1216 W. Healey Street (the home of a family called Robbins), a few blocks away and just across the road from where we had spent Thanksgiving—in what Emma called the Dead Bird House. In January, I had my first experience of an ALA meeting. The midwinter meeting was being held in Chicago. I was still unable to drive a car and was driven to Chicago by Kay Draper, who was accompanied by a PhD student called Ruth Machula—a pretty, reserved woman in her 30s who was very good company on the nearly three-hour drive to the Palmer House on Wabash Avenue, which was the headquarters hotel for the meeting. This historic hotel, which was given to his wife, Bertha, as a wedding gift by the plutocrat Potter Palmer, was slightly frayed at the edges in the mid-1970s, but retained its Gilded Age aura. Though the Palmer House is too small to accommodate ALA's 20,000-plus attendees of today, in 1975 it housed most of the attendees, the official meetings, and the exhibits in a hall in the basement. In the midmorning, the grand foyer was a seething mass of librarians, none of whom I knew, but I pressed on and found a meeting or two in which I was interested. I did not participate actively in that first ALA conference and in truth was more bemused than enlightened. Nevertheless, I have attended all but three of the ALA annual conferences and midwinter meetings since and, though many of those have blurred in my mind, I remember the faded, crowded glamor of the Palmer House in 1976 as if it were yesterday.

The spring semester brought new students and a new class. Wilf Lancaster had completed the manuscript of his book on evaluating library services but was not available to teach a course on the topic, for reasons that I cannot remember. Possibly he was on sabbatical or on one of his numerous overseas consulting trips. I was given the proofs of the book and was asked to teach a course based on it. Fortunately, Lancaster is an accomplished synthesizer and the text was logically arranged, clear, and comprehensive. I did not violate my rule of teaching and lecturing—*never address a group that contains anyone who knows more about the present topic than you do*—and the course went well, as did my repetition of the cataloguing course.

Kay Draper offered to take all four of us to New Orleans by car over the Easter break (which, I was surprised to learn, coincided with the religious festival, as I did not know then how porous the American wall of separation between church and state was). We were keen to go, as it gave us an opportunity to see something of the country outside Illinois and even to take a car journey of a length undreamed of in England. Her car was large even by American standards, and navy blue. We drove south on Interstate 57 towards Memphis and onward. Illinois is a very long state with three parts—Chicagoland, the agricultural middle of soybean and corn fields, and the south (the southernmost part of Illinois is south of Richmond, Virginia). In Champaign, the first signs of spring had appeared, but spring was in full flower once we had crossed Southern Illinois into Kentucky and Tennessee, and the southern accents in the places in which we stopped grew more pronounced. By the time we reached the real South, it seemed like summer. We crossed the Mississippi to visit Vicksburg and then Natchez before taking the road into New Orleans. Somewhere near Vicksburg, I went into a shop to buy some snacks for the children. The man behind the counter asked me where I was from. I intended to say, "We have come from Illinois but I am from England" but could only get "We have come from Illinois" out before he said, "I can tell that you ain't from around here." I found it very difficult being in the South. My sympathies for the civil rights movement were pronounced and had been reinforced by reading about what had happened in this area only a decade before (and was still happening in a less showy way). I am immune to the appeal of "southern chivalry"; am repelled by the yawning gap between the white fences, parasols, etc., and the realities; and to this day am revolted by the sight a decal of the Confederate battle flag on a vehicle. It was hard for me to appreciate the antebellum houses and the historical museums I saw on this journey, so I was very glad to discover that New Orleans was entirely distinct from what we had seen before. I have been there many times since and the appeal of its singularity has grown as I come to appreciate its food, music, and otherness, that manifestation of the "old weird America" that all the tourist kitsch in the world cannot quite conceal. On the way back, we visited Bellingrath Gardens in Alabama and the beaches of imported sand in Biloxi and Pascagoula on Mississippi's Gulf coast. The trip was a glimpse of the size and diversity of America, even with so many regions as yet unseen, and downstate Illinois seemed safe and quiet by comparison—almost "normal"—though it had been a strange land only eight months before.

Cynthia came to visit us for some weeks in the spring, an occurrence that I was surprised to learn much later, had caused much gossip, some hinting at a scandalous relationship. Her return home was the cause of another lengthy car journey. Kay Draper's husband was a faculty member at the University of Guelph, located in that small city some sixty miles from Toronto, and she offered to combine a visit there with a side trip to Toronto, so Cynthia changed her ticket to a Toronto-London flight. I was introduced to another, more congenial America as we drove through Michigan to Detroit and Windsor, Ontario—my first trip to Canada, a country that I have visited very often since, always with great pleasure. The granitic towns of Ontario reminded me of Scotland, not surprising since every other person I met there had a Scottish surname. In Toronto, I went in search of the university in which Robertson Davies taught, and found it though I failed to glimpse the great Canadian author. Cynthia left for England and Kay and I drove back the next day.

During the spring semester, JD organized a trip to Columbus, Ohio, with his systems class in order to visit the Ohio State University Library and invited me to accompany them. The reason for the trip was to see what the OSU Library, under the direction of Hugh Atkinson, was doing with library automation and, incidentally, to see the "Randtriever." The latter was an industrial storage device created by the Remington Rand Corporation in a misguided attempt to apply industrial warehousing techniques to libraries. Ohio State's was the most famous of these devices and was worth seeing if only as a manifestation of the clash of the mechanistic and learning cultures. I remember the first time that I saw Hugh Atkinson, though I am fairly sure my presence did not register with him. Hugh was then in his early 40s, an engagingly informal, fidgety, handsome, red-haired man who exuded both competence and self-assurance. I learned later that he was indeed competent but not as self-assured as he appeared, but then how many of us are? He had installed an electronic materials retrieval system called LCS in Columbus, that I believe stemmed from an early version created in the State University of New York (Hugh's previous appointment was in the library of SUNY Buffalo). Though it would appear primitive to anyone seeing it through the eyes of 2011, it was a considerable advance in library service that Hugh later took to the University of Illinois as the bridge between the card and online catalogues and as the basis of a statewide interlibrary loan system that became the most advanced in the nation.

Sometime in the spring, Herbert Goldhor asked me to teach two courses in the summer school of 1975. I accepted and we decided that Anne and the children would return to Pinner in May as planned after the end of the spring semester. I had some misgivings about staying, but was enjoying the pleasures of college life and thought that summer would be relaxing and informative.

Earlier in the spring, I was asked to visit the library school at the University of Chicago and deliver a speech on cataloguing and the new rules. Art Plotnik, who was then editor of *American libraries,* was in the audience and, after the talk, we renewed our acquaintance made during his visit to England in the 1960s. We have remained friends ever since. He worked with me on two of my books when he was the head of book publishing at ALA. At that time, Art asked me to write an article for the magazine and I worked on that in addition to continuing with my work on AACR2.

After Anne and the children had returned to Pinner in May, I rented an apartment for the summer in a building on the corner of West Green Street and South Busey Avenue in Urbana. The apartment was a semi-basement with brown wooden planking on the walls and dark green shag carpeting on the floor. It was perpetually dark, something I was grateful for when I realized how cool it was—a brown and green refuge from the glaring sun. I lived the life of a college student in between teaching two classes and supervising an individual project. I taught classes on cataloguing (including MARC) and on medical classification and supervised an individual study in the same area. I wrote the article that Art had commissioned and worked on drafts of AACR2, both on a borrowed typewriter in that dark brown, shag-carpeted, and dimly lit room. I attended several parties until late into the night and, in some ways, in the humid greenness of that college town, acted out the adolescent years that I had never had.

I left Champaign-Urbana twice that summer. Once was to go along with a group of students who were driving to Cleveland to attend the Medical Library Association conference. It was a long journey across the flatness of Middle America, but I enjoyed the companionship and seeing new places, even if they each resembled the other. Cleveland was then at the nadir of its fortunes, on a river that was alleged to have caught fire as it emptied into polluted Lake Erie. One of the MLA attendees was mugged and robbed outside the conference hotel at three in the afternoon. I also visited the Case Western Reserve library to the east of the city and attended a reception in the leafy splendor of Shaker Heights—a far cry from the mean streets of Cleveland. I next left town to speak at the ALA annual conference in San Francisco. It was my first visit to California and, despite having to fly there, I was exhilarated to discover the beauty of Baghdad by the Bay. I stayed in the St. Francis Hotel on Union Square and walked around what I later found out was the Tenderloin District, thinking how many ladies and gentlemen of the night there were in this strange city. I had drinks in Lefty O'Doul's and then ate in a nearby grill. I arrived on the Friday and, knowing no one and not being registered for the conference, had two days to climb the hills and explore the piers, narrow streets, and Chinatown alone. The reason I had come was to give a speech on ISBD at 8 p.m. on the Sunday of the conference. I had an early dinner and showed up in the meeting room to meet and exchange pleasantries with the people who had invited me. The room was vast and, to my astonishment, half-full more than forty minutes before the scheduled start of my talk. The number of people already there were more than I had ever spoken to before and, by the time it was 8 p.m., it was standing room only with what I later found out were more than eight hundred people present. It was hot, crowded, and brightly lit and my nerves were calmed only by my certain knowledge that I knew more about the ISBD that any of them. However, the first ten minutes or so of my presentation were suffused with high anxiety, a pattern with which I soon became familiar. Over the next twenty-five years or so, it was only if the symptoms persisted after those first ten minutes that I realized I was in trouble. The simple fact of those more than eight hundred cataloguers turning out on a fine Sunday night in a wide-open city impressed me very much. Here was a large group that took cataloguing seriously and were not afraid to express their opinions, a phenomenon with which I was to become very familiar in the next few years.

The rest of the summer went by quickly and I was, reluctantly, making preparations to return to England. I thought that the past year was to be an interesting interlude in my life and, though I was due to visit the U.S. often on AACR2 business, I would never live there again for an extended period. A dear friend drove me to Indianapolis to board a plane for London in early August. I distinctly remember thinking, as we drove north on Cunningham Avenue to eastbound Interstate 74 and Champaign and Urbana receded behind us, that I would never see those towns again. It was not the last time my ideas about my future were wrong.

11

Back to England, the University of Illinois, 1975–1978

I returned to London in August 1975 and soon realized that it was going to be very difficult for me to resume the life I had before. What I had assumed would be an interesting but ephemeral interlude—a yearlong break—had turned out to be, in some important ways, a life-changing event. Returning to the British Library was a difficult adjustment (for me and for my colleagues) and everything about life in London seemed to be less expansive and life-enhancing. In retrospect, this was an illusion based on contrasting the unreal life of a temporary academic in a foreign country with the realities of my domestic and professional life in my own country, much as a traveler returning from the joys of a Tuscan holiday is likely to find London dreary. Though I was happy that one of my political heroes, Harold Wilson, was still prime minister at the head of a Labour government, this was a difficult time in British politics because of the nation's serious financial problems compounded by the Northern Irish troubles and their explosive fallout in the national capital. The forces (principally a breakdown in the "public good" consensus that had been achieved in postwar "austerity" Britain and the "never had it so good" philosophy that replaced it) that were to culminate in the catastrophe of Thatcher and Thatcherism late in that decade were gathering and there was little hope in the air. On the other hand, I had many opportunities to travel—to Denmark, Switzerland, France, and, most often, to the United States and Canada. These trips were connected with either my being head of the BL's Bibliographic Standards Office or coeditor of AACR2. I had an able colleague in Richard Carpenter in the office, and we worked together and separately on a variety of national and international standardization projects.

As described in chapter 12, work on AACR2 made it plain that we—the Joint Steering Committee—would have to take the initiative in developing a single standard description covering all the formats to which libraries give access and that would be capable of accommodating all future formats. My work on developing this structure—later called the ISBD(G)—resulted in a draft that was considered and approved at a special JSC/IFLA meeting held in Paris in October 1975. This was an interesting trip, quite apart from the substance of the meeting. Anne accompanied me to the meeting; we stayed in the Hotel St. Anne on the Rue St. Anne on the Right Bank near the Louvre and the gardens of the Palais Royale and the Tuileries.

The meetings were held in the Bibliothèque nationale in a grand conference room with great pomp and ceremony. John Byrum attended the meeting, his first trip to Europe, as did Paul Winkler. Neither of them had any French; though mine was no great shakes I was able to use what I had to assist them on two occasions. It transpired that there were two reservations at the hotel in Paul's name. The clerk at the registration desk was a middle-aged man with an air of haughtiness and severity. When Paul appeared, the clerk ran his finger down a list of some sort, and looked up at us. "*Ou est Vinklair?*" (Where is Winkler?) he demanded. I told him that "Vinklair" stood before him as Paul proffered his passport. He snatched the passport without a word, made an entry in his large ledger with great care, then looked up with suspicion after consulting his list again, and asked "*Ou est le deuxième Vinklair?*" (Where is the second Winkler?) It took me more than fifteen minutes to explain in my halting French, of which the clerk clearly disapproved, that this was the one and only Winkler who would grace his establishment.

John Byrum wanted to have a pair of trousers cleaned, so I went with him to a cleaner's in a nearby street. I had written John's name and the name of the hotel on a piece of paper. My handwriting is such that the cleaner interpreted his last name as being "Byruni." This would not have mattered if they had not also managed to mislay the trousers. When I went with John to pick them up two days later, they denied having any articles belonging to anyone called Byrum. It took twenty minutes to establish that there were indeed trousers owing to a customer who they identified in speech as "M'sieu Bee-rooney," but unhappily "*Les pantalon de M. Bee-rooney sont disparu*" (Monsieur Byruni's trousers have vanished). After more discussion, we agreed to return the next day. Happily, John's vanishing trousers—corduroy and of a blue hue—had reappeared, but M Byruni and the Second Winkler were never to reappear.

MG, Paris 1975. Photo by Anne Gorman.

I completed the ISBD(G) on returning to London and worked hard, often into the evenings at home, on the seemingly endless drafts of the various chapters of AACR2 over the next months while dealing with the consequences of the various JSC meetings.

The JSC met in Princeton, New Jersey, in conference rooms of the university, from the 3rd through the 6th of November 1975. I landed at Dulles Airport, located in Virginia to serve the Washington, DC, area and named after the unlamented cold warrior John Foster Dulles. As was fairly common then, the British Airways plane in which I traveled was, at most, half full. I was the only occupant of a middle row of seats, separated by an aisle from two seats only one of which, by the window, was occupied by someone whose face was familiar to me. I had always taken a great interest in American politics and I recognized my fellow passenger as Richard "Dick" Clark, the Democratic senator from Iowa. He was a handsome man with a presence and a healthy, well-coiffed head of hair. I struck up a conversation with him and, after he had finished some paperwork, he was courteous enough to discuss national and state politics with me for more than an hour. It was an act of great kindness, especially when it was evident from the beginning that I was British and could not vote for him even if I lived in Iowa, a state that put candidates above party at that time to the extent of electing two staunch liberals (Clark and John Culver, the father of the present governor of Iowa) despite the state's generally Republican tilt; but theirs was the now outmoded Republicanism of Ike and others and not the kind with which we live today.

The next day, I was driven to Princeton by the Library of Congress' JSC representative, Elizabeth Tait, and her husband. I was surprised to see how rural the area around Princeton was and for the first time understood New Jersey's name—"The Garden State." Elizabeth Tait was very friendly to me away from the meeting tables but, there and at other times, the frustrations of representing LC's then retrogressive positions on code revision and defending the increasingly untenable draft submitted by Paul Winkler frayed her nerves and made for some very tense exchanges, mostly with me since I was producing proposals representing the more progressive ideas coming from the British representatives and the American CCRC. That committee was headed by John Byrum, ALA's JSC representative, who was then working for Princeton's library. John's gift for diplomacy helped at some of the more fraught points of the daylong meetings.

It was a pleasure to leave the meetings and Princeton on the second evening. I went with John on the train via Trenton to New York City. We had dinner in a restaurant near Greenwich Village, then walked through the edgy streets to Washington Square. Knowing nothing of that place other than the Henry James story and its film—*The heiress,* starring the doomed Montgomery Clift—I was quite unprepared for what we found. There were men selling marijuana and other drugs quite openly; women with long, dead-straight hair and layered multicolored garments playing guitars and singing in wispy voices; knots of homeless people muttering or sleeping; men and women for rent; bearded students arguing loudly; couples arm in arm; Hasidim; food vendors; and cops, all ebbing and flowing as if in a dark musical about the Big Apple. We left the park and went to a bar in which the famous, though unknown to me at that time, Maxine Sullivan was singing. The bar was half full and there was chatter in the background as Ms. Sullivan stood, straight and slender and with her head back, in a floor-length dress and sang to a piano accompaniment. I knew little, then and now, of jazz singing but her voice was enchanting in that New York night. After her second set of songs, I approached her and offered her a drink. I was pleased to buy and carry over to her the brandy she requested and for which she thanked me with a quick smile. AACR2 seemed very small beer the next day—down to earth with a thud.

Christmas and New Year's Day came and went to be followed by another tense and crowded meeting of the JSC from February 9 to 13, 1976, in the meeting rooms of the Library of Congress with which I was becoming increasingly familiar.

Thoughts of Champaign-Urbana and my year there began to recede and, though I was still interested in the U.S. and could see myself working there again, the University of Illinois did not figure in those thoughts. Fate, in the person of Professor Divilbiss—JD—intervened. The U of I library school had been holding an annual "Clinic on Library Applications of Data Processing" in Urbana since the early 1960s (they had a good run, the last was in 1998). The early clinics were run by Herb Goldhor and Wilf Lancaster, but the responsibility for the 1976 clinic had fallen to JD. He wrote to me late in 1975 inviting me to present a paper on the economics of catalogue conversion at that clinic in April 1976. This proved to be a momentous event in many ways. First, I returned to downstate Illinois less than a year after leaving for what I thought was the last time. Second, papers at the clinic were given by, among others, Fred Kilgour, the founder of OCLC—then rapidly becoming the major force in librarianship that it remains, for good and ill; the engaging Brett Butler, with whom I was friendly for years until his untimely death; and two young Turks from the New York Public Library, Mitch Freedman and S. Michael Malinconico. Third, I renewed my acquaintance with Melissa Cain, who had been a student in the library school and was then working for the undergraduate library at the U of I, and met her colleague Nancy Allen (then called Nancy Manley), both of whom were very important in my life thereafter.

I landed at O'Hare in the late afternoon and took a taxi to Union Station in downtown Chicago to catch the train (the *City of New Orleans*) south to Champaign. The afternoon gave way to the evening as the train lumbered across the dark prairie and through the little towns that are strung along the tracks all the way between Chicago and Cairo in the far south. I had dinner with JD and Mary Jo in their house in Champaign and then went to my room in the Illini Union—the massive WPA building in what was then the north of the campus. Among the many art works in the union is a mural by Doris and Anna Zinkeisen, the Scottish painters, graphic artists and muralists, who were, when young, fellow students of Marjorie Gillett, Anne Gorman's mother, at Harrow School Art, a school from which my daughter Emma graduated in the 1980s.

I walked across the campus in the morning, enjoying revisiting the campus with eyes anew. Fred Kilgour was an impressive, handsome, slightly dismissive man clad in a dark blue suit and with senatorial white hair. He was beginning to hear the rumblings about AACR2 and lectured me on cataloguing from his point of view, ideas that I found eccentric at best, based as they were on what I saw as the absurd idea that automating catalogues changed the fundamental nature of the catalogue record. It is sad to see the same absurdity perpetrated today without a shred of the excuse that Kilgour could have advanced when online catalogues were aborning and the full impact of MARC and OCLC were yet to be felt. Kilgour was a key figure in the War of AACR2 (see chapter 12) and I was to see much of him in the next years. Brett Butler was that rare bird, a person who grew up in the library vendor world but had a library degree and a deep understanding of the culture and values of libraries. We were, I discovered later, born in the same month (he was two weeks younger) and we had very similar views on libraries and life from the start. He and his partners founded the Information Access Company later in 1976. Mitch Freedman and Michael Malinconico were active in ALA's Information Science and Automation Division (ISAD), which was soon to change its name to the Library & Information Technology Association (LITA). Meeting them at the clinic was to lead to invitations to speak at sessions at ALA conferences and two important institutes sponsored by LITA later in that decade. I also went to the library school to visit Dr. Goldhor, who, among other matters, raised the possibility of my teaching summer school that year. I returned to Chicago on the train and had a splendid time visiting the Art Institute and other attractions before boarding the plane home the next day. During my visit to Champaign, people in the UIUC library told me they were anticipating the arrival of the new university librarian, Hugh Atkinson, with a mixture of emotions. The library was, by and large, settled in its ways and full of strong and contending characters. The fact that Hugh had been hired to bring automation to a vast library that had no automation at the time also caused a great deal of disquiet. I heard later that there was a rumor that Hugh was going to sell the UIUC library's unmatched Milton collection to pay for "computers." In the spring of 1976, all this meant very little to me, though it was to loom large in my life in the not very distant future.

The JSC held its only meeting in the United Kingdom in London, at the headquarters of the Library Association in Ridgmount Street May 24–28, 1976. A week or so later, I was on my way back to Urbana to teach in the library school's summer program. At that time, the country was consumed with celebrations of the bicentennial. In those days, the run-up to the presidential election was of a shorter duration than it is now, though the sudden appearance on the national scene of a one-term governor of Georgia—Jimmy Carter—was of interest to many. Thus, the sunny, bland Gerald Ford was unchallenged as presiding genius of the celebrations that reached their climax on July 4—an arrangement that would be inconceivable in today's bitterly partisan political environment. I rented an apartment in a block on North Neil Street in Champaign from a beautiful Mexican-American woman called Vera (for Elvira) Chavaria. She showed me how to make *mole poblano*—a sauce that, to my amazement, contained bitter chocolate—before she left to spend the summer in Texas. Fortunately, I was to see her again.

One class was "team taught" with the distinguished library historian Michael Harris, who was then, I believe, at the University of Kentucky library school. He turned out to be a boon companion who was, among other things, something approaching a pool shark. We spent many hours in the Deluxe with him showing me how the game was played and me trying to emulate him with, at best, mixed success. The class itself was great fun and, to be honest, apart from a lecture I gave on filing rules and one that he gave on the early feminization of the profession, nothing about its subject matter remains in my memory, though I can recall the relaxed, even cheerful atmosphere of the class and see the room in my mind's eye, dusty with chalk and lit by the fierce summer sun.

I attended the ALA annual conference in Chicago in late June and stayed at the Palmer House. I spoke at two meetings on AACR2 and ISBD, attended lengthy JSC meetings held in conjunction with the conference, and went to a number of ALA Cataloging Committee meetings, drawn-out and contentious but productive affairs. Shortly after returning from Chicago, I watched the bicentennial fireworks and celebrations in the university's Memorial Stadium from a small park in Champaign with Nancy Allen and a number of others. We had a picnic and lay on the grass in the warm, humid July evening. Much as when I watched the fireworks and celebrations on Bastille Day in Paris sixteen years earlier, another country's nationalistic festivities were interesting and impressive even when seen at a slant by a perpetual outsider. It was, I think, at that meeting that someone mentioned that many in the university's library were expecting Hugh Atkinson to replace a number of people in the library's administration and raised the idea that I might wish to apply for one of the to be vacant positions. It seemed improbable and dependent on a number of hypothetical occurrences, but the seed was planted. The rest of the summer went by quickly and I returned to Pinner in August.

My draft of Part 1 was approved at the JSC meeting held in the library of the University of Toronto, October 25–29, 1976. The library building, which incorporated the library school, was then new and of an advanced, asymmetric design. That design was such that some of the rooms, including the one in which we met, were quadrilaterals with walls that appeared to converge. This disconcerting room shape, the lack of windows, and the then fashionable color schemes of russet, gray, and ochre, induced a sense of unreality after hours of complex discussions, raised voices, and unresolved disputes. It would be extreme to compare the JSC meetings to so many Mad Hatter's Tea Parties (still more to match the protagonists of the former with those of the latter) but this meeting had a distinctly hallucinatory effect.

Much of my time in the British Library between the summer of 1976 and the middle of 1977 was taken up with the gathering pace of drafting, redrafting, and proofreading AACR2 rules, circulating those drafts, receiving comments from all and sundry, and doing yet more redrafts. This process resulted in hundreds of handwritten pages that I took to an office in the British Library to be typed, corrected, amended, and otherwise done over until they were ready to be copied and circulated to the interested parties. The one exception to this process was the manuscript of chapter 4 (on the description of manuscripts), which I handwrote with even more neatness than usual and circulated as a photocopy of a manuscript. I spent less and less time on BL projects and European standardization issues and more and more on the incorporation of the ISBD(G) into the almost final Part 1 of the code and rewriting Part 2 after the April 1977 rejection of Paul Winkler's draft by the ALA committee (see below). By the end of this period, work on recasting Part 2 consumed all my time. This was a period of change and turmoil and was, as it turned out, the last year of my working life in England, a time of frequent travel—mostly to the United States—of dealing as best I could with the increasing pressures of completing the code, of dealing with my anxiety and stage fright during my increasing number of presentations, and of a fractured family life anchored only by the steadiness and strength of character of Anne Gorman, a wonderful mother of my then 10- and 7-year-old daughters.

I was in Washington again early in November 1976 to attend meetings connected to AACR2. I stayed with a friend who had moved to the DC area from Champaign-Urbana in Takoma Park, Maryland, and commuted to the meetings by bus. The national election fell on one of the days I was there, and everywhere you went in the world's largest village there was talk of the novelty of the president-to-be from Georgia and the end of the Nixon/Ford era. One day I was having lunch in Jenkins Hill, a bar across the road from the Jefferson LC building, eating crab cakes and reading about the election results in the *Washington post,* and was amused to hear two journalists speculating gloomily about who would have to accompany the new president if he set up a "Southern White House" in Plains, Georgia.

My trip to the ALA Midwinter Meeting in Washington, DC, in January 1977 was memorable in many ways. Once again, I flew to Dulles and took the bus into Washington on what had become familiar roads. In those few days, I participated in a round of JSC and ALA meetings, social events with friends from Illinois, and, most important in retrospect, a meeting with Hugh Atkinson. My friends had told me that what was foretold was coming to pass and that the director of technical services at the U of I library had indicated that he would resign in a few months. It was suggested to me that I might want to apply for the position when it became vacant and that it would be a good idea if I were to meet Hugh informally. I had written to him asking for such a meeting, and he agreed to have breakfast with me in the hotel in which we were staying. I had met him before, in Ohio in 1975, but it was clear that he did not remember me. It was, all in all, not an auspicious occasion. Hugh was ill at ease and fidgety; I was nervous and eager to make a good impression but could tell that this was not occurring. We talked amiably enough and with too few awkward pauses to be really uncomfortable but I left the table convinced that he was glad to see me go and that I should give up all ideas of applying for a post in what was now Hugh's library. As it turned out, Hugh was out of sorts more because it was early morning and he was in the process of giving up smoking than because of me. I heard later that he said he had liked meeting me and that I "wasn't bad for a limey."

Later that month, I distributed the final version of Part 1 of AACR2, and it was approved by all the members of JSC shortly thereafter. In theory, the great majority of my task as coeditor was over. Events did not go according to plan and, as a consequence, more onerous work with even more stringent deadlines was to fall to me (see below). As if this were not enough, I decided, very early in 1977, to apply for the now advertised position of director of Technical Services (essentially cataloguing and acquisitions departments) in the University of Illinois library. In retrospect, my qualifications for the post were patchy; in particular I had very little experience in administration and management. I knew a lot about cataloguing, less about acquisitions, a little about running a cataloguing department and the organization of cataloguing departments in a large library (though whether the lessons of the British Library were applicable to a large university in another country is, to say the least, debatable), and, fortunately for me, nothing at all about the problems peculiar to the University of Illinois library. It seemed a long shot even at the time. I submitted my application and heard, in a relatively short time, that I would be given an interview in March 1977.

Thus it was that, once again, I was back in the place that I had left eighteen months earlier thinking that I would never see again. My friends Melissa Cain and Nancy Allen, both of whom were working in the undergraduate library, met me at Champaign's Willard Airport; I was more than slightly shaken after a short flight from Chicago in a Piedmont Airlines turboprop. Though I had been traveling for many hours and despite the time difference, I met members of the search committee that evening and realized that I was in for a grueling couple of days. I had never undergone the American search experience before and was blissfully unaware of the hoops through which I had to jump in the days to come. I stayed at the Illini Union again and went to bed later that evening exhausted by my travel and less than exhilarated by having been told how well one of the other two candidates, interviewed the week before, had done. The morning brought a breakfast meeting with members of the search committee, followed by an interview with Hugh Atkinson, which went far better than our breakfast in January, and then a round of meetings with various groups and people in the four main Technical Services departments—cataloguing, acquisitions, serials, and the Slavic and Asian libraries—and in the library. Faces and names blurred, I found myself unable to retain even the functions of most of the many people and committees with which I met, uneaten or barely tasted meals came and went, and the endurance test stretched into its third day. I was impressed with the size and complexity of the library—Technical Services alone had about a hundred librarians and three hundred staff members, and there were more serials cataloguers than there were cataloguers in the British National Bibliography—and by the evident problems that the new director would have to face. The most obvious of these were the lack of automation, the inefficient use of OCLC, the enormous backlogs in cataloguing and catalogue card filing, and the generally antiquated and redundant procedures of the departments. Three of the four heads of technical services departments were, at best, suspicious of Hugh and his plans and fearful of the changes to come. From my friends in the library, I learned that one of the librarians in Technical Services who had conceived a dislike of me over events when I was teaching in 1974–75 was telling everyone that I was not a "real librarian" and that I lacked the education for the position. He may well have been right on the second point. I was asked to give a brief talk and answer questions at a meeting of librarians as the penultimate part of the interview. The presentation and questions went well, considering my nervous state. I attributed that to the idea that I felt as though I had nothing to lose, since I had been told that the job was certain to go to the woman who had interviewed the week before. I was asked about my "lack of" education by the vellicating person who had been discussing it with others in the library. I answered him by saying that my library education was as good as any obtainable in the U.S. and that, as to my general education, I could only offer the knowledge I had gained through reading. I tried to make light of the matter by offering to discuss any literary, historical, or political topic they wished and, hearing no takers, offered a synopsis of *Ulysses,* a brief history of France since the Revolution, and the lyrics of "Danny boy." This last levity eased the tension induced in many by embarrassment (I was, after all, the library's invited guest). The interview finished with an hourlong meeting with Hugh that left me feeling hopeful, despite the forebodings of my friends. I flew home the next day wondering, yet again, if I were leaving Champaign and Urbana for the last time.

Soon I was back in America—this time in Washington, DC, for a special JSC meeting precipitated by the gathering dissatisfaction with the lack of progress on Part 2 of AACR2 and the growing realization that, unless there was a radical change, AACR2 would not be the new code that most wanted. I attended the meeting of the ALA cataloguing committee in a hotel south of the Library of Congress, held to discuss Paul's (and LC's) draft of Part 2. The meeting was at times heated and resulted in the complete rejection of that draft, the resignation of Sumner Spalding (the editor of the first AACR) from the position of special "resource person" to the ALA committee. The committee then proposed to the JSC that I should be asked to rewrite Part 2 along the same lines as to structure and style as the already approved Part 1 and with major changes in substance. The ALA committee's proposals were accepted by the JSC at their meeting held in the Jefferson Building of LC in the next days and I was given less about three months to produce a more or less final draft of Part 2, circulate it, and make the necessary changes in time for final agreement on all of AACR2 by August.

It was shortly after my return to London from the Washington meeting that I received the fateful and surprising telephone call from Hugh Atkinson offering me the position of director of Technical Services—a position that I accepted after a brief discussion with Anne and with, alas, very little thought given to the likely impact on my family. I was to start in August 1977, the same month in which a definitive text of AACR2 was to be approved.

The time I had to redraft Part 2 was rendered even shorter by the circumstances in which I worked. I spent many of my days for those eight weeks (all of them for the last four weeks) working at a desk in a very small room adjacent to my young daughters' bedroom in my small house in Pinner. I often worked until late in the night and to this day my daughters talk about "AACR2 music" (the Eagles, Linda Ronstadt, Dobie Gray, the Rolling Stones, the Faces, etc.) they heard as I worked. Given the time pressure and the fact that I was working at home, without the ready online access to library catalogues that we have today, I had to draw examples from my own books, records, maps, etc.—most of these examples have survived into the current iteration of AACR2. It was not until long after the conclusion of the review and amendment process and the delivery of the final version to the printers that I realized that I had handwritten every word in the main body of AACR2 (511 printed pages) at least once, and in many areas several times. I applied the same principles of style and numbering I had used in Part 1 in creating a Part 2 that was internally coherent and consistent with Part 1, and, in addition, took care to eliminate gender and other biases in wording. It seems odd now, but some participants were against such things as substituting "his or her" for "his" in referring to all authors and eschewing the word "tribe" in referring to Native Americans. Largely due to support from the ALA committee, the more enlightened options prevailed. One change that I proposed was rejected—the use of the correct "United Kingdom" for that government instead of "Great Britain," which is merely a geographic expression. Visions of having to change millions of cards in their catalogue danced in the LC representatives' heads and they vetoed the suggestion. It is sad to see this blatant error still perpetuated in modern catalogues.

I followed the same process that I had used for Part 1—writing every rule in longhand, all the while showing the complex indentation and typography found on every page of AACR2; giving the handwritten drafts to BL typists and doing the consequent proofreading, retyping, and circulating of drafts. The difference was in the pace and volume of work for me and the typists. I had suffered from regular migraine attacks since I was about 10 years old. Many of these were incapacitating and accompanied by the classic symptoms familiar to all who are similarly afflicted. Though I had migraines less frequently after I was in my 20s, it is hardly surprising that that I had them quite frequently in the months between my interview at

Illinois and the completion of AACR2. My colleague Derek Austin was a lifelong sufferer and we had talked about migraines and their causes very often, but I was still not sure what triggered mine or how to deal with them. It seemed that they occurred more often when I was away from home. This and the amount of work to be accomplished caused me to be completely housebound, something that posed a major problem when I finished the draft of Part 2. I worked almost nonstop to complete the drafts, to consider suggestions as they came in, and to submit a draft for JSC consideration within weeks before our final meeting. When this work was completed and all that remained was minor editorial work on appendices and the like, I had what can only be described as a nervous breakdown—a prolonged and intense version of the symptoms that first manifested themselves at the time of the Six-Day War ten years before. For two weeks, I was unable to leave my house in Pinner, even for the short walk down Waxwell Lane to the pubs and shops. The most distressing aspects of this time were my inability to talk about what was happening, my deep sense of shame, and my dark forebodings about what was to happen in the future. Gradually, the darkness dispelled but there was a shadow over my life for years to come.

Not long after the worst of this crisis, I traveled to the ALA annual conference being held in Detroit. I was largely unaware of it at the time but ALA was convulsed by a controversy over the film *The speaker*—an ALA-produced film that documented resistance to attempts to suppress the speech of William Shockley, a Nobel Prize–winning physicist and racist. Heaven alone knows why this particular unpopular opinion was chosen by the filmmakers. Perhaps it was to illustrate George Orwell's quotation "*If liberty means anything at all, it means the right to tell people what they do not want to hear*" and its corollary that belief in free speech means that, even when speech is obnoxious or evil, it deserves protection. Most people who say they believe in freedom of speech draw the line at some speech, but the late Judith Krug, one of the prime movers behind *The speaker*, did not. As if illustrating the underlying point, the film tore ALA apart for two years and was a fraught beginning for the incoming president of ALA, Eric Moon, one of only three ALA presidents who were British-born. It may well have scuppered some of the things that Eric had hoped to accomplish during his ALA presidency.

I was too caught up with the battles over AACR2—early skirmishes in the war of AACR2 (see chapter 12) and too unfamiliar with the internal politics of ALA—to pay much attention. I was in the audience at a meeting of the Technical Services Directors of Large Research Libraries (known to many as "the Big Heads") in a room in Cobo Hall when I was called away by Larry Besant, a friend and colleague of Hugh's, then working in Ohio State's library, to come quickly to a meeting in another building at which AACR2 was being discussed. I quickly saw that the degree of heat being generated was in inverse relationship to the amount the various speakers knew about the substance of the code and found myself being called upon to counter inaccurate statements and attempt, mostly unsuccessfully, to fight off attacks on the yet-to-be published new code from progressive cataloguers who distrusted compromises in the text that sullied what they thought of as pure Lubetzkianism; from reactionaries who did not want substantial change; and from assorted nincompoops who thought, to take but one example, that ISBD was "unnatural." My reply to the last was that we would not need cataloguing standards at all if catalogue entries occurred in nature. I had many such discussions at that conference and was glad to leave Detroit at the end of it.

The final JSC meeting to consider the first AACR2 was held in Washington, again at the Library of Congress, August 7–12, 1977. Though this was prolonged, it was far less contentious than previous JSC meetings, its main purpose being to approve the final text and the substantive disputes over various parts of that text having been resolved to varying degrees of satisfaction weeks before the August meeting. What remained were editorial questions, and each of those was decided in the six days of the meeting. AACR2, which had consumed so much of my time and nervous energy in the past four years was, for the time being, settled, and I had time to devote to the details of my move to Urbana-Champaign as it and farewells to the British Library loomed larger.

Since Hugh wanted me to start in August and that did not give us enough time to make the move to America as a family, we decided that I would go on ahead and Anne, Emma, and Alice would follow in the spring of 1978, at which time we would have sold the house in Waxwell Close and could look for a new house to purchase in Champaign or Urbana. I rented another sabbatical house, this time for the academic year, 711 Hamilton Drive in Champaign. I had very few possessions with me apart from clothes and the dark ranch house full of somebody else's furniture and effects near to Hessel Park and the university suited me well enough. I soon had a busy social life away from the library.

I spent my first week at work touring the library and talking to librarians and staff in the four Technical Services departments. My first visit to the Slavic Library was the occasion of a ludicrous misunderstanding. One of the Slavic librarians was a priest in one of the branches of the Ukrainian Orthodox Church. Larry Miller, the affable, scholarly head of that library, introduced me to this gentleman, gave his name, and without turning to me said "He is Ukrainian." Suddenly, I was being embraced enthusiastically with a joyous, heavily accented cry of "Ah, you are UKRANIAN!" followed by some words in what I took to be Ukrainian. Larry, even more flummoxed that I and on the verge of panic, blurted out "NO! *You* are Ukrainian, *he* is English!"

My first important task was to delineate the size and nature of the cataloguing backlog, which amounted to many thousands of volumes, and to devise a way to use OCLC to reduce and, ultimately, eliminate it. This was not easy. Cataloguers are, with good reason, highly resistant to change but, in their hearts, they must have known, as I did, that the only answer to the backlog question was the assembly-line use of cataloguing records from other libraries derived from OCLC without the time-consuming and counterproductive checking, rechecking, and amending those records by cataloguing librarians that was the norm in those times. With the invaluable assistance and prompting of Charlene Renner, a gifted cataloguer who was then in charge of the English Library, we devised a system by which records from OCLC would be matched by a group of library staff and subjected to the minimum alteration. This "copy cataloguing" operation was, not surprisingly, opposed by the head of cataloguing, and whatever hopes she might have had that I would defend their traditional cataloguing practices were dashed. Within two years, the cataloguing backlog was gone and the University of Illinois library was, by far, the largest user of, and contributor to, OCLC. This was but the first of the changes (in cataloguing, catalogue card filing, acquisition procedures, and serials processing) that brought efficiency to technical processing but created more suspicion and antagonism in what was already a contentious and fractured workplace.

I returned to England for Christmas and, though I was delighted to see my daughters and Anne, Pinner seemed already to belong to the past. I left after New Year's Day knowing that my life in England was over, perhaps forever. I attended the Midwinter Meeting of ALA in Chicago in January 1978 and was soon embroiled in all the mounting fuss and anger about AACR2 that was being fomented by, among others, members of the Association for Research Libraries and some elements of LC. These were very trying times and there was, for a while, uncertainty about the future of the new cataloguing rules. It seemed then that Interstate 57, which runs between Chicago and Champaign-Urbana, was the route between one field of battle and another. I returned to the tensions and uncertainties of the University of Illinois library feeling bloodied but, as yet, unbowed on both fronts.

Rain began to fall on Central Illinois in the morning of the eve of Easter weekend, Friday the 24th of March, 1978, and rapidly began to freeze. The freezing rain lasted into the morning of Easter Saturday by which time ice from half an inch to two inches thick coated a ninety-mile-wide belt and caused substantial damage to power lines and trees as well as making driving and even walking hazardous and speculative exercises. At the height of the ice storm, a million people were without power, there were more than a thousand driving accidents, and many millions of dollars' worth of trees were destroyed. Twenty-four of Central and Southern Illinois' counties were declared disaster areas as the ice cover lingered until the Tuesday after Easter. Friends came to my house fleeing the cold of their electricity-less apartments, and meals were moveable impromptu feasts as we sheltered from the consequences of the storm. Outside, the cities were quiet and crystalline, every twig and branch and stone was freaked with ice, shining in the sunlight and clear cold air that followed the freezing rain. The crunch of feet on perilous ice seemingly signaled that the world would break apart unless care were taken.

Two weeks later, Anne, Emma, and Alice arrived to begin a new life in America with then unforeseeable consequences for each of us.

12

The Anglo-American Cataloguing Rules

I have abandoned the generally chronological sequence of this book for three reasons. AACR2 was a major element of my library life of such importance that I feel it merits separate treatment. My involvement with the rules took place over half my professional life and cannot be dealt with adequately in fragments. What follows in this chapter is likely to be of interest mainly to librarians, perhaps even only cataloguers, and more general readers, if any there be, may choose to read, skim, or skip it.

As I write, a bizarrely incoherent and unnecessary draft of a putative successor to the *Anglo-American cataloguing rules, Second edition* (AACR2) is circulating and may well be adopted by our national cataloguing agencies, and the air is thick with talk of metadata (an inferior, unstandardized species of cataloguing done by amateurs); the many fallibilities of search engines and doing "research" using them; electronic finding lists such as that of Amazon.com; and other methods of locating carriers of knowledge and information that appeal to those who know the human and financial cost of real cataloguing but nothing of its value. In addition, many of the successors of library schools do not require their graduates to have taken cataloguing courses and appear to be oblivious to the fact that cataloguing is central to our thought processes, and senior staff at the Library of Congress are talking openly of jettisoning that august institution's historic commitment to providing authoritative cataloguing data to the nation's libraries. *O tempora, o mores!* It might be instructive and useful, at least to a few, to look back at a time when cataloguing (in particular, descriptive cataloguing) was taken seriously by serious people who appreciated the value of authoritative cataloguing to library users in general and scholars and researchers in particular.

The earliest days

The origins of what we now know as Anglo-American descriptive cataloguing lie in the nineteenth century. The small pond of descriptive cataloguing teems with big fish, of whom the biggest in that century were the anglicized Italian Antonio (later Sir Anthony) Panizzi (1797–1879)—the Prince of Librarians (probably the only author of a major cataloguing code to have been condemned to death, albeit in absentia); Maine's Charles Coffin Jewett (1816–1868)—the prophet of the union catalogue; and another New Englander, Charles Ammi Cutter (1837–1903). Melvil Dewey, the American giant of librarianship, never displayed much interest in the topic, being far more interested in classification, the American Library Association (of which he was a founder), and crank spelling. Panizzi, Keeper of the Printed Books at the British Museum, was, in essence, the inventor of the modern national library and a pioneer in many aspects of librarianship—among them national librarianship, library design, and descriptive cataloguing. He turned his busy mind to the problem of ensuring access to the millions of then uncatalogued books in the British Museum and created the first modern code of descriptive cataloguing in his "91 rules" of 1841. Jewett's ideas on cataloguing were embodied in a code that was part of a report he prepared for the Smithsonian (a report that foretold the centralized dissemination of cataloguing data almost half a century before the Library of Congress began its card service). Cutter's *Rules for a printed dictionary catalogue* were originally published as part of a special report on public libraries prepared for the United States Bureau of Education. Panizzi's "91 rules" were narrower in scope than Cutter's rules, which included not only rules on descriptive cataloguing, but also rules for subject headings (an avenue—i.e., a subject headings code—that is largely unexplored to this day) and filing rules. Panizzi's rules were largely confined to the great catalogues of the British Museum Department of Printed Books (part of the de facto national library of the United Kingdom until it was subsumed into the British Library in 1973), and Cutter's rules, though more widely applied in the U.S., never achieved the status of a national, still less international, code. The nineteenth century was the age of single author codes, all of which were influential in different ways but none of which achieved widespread use. The twentieth century was characterized by codes drawn up by committees; codes that, despite their lack of both the concision and clarity of the single author codes, were widely adopted by libraries in Britain and North America. The first of these was the *Anglo-American rules of 1908,* published in separate American and British editions, and the worst was the *ALA cataloging rules* of 1949, which was preceded by a preliminary edition published in 1941. That 1941 draft code was the proximate cause of an article by Andrew Osborn that is one of the founding documents of the Lubetzkian revolution. The rule that will live on in bibliographic infamy in the 1949 publication is rule 116B(3), which applies to, and only to, the Basilian monastery of St. Catherine at Mount Sinai. Thus, the habit of piling up case after case and prescribing rules based on those cases rather than on principle had reached its reductio ad absurdum. The English language codes of the first half of the twentieth century were not only illogical but also lacked utility in practical application. Any cataloguer will tell you that what is needed is a set of general principles that can be applied to new kinds of cataloguing problem, not what amounts to a register of solved cases. (This, of course, is also the fatal flaw of lists of subject headings—they record subjects that have already occurred without giving much guidance on the headings that are needed for new subjects.) The backlash was not slow in coming.

The Anglo-American Cataloguing Rules

The first volumes entitled "Anglo-American catalog[u]ing rules" were published in 1967. The movement that led to these publications began after the disappointment occasioned by the publication, in 1949, of the ALA rules and the LC descriptive cataloguing rules, both of which were adopted grudgingly in North America and ignored elsewhere in the English-speaking world. Seymour Lubetzky, the twentieth century's titan of descriptive cataloguing, wrote devastating explicit and implicit critiques of both. He was also the moving spirit behind the Paris Principles on descriptive cataloguing adopted by a large number of countries in the early 1960s and the author of a draft cataloguing code that embodied his principles. He was appointed editor of the planned new code and worked with the ALA and Library Association cataloguing committees as well as the Library of Congress to design a unified Anglo-American code that based the rules on principle rather than precedent, sharply reduced the number of rules and of variations, and incorporated general, medium-neutral principles of describing library materials of all kinds. Lubetzky's ideas and their consequences (economic and bibliographic) alarmed a sufficient number of mossbacks in the Library of Congress and elsewhere in the U.S. to cause (precipitate?) his removal (resignation?) as editor and replacement by Sumner Spalding of the

Library of Congress, in 1962. Lubetzky had left the Library of Congress to teach at the new library school in UCLA, and it is unclear how or if this is related to his resignation as AACR editor, but the tendency to hew to the LC party line must have lessened when he viewed things from Los Angeles for two years. It is one of the saddest events in cataloguing history that this supremely gifted cataloguing theorist and code writer was unable to be the guiding spirit of a truly revolutionary code that could have avoided all the fuss about, and compromises in, AACR2, a quarter of a century later. This "what if" of cataloguing history is all the more poignant because it would have set us on a path that was unlikely to lead to the chaotic position in which we find ourselves today. The loss to English language cataloguers was the gain of UCLA's library school and its students. The upshot of this murky event was that, though the code as eventually published retained some of the Lubetzkian clarity of thought and reforms, many serious drawbacks remained. First, at a time when the age of international cooperation in cataloguing was dawning, the fudging of the North American text, much of which was not carried over into the, much more Lubetzkian, British text, led to there being continuing major differences between British and American cataloguing practices. Second, the 1967 rules retained many of the outmoded practices and distinctions against which Lubetzky had waged war. Third, in the North American text, the rules on description remained book-centric and inadaptable to the increasing number of other media acquired by libraries. For these and many other reasons, though the first AACR did contain many improvements of the kind recommended by Lubetzky, it soon became clear that it was inadequate to deal with the new realities of international bibliographic cooperation, MARC records, and library automation—the latter represented most significantly by the rapid rise and success of OCLC and the introduction of the first library online systems.

The Anglo-American Cataloguing Rules, second edition

The harmonic convergence of the new realities led to action on several fronts in North America and in the United Kingdom as well as by international bodies. These activities, as far as descriptive cataloguing is concerned, centered on the formulation of the International Standard Bibliographic Description (ISBD) and work toward a truly Anglo-American code for use in all English-speaking countries and, as it turned out, far beyond.

The transition to the new rules in 1968 went well but their imperfections were soon apparent, especially in formulating the British version of the MARC format. The differences in cataloguing rules and practices between

LC and other U.S. and Canadian libraries on the one hand and BNB on the other were, naturally, reflected in the differing U.S. and British MARC formats.

The International Standard Bibliographic Description (ISBD)

For my report commissioned by Anthony Thompson for UNESCO/IFLA (see chapter 8), I compared the descriptive sections (i.e., not the access points) of many hundreds of catalogue records from the eight national bibliographies I had selected and discovered a remarkable affinity in the choice and order of bibliographic data (one difference was the placement of the series data in two of the chosen countries). However, the presentation of the data and the variations in punctuation and abbreviations varied widely, thus making it impossible, when dealing with unfamiliar languages, to decode the descriptions and, crucially at that point, to create programs to translate the data automatically into the emerging machine-readable format. When I had completed the study of the eight national cataloguing agencies, I prepared a report that set out the draft of an international standard that prescribed a standard order of data; standard punctuation separating the elements and subelements of the description; and standard abbreviations. This report was the basis of one of the two working papers at the International Meeting of Cataloguing Experts held in Copenhagen, Denmark, in August 1969. At that meeting, the report was discussed and adopted in principle and given for development into a draft standard to an ad hoc working group chaired by the head of BNB (A. J. "Jack" Wells), of which I was the secretary (the group included the Godmother of MARC—Henriette Avram). I produced the first draft of what was then called the Standard Bibliographic Description in 1969. After about two years of meetings at which the many drafts I prepared were discussed together with many comments on those drafts, the first ISBD was published by IFLA in 1971. This text was adopted by a number of national bibliographies and generated a great deal of comment. Some of the comments verged on the comic, an example being the *Library journal* article that spoke of ISBD's "unnatural punctuation." The Working Group considered and adopted a redrafting of the ISBD(M) based on comments received, and the revised "first standard edition" was published in 1974.

The fundamental ideas in this ISBD, as with all subsequent ISBDs, were that the main parts of the bibliographic description (*areas* in ISBD) and the parts of those areas (*elements*) would be given in an internationally agreed order and set off and delineated by distinctive punctuation. The ISBD also prescribed standard international abbreviations. It is no coincidence that the areas and elements of the ISBD matched the fields and subfields of MARC or that the distinctive punctuation of the standard matched the tags and codes of MARC.

The first ISBD was concerned only with monographs (books), and it soon became apparent that the direction that MARC was taking—work that began in 1974 on the successor to AACR, and the needs of libraries with increasingly diverse collections—required a more general standard, one that brought uniformity to the description of library materials in all formats. We undoubtedly put the cart before the horse in creating the ISBD(M), but there is every reason to believe that step was necessary to demonstrate, on the basis of descriptive data from many countries, that standardization was possible. In any event, the horse and cart were to be put in the correct order in a relatively short time.

Planning AACR2

In 1972, I was seconded to a small group—the British Library Planning Secretariat—to help plan the new national library to be formed from many bodies in the U.K., including the British Museum Department of Printed Books and BNB. That marvelous amalgamation took place in 1973, when the British Library came into being. I was appointed head of the British Library's Bibliographic Standards Office at that time. A number of bodies, including LC, the National Library of Canada, BNB, ALA, and the [British] Library Association (LA) had been engaged for some years in discussions about a replacement for the 1967 AACR as the basis for greatly enhanced international bibliographic cooperation spurred by the rapid spread of the MARC format. These discussions came to a head at a "tripartite" meeting (with representatives from the U.S.A., the U.K., and Canada) at the ALA headquarters in March 1974 (at which I was not present; see chapter 9) to draw up a memorandum of agreement on the creation of a second edition of AACR. That meeting established the Joint Steering Committee (JSC) for the Revision of the Anglo-American Cataloguing Rules—made up of two representatives (one voting, one nonvoting) each from the British Library, LC, ALA, LA, and the joint NLC/Canadian Library Association committee, and the two editors. Despite my nonattendance, I was appointed an editor of the proposed new rules under the title of associate editor. Even then, the Library of Congress in particular and the Americans in general were determined to retain their role as *primus* among the cataloguing *pares*. The role of the associate editor was seen as minor—essentially watching out for the British interests that many felt had been ignored in the formulation of the first AACR. The main objectives of the JSC were to (1) maintain conformity with the Paris Principles; (2) take developments in machine processing of bibliographic data in account; (3) incorporate the ISBD(M) into the chapters on describing library materials; and (4) treat nonbook materials equitably.

I have written about the seven meetings of the JSC and the events surrounding the production of AACR2 in previous chapters. Those meetings considered many drafts and the comments on those drafts from the national libraries and the national cataloguing committees (including ALA's Resources and Technical Services Division's [RTSD's] Catalog Code Revision Committee) and a wide variety of other bodies and individuals. One important early decision of the JSC was to divide the new code into two parts. The first was devoted to description of the resource being catalogued and was therefore concerned with the item (resource) being described. The second was devoted to assigning the name and title access points (headings) and was therefore concerned with the work of which the item was a manifestation. This clear demarcation was not carried out as coherently and consistently in the final text as it should have been but the basic concepts were adopted by the JSC more than thirty years ago, and long before the claim to have invented the distinction by the advocates of the absurdly complicated and theoretical *Functional requirements for bibliographic records* (FRBR, referred to by many as "Fur-ber," a name more suited to a Beanie Baby than an ambitious cataloguing standard). Paul Winkler of the Library of Congress—the American editor of AACR2—was asked to provide the draft for Part 2, and I was asked to provide the drafts of Part 1.

Drafting Part 1 of AACR2

This last assignment made me aware of the limitations of having a standard description confined only to monographs. One of the primary aims of the new code was to treat all library materials equitably, and this led inescapably to the idea that we needed a medium-neutral framework within which ISBDs for individual media could be developed. To this end, I prepared a draft of a general ISBD for consideration by the JSC. The JSC approached the IFLA Committee on Cataloguing with the idea of creating a general ISBD, based on that draft, jointly so that JSC would be able to develop Part 1 of the new rules coherently and in accordance with an international standard, and the IFLA Committee on Cataloguing would be able to develop future ISBDs that conformed to the same standard. A joint JSC/IFLA meeting, held in Paris in October 1975, set up an international

Working Group on the ISBD(G), of which I was the secretary. The meeting achieved agreement on the concept of a general ISBD—the ISBD(G)—that I redrafted for the Working Group a number of times in light of comments received. Because of my close involvement with ISBD(G), I was able to use the ISBD(G) as the basis for drafts of Part 1 of the new code before it was published.

The language and structure of AACR2

I devised a structure for Part 1 that was based on the newly formulated ISBD(G) and that included all the descriptive rules that applied to all materials in chapter 1. Those rules that applied specifically to particular types of material (printed books, cartographic materials, sound recordings, etc.) or to a particular publication pattern (serials) were given in the subsequent chapters (2–12). I created a mnemonic numbering system that told the user in which chapter the rule appeared, then the area of the ISBD with which the rule dealt. For example, rule 1.4 contained general instructions on the Publication, distribution, etc. area applicable to all materials; rule 3. 4 contained instructions on the publication, distribution, etc., area applicable to cartographic materials; and rule 6.4 contained instructions on the publication, distribution, etc., area applicable to sound recordings. This was intended to make reference between chapters easier. Another recommendation that I made and that was adopted in creating this new kind of code was the use of the active voice throughout Part 1 (e.g., "Record a single statement of responsibility as such . . ." rather than "A single statement of responsibility is recorded . . ."). This may seem a relatively minor point but it made the rules easier to understand and teach, reduced ambiguity, and shortened the text. These decisions were later carried over to Part 2 and thus used through AACR2. These two innovations were accompanied by others (improved layout and design; use of more and more current examples; and avoidance of sexist or other prejudicial formulations) all aimed at making AACR2 as easy to understand and use as a necessarily complex text can be. One of the persistent complaints about AACR2 is that it is "too complicated." Those who favor metadata schemes such as the Dublin Core (which is, when all is said and done, no more than a limited subset of the MARC record) tout the simplicity of their system as compared with what they, quite inaccurately, call "MARC cataloguing." The fact is that every rule in AACR2 was framed to deal with a real-world situation encountered by a significant number of catalogers over the years (and every field and subfield of MARC defines a real-world cataloguing element). In other words, the code is complex and

MARC is complex because the bibliographic world is complex. Any scheme that does not take that complexity into account is, at best, simpleminded and, at worst, delusional.

The Catalog Code Revision Committee (CCRC)

The various drafts of the two parts of AACR2 (prepared by Paul Winkler and by me) were circulated to all the constituencies represented on the JSC between 1974 and 1977. Acres of forest were sacrificed to ensure the maximum amount of consultation, participation, and input. The most active of the many bodies involved in this process were the various parts and the whole of RTSD's Catalog Code Revision Committee (an arm of the precursor to ALCTS). The CCRC was ably chaired by my friend John Byrum (of Princeton and later LC) and included such well-known cataloguing experts as Neal Edgar, Åke Koel, Joan Marshall, and Gordon Stevenson. The CCRC enlisted no fewer than thirty-seven "consultants" representing a wide range of other associations as well as ALA committees and divisions. The CCRC and its subcommittees and consultants represented a formidable and, in some ways, dominating force in the AACR2 effort. They were to play an important role in my next AACR2 assignment.

Part 2 of AACR2

By early 1997, I had received the drafts of Part 2 that Paul Winkler had distributed and seen, with some disquiet that the content retained many of the elements of the first AACR that I had thought were to be changed and that, from the editorial point of view, the style and numbering scheme that I had recommended and the JSC approved were not followed in these drafts. I set out my objections to the Part 2 drafts and suggestions as to how it might be harmonized with Part 1 in documents circulated to the JSC and the national cataloguing bodies. I foresaw considerable difficulty in meeting the deadline for completion of the whole project (by the fall of 1977) unless decisions on reconciling these discrepancies were taken quickly. Either the Part 1 that I had just completed would have to be changed utterly or work on Part 2 would have to start afresh with different criteria. Since the JSC had approved Part 1 and LC was seemingly wedded to Paul's approach to Part 2, it was very hard to see how we might proceed. The dilemma was resolved in the way that I favored, principally by the intervention of the ALA cataloguing rules committee.

The rejection of Paul Winkler's drafts of Part 2 by the American CCRC at a preliminary meeting to a JSC meeting held in Washington, DC, in

April 1977 was a major and decisive event in the history of AACR2 (see chapter 11).

The War of AACR2

Long before AACR2 was published in 1978, word of the radical nature of the changes had reached library administrators, in particular administrators of research libraries and large public libraries, and others who had paid very little attention to cataloguing while a revolution was taking place. These fears were stoked by reactionary elements in the Library of Congress, still smarting from the CCRC's démarche, Sumner Spalding's resignation, and Paul Winkler's virtual relegation. MARC, at first used to perpetuate the LC card service and, hence, the card catalogue, was becoming the engine of the doom of both; OCLC had spread from its humble beginnings in Ohio and was on its way to becoming the mainstay of library cataloguing; the first online catalogues and circulation systems were revolutionizing the management of libraries; and ISBD and the looming AACR2 were seen as intolerably expensive engines of change. The arguments raged on the cost of changing access points (headings) that AACR2's Lubetzkianism had supplanted; on the less costly but "foreign" and "unnatural" ISBD conventions; and on LC's policy of "superimposition" (that is, cataloguing new items using the new rules, while leaving previously catalogued works under headings derived from the old rules). The really sad thing about these furious and sometimes theological discussions is that every changed heading represented a move toward user-friendliness and, hence, increased accessibility for catalogue users. However, the discussions, as is usual with administrators, centered on costs rather than increased service to users. I remember all too clearly the sessions at the ALA Annual Conferences and Midwinter Meetings in that time at which cataloguing conservatives railed against the cost of implementing AACR2 and catalogers called for its immediate implementation. There were a number of articles and papers both pro and con. Probably the most valuable articles in favor of AACR2 were contributed by Arlene Taylor, who had, unlike most of the other contributors to the debate, done some research that showed it was cost-effective to implement AACR2 if the library changed headings when there were five or fewer entries to a heading and made references between the old form and the new when there were more than five. This was, of course, before the contents of card catalogues were digitized and added to online catalogues. At that time, card catalogues and online catalogues coexisted uneasily (not every card catalogue has been digitized even to this day). The upshot of the brouhaha over AACR2 was that the Library of Congress (let it not be forgotten that LC was one of the "authors" of AACR2 and party to all its collective decisions), at the urging of the reactionaries of the Association of Research Libraries, delayed the implementation of AACR2 for a year, thus ensuring the creation of many thousands of MARC records that would need to be upgraded later at a great cost in time and money. In the end, the War of AACR2 was over, the new code was adopted, and a new age of cataloguing was born.

> "But what good came of it at last?"
> Quoth little Peterkin
> "Why that I cannot tell," said he
> "But 'twas a famous victory!"

The Tallahassee conference, 1979
In April 1979, the library school of Florida State University held an international conference on AACR2. The speakers were all members of either the Joint Steering Committee or one of the national committees, with the shining exception being the paper given by Seymour Lubetzky on "The fundamentals of bibliographic cataloging and AACR2." It was the first time that I had met Dr. Lubetzky—an honor to which I had looked forward for many years. He, then two weeks short of his 81st birthday, was gracious and very correct but was concerned about some fundamental issues connected with corporate authorship and the treatment of serials. He described AACR2 as the product of "meticulous craftsmanship," praise that meant a great deal to me, but was not convinced that it would be successful in application. On examination, his objections all relate to theoretical questions about authorship and the main entry that, as things turned out, did not affect the actual application of AACR2 because the idea of the "main entry" has been largely sidelined by changes in cataloguing technology. I inscribed the copy of AACR2 I gave to Dr. Lubetzky with my signature and the words *il miglior fabbro* ("the better craftsman").

The Tallahassee conference is memorable to me for many reasons, not least the opportunity to meet and discuss cataloguing matters with the person to whom I had looked up for so many years.

The revised AACR2 of 1988
When the War of AACR2 was over, the rules rapidly found acceptance in the English-speaking world and far beyond. By the time the revision of AACR2 was published, it had been translated into, among other languages,

Left to right: Mitch Freedman, Phyllis Richmond, Jean Weihs, Joe Howard, Michael Malinconico, MG, Seymour Lubetzky, John Byrum, Paul Fasana, Sanford Berman. Tallahassee, Florida, April 14, 1979. Photo by Maurice J. Freedman.

Arabic, Chinese, Danish, French, Spanish, Turkish, and Urdu and was in use in many shared cataloguing networks around the world. AACR2 also influenced many national and regional cataloguing codes developed in that period. Despite this ringing success, it was apparent that there were rules in AACR2 that should be changed because they were internally inconsistent or because new cataloguing problems (specifically those associated with computerized catalogue records and databases) had presented themselves. The Joint Steering Committee was reconstituted to include a representative from the Australian Committee on Cataloguing and solicited suggestions for revisions from the national cataloguing committees and national libraries that were represented on the JSC. These suggestions were considered by the JSC at nine meetings held in the U.S., the U.K., and Canada between 1979 and 1986. I drafted revised rules based on the decisions taken at those meetings. Understandably, the most extensive revisions were to the descriptive rules contained in chapter 9, now retitled "Computer files." By this time, I had become acquainted with word processing so the process of revising AACR2 was speedier and more efficient than the first time around. In addition, there was far less controversy over the revision and, when what became known as AACR2R was published in 1988, there was no repeat of the War of AACR2. I was almost disappointed that there was not even the Skirmish of AACR2R but was pleased to be able to end my twenty-year involvement with AACR on a tranquil note.

The future . . . ?
I would argue, and believe the facts show, that AACR2 is well on the way to being a global cataloguing code in that its first part is based on the ISBD—the most successful international bibliographic standard of all time—and its second part contains within it a distillation of the Lubetzky approach to access points. Further, I believe that AACR2 should be stripped of all the special case-law rules that were imported into Part 2 from previous codes (for example, the numerous cases of special religious materials and laws) and that Part 1 should be stripped of overelaborations in particular cases—those that are insufficient for the specialist cataloger and too much for the general cataloguer (for example, in the rules for music and maps). These rules should be incorporated in specialist cataloguing manuals that are supplementary to AACR2. The resulting "essential AACR2" could then be used as the basis for a universal cataloguing code that, in turn, would become the basis of national and linguistic iterations of the universal code. Others think differently and are prepared to hew to a "standard" (the RDA) that is radically different from all other national codes—the vast majority of which are congruent with AACR2.

The JSC made a fundamental, if politically understandable, mistake when it presented the new rules as the second edition of the 1967 AACR. It was nothing of the sort—it was a clean break with the past as was recognized in Dr. Lubetzky's paper in the Tallahassee conference in which he described AACR2, without unqualified approval, as "a transformed code." It should have been called something like the "English language descriptive cataloguing rules" and the subsequent revisions presented as what they were—new editions of the basic work. Instead, the talk used to be of AACR3 and now is of the Resource Description and Access (RDA)—revolutionary breaks with AACR2 justified in the minds of their proponents by the changed nature of the bibliographic world and the difficulty of cataloguing electronic resources. This view is never expressed with clarity and is largely based on trendy chatter, gaseous assertions, and untested assumptions or on the search for the philosopher's stone of bibliography—high-quality cataloguing with no or little expense. These are poor foundations for the complex, lengthy, and expensive process of cataloguing code revision.

My long involvement with AACR was fun, if not unalloyed fun, while it lasted and the twenty years since have never afforded such a remarkable professional opportunity as the chance to be in the thick of a very important change in descriptive cataloguing.

epilogue

The way in which we become reconciled to dying is that the world becomes increasingly unrecognizable.

—Jonathan Miller

The uncontrolled growth of technology destroys the vital source of our humanity. It creates a culture without moral foundation. It undermines certain mental processes and social relations that make life worth living.

—Neil Postman

I have lived half my life in a country not my own, and the country that is my own is increasingly strange to me. I was 70 in March 2011 and one of the great surprises of my life is that, after many years of being the youngest person in most groups, I have grown old. It is as if, on some unknowable and unrecognized day, youth gave way to age, and the turbulence and glories of the former, those unbearable, unforgettable highs and lows, were memories of another person looked back on by the person I have become—a person who can only recall, not experience, the passions and despairs of that young man, the intense joys or the bitter griefs.

The years have gone by, like the pages of a calendar blown by winds into oblivion in the opening sequence of many an old film. The Decade of This has given way to the Age of That; those who were young are now old, children have become middle-aged men and women, and the old and not so old are dead. I have reached the age in which many dreams are fitful or unwelcome, and there is more inclination to look back than forward, more of a temptation to see what is wrong or in decline than what is right and good. I can no longer step out on the daily tightrope with the heedlessness of youth, that wonderful lack of fear that lends our early decades much of their beauty, terror, and fascination. To know more is to fear more, and to fear more is always to see the lurking darkness. The library culture in which I grew and was fashioned seems, some of the time, to be a distant memory, and the changes that have been are as nothing when compared to the changes that are to come—or so we are told. The artifact that has been at the heart of our culture and the learning that sustains it—the printed book—is said to be obsolescent and soon to be obsolete. University library administrators, of all people, talk of "legacy collections" in dismissive terms as if the collective record of the thoughts, discoveries, and desires of humanity presented in authentic and immutable form were something to be disposed of once the funeral rites of the printed book were over. The digital life, as generally experienced, is lived in the now with little regard for the past and no concern for the future—it is a superficial, skimming, skittering sort of life in which the most profound text is awarded the same importance as a video of a kitten playing the piano and in which "multitasking" (doing several inconsequential things at the same time) is a skill on a level with those needed for the concentrated, sustained reading of texts that can, with effort, lead to the attainment of understanding and, with luck, wisdom. Terms too hollow to rise to the status of clichés such as "the age of information," "our busy lives," and "information wants to be free" are the unquestioned bywords of those who aspire to be leaders and seers. Despite all this and in face of much of the evidence, I remain optimistic about the future of learning; the onward transmission of the human record; the prospects for coordination of the human record with other aspects of the cultural record. With that coordination, the related disciplines of librarianship, archival work, museology, and the work of those concerned with the scholarship and preservation of works of art can be seen as branches of the same great endeavor—ensuring current access to, and organization, preservation, and onward transmission of, the cultural creations of humankind. I have a vision of a librarianship that has rejected the alien cultures of information technology and scientific management (without abandoning the use of technology as a tool or the use of cost-efficient administrative techniques) and embraced the role of stewards of the human record while working with other professions and institutions that are concerned with other aspects of the cultural heritage. Beyond that I have other visions of libraries today and in the future.

As I write, somewhere, there is a 10-year-old boy who has encountered for the first time an author whose books set his brain on fire in an underfunded public library in a small town because a librarian who has befriended him recommended that author. Somewhere in a depressed area of a big city, a librarian is helping a woman who can barely speak English to learn to read and write in that language. Somewhere a student who is the first person in her family to attend college is receiving friendship and help that will make the all the difference in her studies from an experienced and qualified librarian. Somewhere a scholar is "discovering" a manuscript that will change her subject because an unknown cataloguer created a record for it forty years ago and a conservator stored it in optimal conditions for all those years. Somewhere a person who is housebound is reading the books or viewing the videos that were chosen and delivered by librarians working in their stressed suburban library's services to shut-ins. Somewhere a scholar is learning of a new line of inquiry from a subject-specialist librarian in a public college. Everywhere, selfless, skilled public servants who work in libraries are finding joy in their work because they know that their knowledge is helping individuals become more empowered, more autonomous, and more able to deal with life.

The lens into the future is fogged by the miasma of nonsense about video gaming, twittering, the faux friendships of social networking, and the rest of the vain, and often ridiculous, attempts to clasp the shiny, evanescent culture of digital youth that are currently so popular among some librarians. However, through the murk I can see the librarians of the future continuing to be inspired by enduring spirit of service, devotion to literacy and learning, and commitment to education and democratic values that has sustained us for so long. It is that that makes me proud to have had a library life and full of hope for the days to be for libraries, for our profession, and for the communities we serve.

notes

Chapter 1, "Et in Arcadia Ego, 1941–1945"

p. 1, *The building was refurbished . . .* : See a description at the VisitLondon website published by the Mayor's Office, www.visitlondon.com/attractions/detail/220251 (consulted February 2, 2010).

p. 3, *Though my father was present . . .* : His service record says he was at "home" (probably in the Middlesex Regiment barracks in Mill Hill) from August 19, 1939 (two weeks before war was declared on Germany) to June 17, 1942.

p. 5, *a north London Catholic church*: The church of St. Paul the Apostle, 22 Bradley Road, Wood Green, London N22.

p. 5, *Charles Stewart Lawrence Gorman*: Private C. S. L. Gorman, an infantryman in the Machine Gun Corps, was killed on November 2, 1918, nine days before the Armistice, and is buried in the Kezelberg military cemetery near Ypres, Belgium.

p. 5, *Desmond Thomas Gorman*: D. T. Gorman is commemorated on a memorial in Pozieres near the Somme.

p. 7, *Unfortunately, the building was destroyed . . .* : "The first day of the month of October found the people under continuous bombardment . . . Another raid commenced before midnight. Incidents were reported, including a parachute mine on North End Village . . . ten people were killed and 26 treated for injuries." Hampstead at War / Hampstead Borough Council, 1946 (reprinted by the Camden Society, 1977), p. 9.

p. 7, *. . . after my father returned from the war in late 1945*: His service record says he returned "home" from North Africa on August 10, 1945, and was discharged from active duty (in Taunton, Somerset) on November 12, 1945. I have no idea if he came to Oxfordshire after or before the latter occasion, but my brother David's birth date would seem to indicate an August arrival.

Chapter 2, "London, 1946–1947"

p. 11, epigraph: Grayling, A.C. Towards the light: the story of the struggles for liberty and rights that made the modern West. *London: Bloomsbury, 2008. p. 61.*

p. 12 *in the Middlesex Regiment—the "Diehards"*: It is common for British regiments to be given nicknames. The Middlesex were called the "Diehards" because of their indomitable performance in the Peninsular Wars of the early nineteenth century.

p. 12: *His commendation on his demob . . .* : This encomium was signed "Major E. Crossley, Camp Commandant, 144 Transit Camp" and dated July 12, 1945.

Chapter 3, "On the Move, 1948–1952"

p. 23, *Canon Clement Henry Parsons (1892–1980)*: Canon Parsons died on my 39th birthday (March 6, 1980) at the age of 88 in the Hospital of St. John & St. Elizabeth, the place in which two of my siblings were born and in which my father died three months after the Canon.

p. 26, *a "Christmas box"*: A Christmas box is a kind of tip that was given to delivery people (coalmen, milkmen, dustmen, paperboys, etc.), traditionally on December 26th—a day still known as Boxing Day for that reason.

p. 27, *. . . fascinated by the Lady's taut, shiny, bare body*: The "Naked Lady," as we all called it, is a statue called "La Delivrance" made by the Frenchman E. Guillaume as a monument to the soldiers of the Battle of the Marne and presented to the borough by Viscount Rothermere, the right-wing newspaper magnate.

p. 28, *The charging system they used . . .* : It was invented by an American librarian called Nina Browne in the 1890s. The system is commonly misspelled as Brown.

p. 29, *. . . the signed copy I have of her 2000 autobiography*: Colwell, Eileen. *Once upon a time.* Hebden Bridge, Yorkshire: Pennine Pens, 2000.

Chapter 4, "Finchley Catholic Grammar School, 1952–1957"

p. 38, *a parody of an English public school*: For a discussion of the Eleven Plus and the grammar school phenomenon, see Kynaston, David. *Austerity Britain, 1945–1951.* London: Bloomsbury, 2007. Part 2: Smoke in the valley, chapter 12.

p. 38, *the onetime cardinal-archbishop of Westminster*: Francis Alphonsus Bourne, 1861–1934.

p. 39, *. . . in a newsletter from the school*: I stayed away from all contact with, or knowledge of, the school between 1957 and 2007. Seeking information as background to this memoir has necessitated some slight encounters since, including reading the newsletter of the "Old Albanians" (the ridiculous name of the former pupils' association).

p. 41, *the historic Hendon Aerodrome*: Hendon Aerodrome (now occupied by a charmless housing estate and Hendon Police College) was a fabled center of aviation. It was the site of the first parachute drop from a powered aircraft; the first place from which airmail was sent and at which received; the first night flights; and the first aerial defense of a city. When I was young, you could view the annual Hendon Air Show from the slopes of Sunnyhill Park.

p. 46, *the "Family of man" exhibition*: *The family of man: the greatest photographic exhibition of all time* . . . New York: Maco Magazine Corp. for the Museum of Modern Art, 1955, p. 27.

Chapter 5, "Hampstead Public Library, 1957–1960"

p. 51, epigraph: Roy, Kenneth. "Hampstead is a state of mind." *The Observer*, 10 December 1995, p. 10 (Kenneth Roy's Britain, 15).

p. 52, *The latter included, incredibly,* Forever Amber: *Forever Amber* was a romance novel by Kathleen Winsor set in Regency England. It was first published in 1944 and was of the type that is known today as a bodice ripper—tame stuff indeed by twenty-first-century standards.

p. 53, *a fearsome cast-iron machine (an Adana)*: The Adana Company (1922–1999) made a variety of printing machines. This model impressed letters on metal plates.

p. 55, *though since this is the title of a novel by Jack Kerouac*: Kerouac, Jack. *Dr. Sax: Faust part three*. New York: Grove Press, 1959

p. 55, *misprinted in the local paper*: *The Hampstead & Highgate Express,* known universally as "The Ham & High."

p. 62, *In 1820 Keats, seriously ill with tuberculosis . . .* : I have a copy of the definitive edition of the poems of John Keats, edited by Jack Stillinger (Cambridge, Mass.: Harvard University Press, 1978), signed by the editor whom I came to know at the University of Illinois, in which he was one of its illustrious professors.

p. 62, *Sir Charles Dilke*: See Jenkins, Roy. *Sir Charles Dilke: A Victorian tragedy*. 1965.

p. 63, *I read books about Joyce and* Ulysses, *most notably . . .* : Gilbert, Stuart. *James Joyce's* Ulysses: *A study*. Revised ed. London: Faber, 1952; and Budgen, Frank. *James Joyce and the making of* Ulysses. New York: Harrison Smith and Robert Haas, 1934.

p. 63, *children's versions of the Arthur stories*: Notably Roger Lancelyn Green's *King Arthur and his knights of the Round Table* (1933).

p. 63, *More important, I read William Gaunt's brilliant books . . .* : Gaunt, William. *The Pre-Raphaelite tragedy*. London: Cape, 1942; and Gaunt, *The aesthetic adventure*. London: Cape, 1945.

p. 64, *the West Hampstead Women's Centre*: See www.whwc.co.uk.

p. 66, *"How about lyonch?"*: This invariable waggery was a reference to an advertising campaign for Lyon's teashops in the 1930s with the slogan "Where's George? Gone to Lyonch!" accompanied by a drawing of George Robey, the famous music hall comedian.

p. 66, *a NALGO convalescent home*: National Association of Local Government Officers—the trade union for local government employees.

p. 73, *. . . Orwell's bleak warning—"If you want a vision of the future . . ."*: Orwell, George. *Nineteen eighty-four*. 1949.

Chapter 6, "Paris and Afterwards, 1960–1962"

p. 78, *"KROUTCHEW"*: Nikita Khrushchev was visiting Vienna and being given the cold shoulder by his hosts, partly because of the U2 incident of May 1, 1960, in which Gary Powers, piloting a spy plane, was shot down by the USSR. He was to be put on trial in Moscow—the reason for the trip by Tom, Bob, and John.

p. 78, *"LUMUMBA"*: Congo had just gained its independence from Belgium (perhaps the cruelest of the imperial powers), and Patrice Lumumba, the prime minister of the new country, had assailed colonialism at the independence ceremony.

p. 87, *. . . leading to the great gallery*: Now, ludicrously, renamed "Tate Britain" (a name that makes neither artistic nor logical sense) to differentiate it from "Tate Modern" in what used to be Battersea Power Station.

p. 91, *philosophical anarchism typified by Kropotkin*: Kropotkin, Petr Alkseevich, 1842–1921, was a biologist who believed that evolution was made possible by cooperation, and the father of philosophical anarchism.

p. 91, *. . . of which Blanqui and Bakunin were the inspiration*: Louis-Auguste Blanqui, 1805–1881, was the leader of a violent faction in the Paris Commune of 1871. Mikhail Aleksandrovich Bakunin, 1814–1876, was a thinker and revolutionary whose lines "freedom without Socialism is privilege and injustice . . . Socialism without freedom is slavery and brutality" foreshadowed much of the twentieth and twenty-first centuries.

p. 92, *Bergman's films being what they are . . .* : The great Stephen Potter, in a series of books beginning with *The theory and practice of gamesmanship* (1947), expounded on how to seem superior without actually cheating.

p. 93, *especially the Joint Fiction Reserve system*: The Joint Fiction Reserve (JFR) of London's public libraries was an incredibly simple and administratively inexpensive system basing on each library agreeing to buy and keep all the novels by authors whose last names fall within a certain alphabetic range. Hampstead's range was GO-GRA, so a library wishing to borrow, for example, any novel by the obscure American author Herbert Gorman would apply to Hampstead without having to consult any catalogue. In all my long career, I never came across a simpler or more effective system.

Chapter 7, "Marriage and Library School, 1962–1964"

p. 102, *a standard book on the nearly forgotten art of historical bibliography*: Binns, Norman E. *An introduction to historical bibliography*; with a preface by Arundell Esdaile. London: Association of Assistant Librarians, 1953.

p. 102, *"not over ambitious for himself . . . "*: Wade, A. J. *Update* (2007) vol. 6, issue 5.

p. 109, *. . . and with the Great Names associated with them . . .* : Charles Ammi Cutter (1837–1903), Melvil Dewey (1851–1931), Henry Evelyn Bliss (1870–1955), James Duff Brown (1862–1914), and Shiyali Ramamrita Ranganathan (1892–1972)—all of whom created codes of descriptive cataloguing and/or library classification schemes. The first three were American, Brown a Scot, and Ranganathan an Indian. Seymour Lubetzky (1898–2003) was the foremost cataloguing theorist of the twentieth century. He was an American, though born in what is now Belarus.

p. 111, *Licklider's futuristic ideas about technology and libraries*: Licklider, J. C. R. *Libraries of the future*. Cambridge, Mass.: MIT Press, 1965.

p. 111, *the philosophical polymath Bar-Hillel's essays on information and language*: Bar-Hillel, Yehoshua. *Language and information: Selected essays*. Reading, Mass.: Addison-Wesley, 1964.

p. 112, *This honor was named after Albert Cawthorne . . .* : Black, Alistair. "Man and boy: Modifying masculinities in public librarianship, 1850–1950, with a case study of the interwar Librarianship Masonic Circle." In *Gendering library history* / edited by Evelyn Kerslake and Nickianne Moody. Liverpool: John Moores University, 2000.

p. 114, *Her parody of Lewis Carroll on cataloguing and classification . . .* : Williams, Diana R. "Twinkle, twinkle, little scientific & technical aerospace reports, or, Alice's adventures in bookland." *Assistant librarian*, vol. 59, pp. 234–6 (December 1966). Reprinted under Gorman, Diana R. In *Library humor: A bibliothecal miscellany to 1970* / edited by Norman D. Stevens. Metuchen, NJ: Scarecrow Press, 1971.

Chapter 8, "BNB, Children, Cataloguing, and a Crisis, 1966–1969"

p. 115, *the new Anglo-American cataloguing rules . . .* : *Anglo-American cataloguing rules*. British text. London: Library Association, 1967.

p. 117, *This was long before 1950 . . .* : This account of BNB is my impressionistic sketch. For an authoritative history, see Stephens, Andy. *The history of the British National Bibliography, 1950–1973*. Boston Spa (Yorkshire): British Library, 1994.

p. 117, *. . . to use the legal deposit laws . . .* : Legal deposit laws date back to sixteenth-century France with the *Ordonnances de Montpellier* of 1537.

p. 118, *a variant of the 1908 Anglo-American cataloguing rules (AA1908)*: Anglo-American cataloguing rules. British text. London: Library Association, 1908.

p. 118, *. . . according to the rules drawn up . . .* : British Museum Department of Printed Books. *Rules for compiling the catalogues of printed books, maps and music in the British Museum*. Rev. ed. London: British Museum, 1936.

p.119, *On my first day, I met Richard "Dicky" Bird . . .* : From the Lorenz Books 2006 catalogue: "Richard Bird has been gardening since childhood and currently maintains a large garden where his abiding passion for plants is very evident. He has contributed to numerous publications and has been magazine editor for Focus on Plants, the Hardy Plant, Alpine Gardening and the Alpine Garden Society's magazine Bulletin. He is also a full-time author on gardens and plants and has written nearly 30 books on subjects as diverse as alpines and rock gardens, lilies, perennials, organic gardening and window boxes. He is the author of *Sensational Shrubs and Glorious Climbers* (Lorenz Books) and *A Gardener's Guide to Annuals and Perennials* (Lorenz Books)."

p. 120, *. . . an influential book on classification*: Mills, J. (Jack). *A modern outline of library classification*. London: Chapman & Hall, 1960.

p. 120, *He later tried to revive the nineteenth-century tradition . . .* : See, for example, Croghan, Antony. *A bibliographic system for non-book media*. 2nd ed. London: Coburgh Publications, 1979; *and* Croghan, *A faceted classification for, and an essay on the literature of, the performing arts*. London: A. Croghan, 1968.

p. 120, *a report, initially for internal use and later published . . .* : Gorman, Michael. *A study of the rules for entry and heading in the* Anglo-American cataloguing rules, *1967 (British text)*. London: Library Association, 1967. The summary of pre-1967 BNB cataloguing practice was given as an appendix in this publication.

p. 122, *Stephen Spender, who lived in a house in Loudoun Road . . .* : Spender, Stephen, 1909–1995, English poet and critic. See www.poetryfoundation.org/archive/poet.html?id=6465 (consulted July 4, 2010).

p. 126, *I published an article . . .* : Gorman, Michael. "A-A 1967: The new cataloguing rules." *Library Association record,* vol. 70, no. 2 (February 1968), pp. 27–32; and Gorman, "Decision flow diagram of the *Anglo-American cataloguing rules.*" *Catalogue & index,* no. 9 (January 1968), pp. 8–9.

p. 127, *. . . a national conference on the rules . . .* : Seminar on the *Anglo-American cataloguing rules (1967)* / edited by J. C. Downing and N. F. Sharp. London: Library Association, 1969.

p. 128, *"The Metropolitan Railway"*: Betjeman, John. *A few late chrysanthemums.* London: John Murray, 1954, p. 38.

p. 129, *Leni Riefenstahl's* Triumph of the will: *Triumph des Willens,* a notorious 1935 propaganda film documenting the infamous Nazi Nuremberg Rallies of 1934.

p. 130, *John and I wrote the first British MARC format manual . . .* : Gorman, Michael, and J.E. Linford. *Description of the BNB MARC record: a manual of practice.* London: Council of the British National Bibliography, 1971.

p. 131, *Herman Liebaers . . . described him . . .* : Liebaers, Herman. *The Dutch Tea Party of IFLA in the Seventies.* A speech at the 68th IFLA Council and General Conference, Glasgow, Scotland, August 2002.

p. 132, *My report was circulated widely . . . .* : For detailed comments, see Domanovsky, Ákos. *Digest of the comments received on* Bibliographical data in national bibliography entries *by Michael Gorman (DE2).* (International Meeting of Cataloguing Experts. Working paper; 2). Mimeographed typescript.

p. 134, *a conference called the International Meeting of Cataloguing Experts (IMCE) . . .* : For an account of the genesis and proceedings of the IMCE, see Chaplin, A. H., and Dorothy Anderson. Report of the International Meeting of Cataloguing Experts, 1969. *Libri.* Vol. 20, no. 1 (1970), pp. 105–122.

Chapter 9, "BNB, The British Library, 1970–1974"

p. 139, *the EUDISED project*: The European Documentation and Information System for Education.

p. 140, *. . . the marvelous Russian film of* Hamlet *. . .* : *Gamlet* / directed by Grigori Kozintsev, with a screenplay based on a translation of the play by Boris Pasternak. 1964.

p. 144, *the Parry report*: United Kingdom University Grants Committee. *Committee on Libraries, Report.* London: HMSO, 1967. Chaired by Thomas Parry.

p. 144, *the Dainton report*: United Kingdom Department of Education & Science. *National Libraries Committee. Report.* London: HMSO, 1969. Chaired by Frederick Dainton. (Cmnd. 4028)

p. 144, *a white paper . . . published in 1971*: United Kingdom Paymaster General. *The British Library.* London: HMSO, 1971 (Cmnd. 4572).

p. 146, *By the latter he meant the idiosyncratic, largely unrecorded practices* . . . : British Museum. *Rules for compiling the catalogues of printed books, maps, and music in the British Museum*. Revised ed. London: The Museum, 1936.

p. 146, . . . *academic achievement and indisputably high levels of scholarship*: Richard Sydney Pine-Coffin, a Peterhouse man, was the translator and editor of, among others, a standard edition of the *Confessions* of St. Augustine of Hippo and *Galateo* by Giovanni dell Casa.

p. 148, *Anthony Baker published an article on Morris in 1969*: Baker, Anthony. "The quest for Guido." *Private library*, 1969

p. 149, *Officina Mauritiana*: This was probably a tip of Guido's hat to the Officina Bodoni, the acclaimed early twentieth-century press of Giovanni (né Hans) Mardersteig, itself named after the great Italian printer Giambattista Bodoni, 1740–1813.

p. 149, *only one of which I still possess, a poem* . . . : Rolfe, Fredk. W. *Ballade of boys bathing*. Holborn: apud Guidonem Londinensem impressa, October 1972. 4 pages. A limited edition of 200 copies; mine is no. 148.

p. 149, . . . *whose late husband Reginald, the grandson of the 3rd Earl of Bradford* . . . : Reginald Francis Orlando Bridgeman, MVO, CMG (1884–1968).

p. 150, *"parish of enormous hay fields"*: Betjeman, John. "Middlesex." In his *A few late chrysanthemums*, 1954.

Chapter 10, "Illinois, 1974–1975"

p.158, *The policy on the size and scope of the library collection* . . . : University of Illinois Library. History of the Library. www.library.illinois.edu/learn/basics/history.html (dated July 3, 2009, consulted April 1, 2010).

p. 159, . . . *and opened in 1897 as the University Library*: Melvil Dewey spoke at the opening of the University Library in 1897. I had the honor of being the speaker at the centenary of that opening in 1997.

p. 159, *the socialist John Peter Altgeld—"the forgotten eagle"*: Altgeld, the German immigrant who was governor of Illinois, 1893–1897, was so called in the poem "Altgeld the Eagle" by Vachel Lindsay: "Sleep softly—eagle forgotten—under the stone. / Time has its way with you there, and the clay has its own."

p. 159, *Katharine Sharp, the founder of the school*: Katharine Lucinda Sharp (1865–1914), a pupil and disciple of Melvil Dewey, founded the Illinois State Library School in Urbana in 1897.

p. 167, *Since the Illini were the original inhabitants of the state* . . . : After years of resistance from the people who thought this insulting display a fine old tradition, the last dance of Chief Illiniwek took place in 2007.

p. 169, *This historic hotel* . . . : The original gift hotel was destroyed in the Chicago Fire shortly after its opening and was rebuilt by Palmer with even more opulence and expense than the original, opening in 1873.

p. 169, *Wilf Lancaster had completed the manuscript . . .* : Lancaster, F. Wilfrid. *The measurement and evaluation of library services* / [written] with the assistance of Marcie Joncich.—Washington, DC: Information Resources Press, 1977.

p. 171, *The latter was an industrial storage device . . .* : After limping along for years of increasingly expensive maintenance, the Randtriever was decommissioned in 1992.

p. 172, *I wrote the article that Art had commissioned*: Gorman, Michael. "Osborn revisited, or, Four catalogers, only one of whom shall save us." *American libraries*. Vol. 6, no. 10, pp. 599–601 (November 1975).

Chapter 11, "Back to England, The University of Illinois Library, 1975–1978"

p. 177, *Richard "Dick" Clark, the Democratic senator from Iowa*: Richard Clark, 1928–, was elected to the Senate, defeating the Republican incumbent, in 1972. He was defeated in his bid for reelection by another Republican in 1978.

p. 178, *Maxine Sullivan was singing*: Maxine Sullivan, 1911–1987. See www.swingmusic.net/Sullivan_Maxine.html (consulted May 4, 2010).

p. 180, *Meeting them at the clinic*: *Closing the catalog: Proceedings of the 1978 and 1979 Library and Information Technology Association institutes* / edited by D. Kaye Gapen and Bonnie Juergens. Phoenix, AZ: Oryx, 1980; and *Authority control: The key to tomorrow's catalog: Proceedings of the 1979 Library and Information technology institute* / edited by Mary Ghikas. Phoenix, AZ: Oryx, 1982.

p. 186, *Largely due to support from the ALA committee . . .* : See "Gorman, Michael. "AACR2: Main themes." In *The making of a code: The issues underlying AACR2* / edited by Doris Hargrett Clack. Chicago: ALA, 1980. pp. 41–50.

p. 186, *the use of the correct "United Kingdom" . . .* : There are a number of islands west of the European landmass. Most of them are occupied by two countries—the United Kingdom and the Republic of Ireland. The largest of these islands is called Great Britain or Britain; it contains most of the nations of England, Scotland, and Wales (other parts of those nations being on smaller islands), which form the United Kingdom, together with Northern Ireland, six counties in the northeast of the island of Ireland, the second largest island.

p. 187, *. . . a controversy over the film* The speaker *. . .* : For a full description of this controversy, see Kister, Kenneth F. *Eric Moon: The life and library times*. Jefferson, NC: McFarlane, 2002, pp. 334–350.

p. 187, *George Orwell's quotation "If liberty means anything at all . . ."*: From the unpublished preface to the first edition of *Animal farm* (1945). The preface was first published in the *Times literary supplement* in 1972.

p. 190, *Rain began to fall on Central Illinois . . .* : Changnon, Stanley A., and

David Changnon. *Record winter storms in Illinois, 1977–1978*. Urbana, IL: Illinois State Water Survey, 1978 (ISWS RI 88/78).

Chapter 12, "The Anglo-American Cataloguing Rules, 1968–1988"

p. 191, *What follows in this chapter* . . . : This chapter is based on my "True history of AACR2 / By One Who Was There," published in *Commemorating the past, celebrating the present, creating the future* / Pamela Bluh, editor. Chicago: ALA, 2007. pp. 60–74.

p. 191, *As I write, a bizarrely incoherent and unnecessary draft* . . . : Joint Steering Committee for the Revision of AACR2. *RDA: Resource description and access*. Part 1 (5JSC/RDA/Part 1) December 2005, and numerous other documents.

p. 191, *O tempora, o mores!*: "O the times, o the manners!" Marcus Tullius Cicero. In *Catilinam*.

p. 191, *in particular, descriptive cataloguing*: A preliminary definition is necessary. *Descriptive cataloguing* is used in library literature with two meanings. In the first sense, it means creating the description of the resource (book, electronic resources, map, etc.) being catalogued and assigning name and title (but not subject) access points. In the second sense, it means only creating the description. I use the term in its first, broader sense, except when, as in the Library of Congress rules for descriptive cataloguing, the context implies the second sense.

p. 192, *Antonio (later Sir Anthony) Panizzi (1797–1879)—the Prince of Librarians*: Miller, Edward. *Prince of librarians: The life and times of Antonio Panizzi of the British Museum*. London: Deutsch, 1967.

p. 192, *Charles Ammi Cutter (1837–1903)*: Miksa, Francis L., ed. *Charles Ammi Cutter, library systematizer*. Littleton, CO: Libraries Unlimited, 1977.

p. 192, *Jewett's ideas on cataloguing* . . . : Jewett, Charles Coffin. *On the construction of catalogues of libraries, and of a general 1852 catalogue; and their publication by means of separate, stereotyped titles*. Washington, DC: Smithsonian Institution, 1852.

p. 192, *Cutter's* Rules for a printed dictionary catalogue . . . : Cutter, Charles Ammi. *Rules for a printed dictionary catalog*. Washington, DC: Government Printing Office, 1876. (*Special report on public libraries* / United States Education Bureau; part 2)

p. 193, *The first of these was the* Anglo-American rules of 1908: AA 1908. *Catalog rules, author and title entries* / compiled by committees of the American Library Association and the [British] Library Association. American ed. Chicago: ALA, 1908.

p. 193, *the worst was the* ALA cataloging rules *of 1949*: ALA 1949. *A.L.A. cata-*

loguing rules for author and title entries / prepared by the Division of Cataloguing and *Classification of the American Library Association*. 2nd ed. / prepared by Clara Beetle. Chicago: ALA, 1949.

p. 193, *a preliminary edition published in 1941*: A.L.A. *catalog rules, author and title entries* / prepared by the Catalog Code Revision Committee of the American Library Association, with the collaboration of a committee of the (British) Library Association. Preliminary American 2nd ed. Chicago: ALA, 1941.

p. 193, *. . . one of the founding documents of the Lubetzkian revolution*: Osborn, Andrew D. "The crisis in cataloging." *Library quarterly*, vol. 11, no. 6 (October 1941), pp. 393–411.

p. 193, *The rule that will live on in bibliographic infamy . . .* : ALA 1949. *Op. cit.* p. 174.

p. 193, *The first volumes . . .* : AACR. *Anglo-American cataloguing rules* / prepared by the American Library Association, et al.(North American text). Chicago, ALA, 1967. And *Anglo-American cataloguing rules* / prepared by the American Library Association, et al. (British text). London: Library Association, 1967.

p. 193, *. . . the ALA rules and the LC descriptive cataloguing rules . . .* : *Rules for descriptive cataloguing in the Library of Congress*. Washington, DC: LC, 1949.

p. 193, *. . . wrote devastating explicit and implicit critiques of both*: Lubetzky, Seymour. *Cataloguing rules and principles*. Washington, DC: Library of Congress, 1953; and "Some observations on revision of the cataloguing rules." *Library quarterly*, vol. 26, pp. 362–366.

p. 193, *He was also the moving spirit behind the Paris Principles . . .* : International Conference on Cataloguing Principles, Paris, 1961. Statement of principles: adopted at the International Conference on Cataloguing Principles, Paris, October 1961. Annotated ed., with commentary and examples by Eva Verona assisted by [others]. Definitive ed. London: Department of Printed Books, British Museum for the International Federation of Library Associations (Committee on Cataloguing), 1971.

p. 193, *. . . a draft cataloguing code that embodied his principles*: Lubetzky, Seymour. *Code of cataloguing rules: author and title entries: an unfinished draft . . .* Chicago: ALA, 1960.

p. 194, *. . . their imperfections were soon apparent . . .* : Gorman, Michael. *Description of the BNB/MARC record: a manual of practice* / with the assistance of John Linford. London: BNB, 1971.

p. 195, *At that meeting, the report was discussed and adopted . . .* : Gorman, Michael "International Meeting of Cataloguing Experts: a report from Copenhagen," *Catalogue & index* 16 (Oct. 1969):12.

p. 195: *I produced the first draft of what was then . . .* : Gorman, Michael. *Standard*

220 • BROKEN PIECES

bibliographic description: A proposal for a standard comprehensive international system for the recording of bibliographic data / revised draft proposals for consideration by the IMCE Working Party on the Standard Bibliographic Description prepared by Michael Gorman. [London: BNB], 1969.

p. 195, *After about two years of meetings at which the many drafts* . . . : International Standard Bibliographic Description: for single volume and multivolume monographic publications; recommended by the Working Group on the International Standard Bibliographic Description set up at the International Meeting of Cataloguing Experts, Copenhagen, 1969. London: IFLA Committee on Cataloguing, 1971; and Gorman, Michael. "Standard bibliographic description." *Catalogue & index,* no. 22 (Summer 1971), p. 3–5.

p. 195, *. . . and generated a great deal of comment*: See, for example: "More ISBD discussion: Articles and a forum." *Library journal,*vol. 98 (Feb. 15, 1973), p. 495–496.

p. 195, *Some of the comments verged on the comic* . . . : Swanson, Gerald. "ISBD: standard or secret?" *Library journal,* vol. 98 (Jan. 15, 1973), p. 124–130; and Gorman, Michael. "Soothing the ISBD jitters (Letter in reply to G. Swanson)," *Library journal,* vol. 98 (March 15, 1973):811.

p. 195, *The Working Group considered and adopted* . . . : ISBD(M)-International Standard Bibliographic Description for monographic publications. 1st standard ed. London: IFLA Committee on Cataloguing, 1974.

p. 197, *The main objectives of the JSC were* . . . : See *AACR2. Anglo-American cataloguing rules.* 2nd ed. Chicago: ALA, 1978. p. vii.

p. 198, *Because of my close involvement* . . . : *ISBD(G): General International Standard Bibliographic Description: annotated text.* London: International Office for UBC, 1977.

p. 198, *avoidance of sexist or other prejudicial formulations*: See, for example, the use of the term *Native American nations* rather than *tribes* in AACR2 op. cit. rule 21.35.

p. 198, *. . . as compared with what they, quite inaccurately, call "MARC cataloguing"*: MARC is, of course, a framework standard that is complex because of the complexity of the data prescribed by content standards such as AACR2.

p. 200, *The arguments raged on* . . . : McCallum, Sally. "Some implications of desuperimposition." *Library quarterly,* vol. 47 (April 1977), p. 111–127.

p. 200, *Probably the most valuable articles in favor of AACR2* . . . : Taylor, Arlene. "The impact of LC's implementation of AACR2." *Technicalities* (December 1980): p. 4–6; "A five-year projection of the impact of the rules for form of heading in AACR2 upon selected academic library catalogs." *SPEC* kit 68 (October 1980), p. 1–19 (also in *Alternative catalog newsletter,* nos. 24–26

(December 1980); "What if we had a crisis, but nobody noticed? The impact of AACR2." *Georgia librarian* (May 1980), p. 5–8.

p. 201, *In the end, the War of AACR2 was over . . .* : Martell, Charles. "The war of AACR2." *Journal of academic librarianship*, vol. 7, issue 1, pp. 4–8, 19??.

p. 201, *"But what good came of it at last?"*: Southey, Robert. *The battle of Blenheim.* 1797.

p. 201, *In April 1979, the library school of Florida State University . . .* : *The making of a code: the issues underlying AACR2* / edited by Doris Hargrett Clack. Chicago: ALA, 1980.

p. 201, *He described AACR2 as the product of "meticulous craftsmanship," . . .* : Ibid. pp.16–25.

p. 201, *I inscribed the copy of AACR2 I gave to Dr. Lubetzky . . .* : T. S. Eliot dedicated "The wasteland" (1922) "for Ezra Pound *il miglior fabbro*."

p. 201, *By the time the revision of AACR2 was published . . .* : AACR2R. *Anglo-American cataloguing rules.* 2nd ed., 1988 revision. Chicago: ALA, 1988. p. xiii.

p. 203, *. . . specialist cataloguing manuals that are supplementary to AACR2*: Gorman, Michael and Pat Oddy. "The Anglo-American cataloguing rules. Second edition: Their history and principles." In *The principles and future of AACR : Proceedings of the International Conference on the Principles and Future Development of AACR, Toronto, Ontario, Canada, October 23–25, 1997*/ edited by Jean Weihs. Chicago : American Library Association, 1998.

p. 203, *. . . in Dr. Lubetzky's paper in the Tallahassee conference . . .* : *The making of a code*, op. cit. p. 25.

p. 203, *. . . and is largely based on trendy chatter, gaseous assertions, and untested assumptions*: See, for example: Coyle, Karen, and Diane Hillman. "Resource Description and Access (RDA): Cataloguing rules for the 20th [sic] century." *D-Lib Magazine*, 13(1/2). January/February 2007. www.dlib.org/dlib/january07/coyle/01coyle.html (consulted Feb. 2, 2007).

epilogue

p. 206, *I have a vision of a librarianship . . .* : Gorman, Michael. "The right path and the wrong path: The role of libraries in access to, and preservation of, cultural heritage." *Progressive librarian*, no. 28 (Winter 2006–2007), pp. 87–99.

index

In this index, MG=Michael Gorman. Page numbers in italic indicate photographs.

"91 rules." *See* Panizzi, Anthony

A
AACR *(Anglo-American Catalog[u]ing Rules)* (1967), 119–20, 151, 193–94
AACR2 *(Anglo-American Cataloguing Rules, 2nd edition)* (1977), 197, 198
    as clean break with the past, 203
    complexity of, 198–99
    and deficiencies of AACR, 194–95
    examples in, 186, 198
    as global cataloguing code, 202–3
    language and structure of, 198–99
    need for revision of, 202
    and nonbook materials, 176
    numbering system of, 198
    war of, 200–201
    See also Gorman, Michael, as editor of AACR2; Joint Steering Committee (JSC)
AACR2 *(Anglo-American Cataloguing Rules, 2nd edition)* (1977), part 1 (descriptive cataloging), 183, 194, 197–98, 203
AACR2 *(Anglo-American Cataloguing Rules, 2nd edition)* (1977), part 2 (access points)
    CCRC's rejection of Winkler's draft, 182
    elimination of special case rules, 203
    MG asked to rewrite, 185–86
    Winkler's drafts of, 185, 197, 199–200
"AACR2 music," 186
AACR2R *(Anglo-American Cataloguing Rules, 2nd edition)* (1988), 202–3
Abbey Road, 108
Abse, Danny, 92
access points
    debate over cost of changing, 200
    MG learns about, 53
    MG report on for BNB, 120–21
    See also AACR2 *(Anglo-American Cataloguing Rules, 2nd edition)* (1977), part 2 (access points)
accountancy, MG considers as career, 93
ALA. *See* American Library Association (ALA)
ALA cataloging rules (1949), 193–94
Allen, Nancy, 181, 184
Allen, Walter, 160
America, impressions of
    from books and films, 71, 94
    Champaign-Urbana, Illinois, 157–58
    Chicago, 154–55
    deep South, 169–70
    Illinois, 151–52
    job interviews in, 116
    New York City, 178
American holidays
    Fourth of July celebration, 181
    Thanksgiving, 167

• 223

American Library Association (ALA)
    ALA cataloging committee (*See* Catalog Code Revision Committee (CCRC), ALA)
    membership on JSC, 196
    MG's first meeting, 168–69
anarchism, MG's interest in, 91, 104
Anderson, Dorothy, 132, 134
Angel family (neighbors in Hendon), 30–31
Anglo-American catalog rules of 1908, 118, 119, 193
Anglo-American Cataloguing Rules, 2nd edition. See AACR2 *(Anglo-American Cataloguing Rules, 2nd edition)* (1977)
Anglo-American Cataloguing Rules, 2nd edition, Revised) (AACR2R)(1988), 202–3
Anglo-American Catalog[u]ing Rules (AACR) (1967). See AACR *(Anglo-American Catalog[u]ing Rules)* (1967)
Arabella (paying guest), 41
art, experience of, 9–10, 23, 63
Association of Research Libraries, 189, 201
Atkinson, Frank, 55, 56
Atkinson, Hugh
    hires MG at U of Illinois, 183, 184, 185, 186, 188
    at Ohio State University Library, 171
    at University of Illinois, 159, 181
Austin, Derek, 119, 187
Australian Committee on Cataloguing, 202
Avram, Henriette, 130, 136, 140, 195–96

B
Babington, Anthony, 55
backlogs
    in British Museum Department of Printed Books, 146–47
    at U of I library, 184, 189
Bagnall, Malcolm, 56
Balling, Eigil, 136, 140
Barrett, Alice Kitchen (grandmother), 4, 5, 21
Barrett, Jack (uncle), 4, 5, 13, 35, 36
Barrett, Joseph (grandfather), 14
Barrett, Margaret (aunt), 4, 5
Barrett, Mary (aunt), 4, 5
Barrett, Mavis (Uncle Jack's wife), 36
Barrett, Tony (uncle), 4, 5, 13
Barrett family, 6
Bartram's school, 16–17
Berman, Sanford, *202*
Besant, Larry, 188
Bevan, Aneurin "Nye," 46

Bibliographic Standards Office (British Library), 151, 175, 196
Binns, Norman, 102
Bird, Richard "Dicky," 119, 126, 127, 214n
BL. *See* British Library
Blair, Tony, 104
Bliss, Henry E., 109, 213n
BNB. *See* British National Bibliography (BNB)
bookbinding, class on, 111
bookplates, commissioned by MG, 148
bookshops and MG, 31–32
Borges, Jorge Luis, 131
Bridgeman, Olwen Jones, 149–50
Bridgewater, Bentley, 118
British Cataloguing Rules Committee, 134
British Library (BL)
    Bibliographic Standards Office, 151, 175, 196
    contrast with U of Illinois, 175
    history, 144, 151
    on JSC, 196
British Library Planning Secretariat, 145, 151, 196
British Museum Department of Printed Books and BNB, 117–18
    cataloging codes, 118, 146, 214n, 216n
    use of Panizzi's rules by, 192
British National Bibliography (BNB)
    absorbed into British Library, 145, 151
    history of, 116–18
    MG's work at, 115, 126
    moves to larger quarters, 126, 128
British politics, 175
Brown, Bob, 154
Brown, James Duff, 109, 213n
Budapest, impressions of, 143
Bungay, Fred, 87
Burgess, Katherine, 6
Butcher, Joan Gillett (sister-in-law), 91, 147
Butcher, Paul (nephew), 147
Butcher, Peter (brother-in-law), 129, 147
Butcher, Stanley, 52–53
Butler, Brett, 179
Byrum, John, 166, 176, 178, *202*

C
Cain, Melissa, 179, 184
camel, brought back by father, 43
Campaign for Nuclear Disarmament (CND), MG's interest in, 91, 123
Canada
    impressions of, 170–71
    MG applies for job in, 151

Canadian Library Association, 196
Carpenter, Richard, 175
Catalog Code Revision Committee (CCRC), ALA
   discussions on revising AACR2, 196
   and gender neutral language, 186
   and lack of progress on AACR2, part 2, 185, 199
   rejection of draft of AACR2 part 2, 182
   resignation of Spalding from, 185
   role in AACR2, 178, 197, 199
   work with Lubetzky, 193
catalogue cards, filing of, 70
catalogue drawer rods, dueling with, 70
cataloguing
   centrality to librarianship, 162, 191
   MG's interest in, 109
cataloguing codes
   ALA cataloging rules (1949), 193–94
   Anglo-American catalog rules of 1908, 118, 119, 193
   international codes, 202
   MG's first interest in, 110, 113
   Resource Description & Access (RDA), 191
   single-author codes, 120, 192
   See also AACR *(Anglo-American Catalog[u]ing Rules)* (1967); AACR2 *(Anglo-American Cataloguing Rules, 2nd edition)* (1977); standards for cataloguing
Catholic Church, MG's relation to, 99–100
Cawthorne (Albert) Prize, won by MG, 112
CCRC. *See* Catalog Code Revision Committee (CCRC), ALA
chain indexing, 118
Champaign-Urbana, Illinois, impressions, 157–58
Chaplin, Arthur Hugh, 132, 134, 136
Chicago, impressions, 154–55
chickenpox, MG contracts, 35
children's services at Hendon library, 29
Christensen, Karen Lunde, 140
Churchill, Mr. (milkman), 32–33
cinema
   during courtship, 91–92
   effect on MG/early memories of, 8–9
   in Paris, 86
   and smoking, 122
   The war game, 123
   in Wembly, 101
circulation services and photocharging machines, 59, *60*

Clark, Richard "Dick" (senator from Iowa), 177–78, 217n
Clarke, Richard, Fr., 100
Clinic on Library Applications of Data Processing, 179
Coates, Eric, 117, 118
Cole, John Y., 127
collection development, 69
Colwell, Eileen, 29
Compton, Denis Charles Scott, 26
computers, discussions at BNB about, 126, 130
   See also library automation
Cooperative Permanent Building Society, 88–91
Coote, Canon, 42
Copenhagen, visit to, 134–35
Cotswold, memories of, 8–9, 35–36
Coward, Richard, 119, 126, 130, 145, 147
Craigen, Billy, *4, 5*
cricket at St. Albans, 25
Croghan, Antony, 120
Cuban missile crisis, 104
Curwen, Tony, 139
Cutter, Charles Ammi, 109, 192, 213n
Cynthia. *See* Paterson, Cynthia

D
Dainton report on British Library, 144, 215n
democratic values, commitment to, 207
Denmark, visit to, 134–35
Dennis, Dick, 58
Derry, John, 30–31, 112
descriptive cataloguing
   definition, 110, 218n
   history, 192
   UNESCO/IFLA report on, 132
   work on with Mary Piggott, 121
   See also AACR2 *(Anglo-American Cataloguing Rules, 2nd edition)* (1977), part 1 (descriptive cataloging)
Dewey, Melvil, 109, 192, 213n
Dewey decimal classification, 118
digital life, superficiality of, 206
Divilbiss, James L. "JD," 160, 161, 165, 171, 179
Domanovsky (Hungarian library educator), 133
Donald, Roger, 55
Dowley, Mr. (porter at Kilburn), 64–65, 75
Downing, Joel, 116, 117, 118, 134, 139
Downs, Robert Bingham, 159
Drabble, Margaret, 124
Draper, Kay, 163–64, 169–71

dress codes for librarians
    at Ealing Library, 58, 103
    at Hampstead Library, 58
    at IFLA meeting in Grenoble, 140
    at University of Illinois, 161
Dublin Core, 198
Dudley, Edward, 58, 116, 127

E

Ealing Public Library, 101–2
Ealing Technical College, 104
Edgar, Neal, 199
Eleven Plus exam, 24, 35
Elsinore, meeting at, 140
EUDISED (European Documentation and Information System for Education) project, 139, 151, 215n
Evans, Margery, 55

F

family as idea, 3
Farnborough Air Show, 31
Fasana, Paul, *202*
fascists, MG's acquaintance with, 129
Festival of Britain, 31
filing of catalogue cards, 70
Finchley Catholic Grammar School, 35, 37–41, 45, 47–48
Finerty, Eric, 117, 118–19, 132
Finland, impressions of, 142
Fodder, "Bill," 102
football (American), 166–67
Fourth of July celebration, Chicago, 181
France
    first impressions, 77–78
    political situation in 1960, 79–80
    See also Paris
Frank, Mr. (customer for ration coupons), 27
FRBR (Functional requirements for bibliographic records), 197
Freedman, Mitch, 179, *202*
Functional requirements for bibliographic records (FRBR), 197
"Fur-ber," 197

G

gardens
    and horse manure, 32–33
    in house at Sunny Gardens Road, 41
    at Waxwell Close, 149
Garforth, John
    at Hampstead library, 56, 57
    influence on pacifism, 73
    recreations with, 71, 91, 105, 129
Garforth, Susanna, 105, 129
Gayler, Bob, 117, 118, 119–20, 126, 132
gender-neutral language in AACR2, 186, 198
Geoghegan, Miss (teacher), 25, 35
George VI, death of, 35
Germany, impressions of, 141
Gillett, Anne
    courtship of, 91, 92
    at Hampstead library, 58
    letters from, 79, 86
    meets train in London, 87
    starts going out with, 75
    See also Gorman, Anne Gillett (wife)
Gillett, Herbert (father-in-law), 91, 93
Gillett, Joan. *See* Butcher, Joan Gillett (sister-in-law)
Gillett, Marjorie Cracknell (mother-in-law), 91
Gilli, Herman, 84
girlfriends
    Isabel Thomson, 58
    at Kilburn, 71, 75
    Lothian, Katie, 45
    Richardson, Priscilla, 21
    See also Gillett, Anne
Golders Green, London, 21, 28
Goldhor, Herbert
    advice on teaching, 162
    Clinic on Library Applications of Data Processing, 179
    hires MG to teach at U of Illinois, 151, 153, 158, 171
Google, anticipation of, 145
Gorman, Alice Clara (daughter), 131, 137
    See also Gorman daughters
Gorman, Alicia Felicia Barrett (mother), *4, 133*
    background and family of, 3, 5–6
    character of, 13–14, 17, 94–96
    cleft palate of, 13, 43, 94
    eulogy for, 96–97
    holiday in Ireland, 112–13
    objections to MG's marriage, 99, 100
    remote and physically frightening figure, 25, 38
Gorman, Anna Clara (daughter)
    See also Gorman daughters
Gorman, Anne Gillett (wife), *133*
    accompanies MG to Paris, 176
    garden of, 149
    and job at U of I, 186
    move to Urbana-Champaign, 188, 190

returns to England, 171
steadiness and strength of character of, 182
strains on marriage, 131
takes MG to airport, 153–54
trip to Wales with, 124
See also Gillett, Anne
Gorman, David John (brother), 7, 114, 148, 150
Gorman, Diana Williams (sister-in-law), 133, 150
Gorman, Emma Celeste (daughter), *133*
   birth of, 121–22
   trip to Wales with, 124
   as vegetarian, 167, 169
Gorman, Joanna Susan (sister), 7, *133*
Gorman, Michael, *133, 202*
   on aging, 205
   articles written, 126–27, 171–72, 214n, 217n
   childhood, 1–9
   at Cooperative Permanent Building Society, 88–91
   decision to go to library school, 87–88
   education of, 16–18, 38–49
   lack of visual intelligence, 2
   as "mad, bad, and dangerous to know," 57
   marriage to Anne, 58, 99, 131
   migraine headaches, 186–87
   National Service, avoidance of, 49–50
   nervous disorders, 132, 150, 161, 187
   pacifism of, 72–73, 123
   panic attacks of, 123–26
   paper route of, 26
   and photocharging machine, 59, *60*
   plane phobia, 112–13, 124, 152–53
   poetry writing by, 140–41
   political positions, 16, 46, 91, 92–93
   radical socialism, interest in, 104
   sex education of, 25, 27, 45, 47, 51–52
   smoking given up for daughter, 122
   stage fright, 125, 172–73
   as teacher, 115, 120, 150, 161, 168–69
Gorman, Michael, as editor of AACR2
   appointed coeditor of AACR2, 152, 196
   asked to rewrite Part 2 of AACR2, 185–86
   travel connected with, 175
   work process for AACR2, 182, 186
   work process for AACR2R, 202
   working on, 165–66, 171–72, 177
Gorman, Michael, reading of, 29–30
   Arthurian myths, 63
   Bar-Hillel, 111
   and bookshops, 31–32
   on busses, 51
   at Cooperative Permanent, 90
   effects of, 46
   during lunch at Kilburn, 71
   Macaulay, 40
   Pre-Raphaelites, 63
   Trollope, 93–94
   Ulysses/James Joyce, 62–63
   while recuperating from chickenpox, 36
   while truant, 44
Gorman, Michael, travels of
   Budapest, 143
   Canada, 170–71
   Germany, 141
   Helsinki, 142
   Ireland, 112, 132
   Italy (Lucca), 37, 105–7, 135
   for library-related projects, 139, 140, 175
   Paris, 75–87
   reflections on, 37, 77, 141–42
   Wales, 124
   See also America, impressions of
Gorman, Norah (aunt), 9–10
Gorman, Paul Justin (brother), 8, 87, 112, *133*
Gorman, Philip Dennis (father), 2, *4*, 5–6, *133*
   after war, 13, 15
   effect on pacifism of MG, 123
   as gardener, 32–33
   holiday in Ireland, 112–13
   military career of, 11–12, 17
   places MG at North Finchley, 21
   as salesman for curtain materials, 26
   sense of humor, 43–44
   "sod them" antiauthoritarianism, 15, 48
Gorman, Philippa Mary (sister), 7
Gorman, Timothy James (brother), 8
Gorman daughters
   as light of life, 137, 142
   return to England, 171
   in school in Champaign, 163–64
   in United States, 152–54, 163, 168, 188–90
   See also Gorman, Emma Celeste (daughter)
Gorman family, 5
Gower, John, 67–68
Guiles, Kay, 136

H

Halliwell, Kenneth, 67
Hammond, Valerie, 53
Hampstead Heath, 20–21
Hampstead Public Library, 1, 49, *52*, 58, 59, 61–65

Hans Hill Farm, 35–36
hares dancing in English countryside, 37
Hawkins, Lilian, 24–25, 35
Haynes, Christine, 55–56
Helsinki, travel to, 142
Hendon Central, 26, 41
Hendon Public Library, 28–29, 88
Höhne, Heinz, 136
Holland, Steve, 148
Holt, Brian, 119
Honoré, Suzanne, 136
Hookway, Harry, 144
horse manure, 32–33
Hospital of Saints John & Elizabeth, 94–96
Howard, Joe, *202*
Howard, Tom, 64, 65, *67*
Huggett, Annie, Miss, 64, 66, 67, *67,* 70
Hungary National Library, visit to, 143
Hunter, Eric, 139

I

IFLA (International Federation of Library Associations and Institutions)
    commissions MG to write report comparing descriptive cataloging practices, 131–32
    and ISBD, 195, 197–98
    meetings of, 140, 143
    participation in, 139
    Universal Bibliographic Control committee, 132
Illinois, impressions of, 151–52
image of librarians, not of interest to MG, 103, 111
IMCE (International Meeting of Cataloguing Experts), 134, 136, 139, 195
Institute of the Blessed Virgin Mary, 48
interlibrary cooperation, technology as hindrance to, 110
interlibrary loan
    and formation of British Library, 144
    Joint Fiction Reserve system, 93, 213n
    MG's uses of, 54, 93
International Meeting of Cataloguing Experts (IMCE), 134, 136, 139, 195
International Standard Bibliographic Description. *See* ISBD (International Standard Bibliographic Description)
interviews, American-style, 184–85
Ireland, holidays in, 112, 132
ISBD (International Standard Bibliographic Description), 195–96
    debate over costs of, 200
    ISBD(G), 176–77, 182, 197–98
    ISBD(M), 153, 195, 197
    meeting in Estoril on, 140
    as MG responsibility at Bibliographic Standards Office, 151
    most successful international bibliographic standard of all time, 203
    speech on at 1976 ALA, 172–73
    Standard Bibliographic Description Working Group, 139, 195, 198
    as "unnatural," 188
Italy (Lucca), impressions of, 37, 105–7, 135

J

Jacobs, Mr., 88, 90, 94
Japanese basketball players, encounter with, 137
JD. *See* Divilbiss, James L. "JD"
Jean W., 82–83
Jeffries, Alan, 139
Jewett, Charles Coffin, 192
Joanna, Mother, 48–49
Johnson-Laird, Maureen Sullivan, 105
Johnson-Laird, Philip, 73, 105, 123
Joint Fiction Reserve, 93, 213n
Joint Steering Committee (JSC)
    approval of final text (Aug 1977), 188
    approves AACR2, part 1 (Jan 1977), 183
    divisions in, 166
    error in presenting AACR2 as revision of AACR, 203
    establishment of (1974), 152, 196–97, 202
    meeting on AACR2, part 2 (1977), 185, 199
    meetings (1975-1976), 165, 177, 181, 188
    meetings (1978), 189
Jolley, Leonard, 136
Jones, Mr. (librarian at Hampstead), *52,* 64, 65–66, *67,* 70
JSC. *See* Joint Steering Committee (JSC)

K

Karina, Anna, 135
Keats, John, 61
Kerr, Ross, 136–37, 140
Kierkegaard, Preben, 136
Kilburn Branch Library, *65*
    Anne as librarian of, 101
    MG at, 52, 54, 57, 64–68
Kilgour, Fred, 179
Knowles, Ernie, *52,* 65
Koel, Åke, 199

Kovacs, Ilona, 143
Krug, Judith, 187

L

Laing, J. D., 46–47, 48
Laker, Jim, 46
Lancaster, Cesaria Volpe, 161
Lancaster, F. Wilfred, 160–61, 165, 169, 179
Larsen, Birgit, 136, 140
learning, future of, 206–7
legacy collections, 206
legal indexing, need for, 120
Lewis, Peter, 139, 152, 153, 166
librarianship
    cataloguing as basis of, 162, 191
    as stewards of the human record, 206–7
    values of, 109, 111
library as social center at Kilburn, 68
Library Association
    Cataloguing and Indexing Group, 139
    and library school curriculums, 87, 104, 108, 109
    membership on JSC, 196
    MG becomes Associate of, 114
library automation
    AACR inadequate for, 194
    catalogue card printers, 53
    and debate over cost of changing access points, 200
    at Ohio State University Library, 171
    photocharging machine, 59, *60*
library education
    absence of cataloging courses in, 191
    conflict between vocation training and academic education, 163
    gulf between librarians and library educators, 159
    infestation by information scientists, 109
    MG as student, 104, 111–12, 113–14
    MG as teacher, 115, 120, 150, 161, 168–69
    school curriculum, 108, 109
Library of Congress
    alarmed by Lubetzky's ideas, 193
    card service, 200
    as leader in revision of cataloguing codes, 196
    on MARC format, 130
    opposition to AACR2, 189, 200
    as retrogressive force in cataloguing, 132, 165–66, 191
    and revision of 1949 code, 193
    superimposition policy of, 200
    visions of having to change millions of cards, 186
library schools. *See* library education
Licklider, J. C. R., 111
Liebaers, Herman, 131, 215n
Linford, John, 129–30, 139, 147
Lipitsch (schoolmate), 39
literacy, decline of, 2
Lock, Tony, 46
London, 13–16, *14*
London fog, 27–28
Lothian, Katie, 45
Lubetzky, Seymour, *202*
    criticism of 1949 ALA rules, 193–94
    foremost cataloguing theorist, 110, 134, 213n
    influence on AACR, 194
    influence on AACR2, 200, 203
    influence on ISBD, 203
    MG meets at Tallahassee conference, 201
    opposed by Spalding, 165

M

Mac (friend). *See* McEnroe, Bryan "Mac"
Mac, Miss (coworker at BNB), 119
Machula, Ruth, 169
main entries and added entries. *See* access points
Malinconico, S. Michael, 179, *202*
Maltese, Diego, 133, 136
Manley, Nancy. *See* Allen, Nancy
MARC format
    differences between U.S. and British practice, 194–95
    introduced at BNB, 145
    and ISBD, 195–96
    manual, British, 130, 215n
    and need to revise AACR, 194, 196
MARC project at BNB, 130, 145, 215n
Marshall, Joan, 199
McEnroe, Bryan "Mac"
    as best man, 99
    recreations with, 37, 71, 91
    trip to Paris with, 75, 87
McKeown, Carmel, 45
McLeod (school friend), 25
Medical Library Association conference, 172
Melville (coworker at Ealing), 103
Menuhin, Yehudi, 108
metadata schemes, 198
microfiche BNB, 145
Miller, Larry, 189
Mills, Jack "Dark Satanic," 120, 214n

Mochrie, Jo, 100
Moon, Erik, 187
Morgan, Tom, 120
Morris, Guido, 148–49
Morris, Wilma, 127
Morsch, Lucille, 132, 133
multitasking, 206
Murphy, Damian, 32

N

"Naked Lady" statue, 27, 210n
national bibliographies, history of, 116–18
National Lending Library, cataloguing scheme of, 145–46
National Library of Canada, 196
National Reference Library of Science and Information (NRLSI), 145, 146
nature, memories of, 36–37
New York City, impressions, 178
Nixon, Richard, 153
NLC/Canadian Library Association, 196
nonbook materials in AACR2, 197
Norsted, Marilyn, 162
North Western Polytechnic
    MG teaches at, 115, 120
    takes classes at, 87
NRLSI (National Reference Library of Science and Information), 145, 146
nuclear weapons, 104, 123–24

O

OCLC
    and backlog at U of Illinois, 189
    as mainstay of library cataloging, 179, 200
O'Connor, Armel, 25, 35
O'Connor, Miss (teacher at St. Albans), 25
Oddy, Paul, 61
OEEC (Organisation for European Economic Cooperation), 83–85
Ohio State University Library, 171
O-level exams, 47
Organisation for European Economic Cooperation (OEEC), 83–85
Orton, Joe, 67
Osborn, Andrew, 193
Our Lady of Dolours Catholic Church, 42
Outlaw family, 16

P

Palmer House, Chicago, 169, 216n
Panizzi, Anthony, 118, 146, 192
Paris, 75–87
    Americans on train to Paris, 76, 78, 127
    employment at OEEC, 83–86
    library in, 86–87
    lodgings in, 80–81
    meals, 83
    memories, 78–79, 86
    Metro, *81,* 82
    trip to, 75–87
Paris Principles, 134, 136, 193, 197, 219n
Parry report on British Library, 144, 215n
Parsons, Clement Henry, 23, 210n
Paterson, Cynthia, 126, 152–53, 170–71
patrons
    at Hampstead PL, 54
    at Kilburn branch, 67–69
"paying guests," 26, 33, 41, 59
Peace Pledge Union, 123
Phelan, Anna Cortopassi, 105
Phelan, Geoffrey, 105–7
Phillips, Andrew, 147, 151
photocharging machines, 59, *60*
physical abuse in schools, 38, 39–40
Piaf, Edith, 79
Pierrot, Roger, 136
Piggott, Mary, 121, 139
Pine-Coffin, R. S., 146, 216n
Pinner, 128–29
plane crashes, memories of, 31, 112, 123
Plotnik, Art, 127, 171
poetry, effect on MG, 2, 140–41
Potter, Bill, 161–62, 165, 166–67
poverty of Gorman family, 25–26
prayer, power of, 49–50
Price, Ken, 148
principles as basis for cataloging codes, 193
printed book as obsolete, 206
publishing, MG considers as career, 93

Q

Quill, Patrick, 139

R

radio programs, 32
Ranganathan, S. R., 109, 113, 118, 213n
Rather, Lucia, 136, 140
RDA. *See Resource Description & Access* (RDA)
Redfern, Brian, 116, 120
reference services, MG's introduction to, 54
Reilly, Paddy, 45
religion
    Catholic Church, 99–100
    Catholic youth group, 44–45

Methodist church service, 124
Our Lady of Dolours Catholic Church, 42
power of prayer, 49–50
Renner, Charlene, 189
Resource Description & Access (RDA)
    bizarrely incoherent and unnecessary draft of, 191
    radically different from all other national codes, 203
Resources and Technical Services Division. Cataloging Code Revision Committee. *See* Catalog Code Revision Committee (CCRC), ALA
Richardson, Priscilla, 21
Richmond, Phyllis, *202*
Rickmansworth, Hertfordshire, 99
Rix, T. J., 102
Roberts, Julian, 146–47
Ronalds, Alan, 56
Rule 116B(3), 193
Rules for a printed dictionary catalogue (Cutter), 192

S

San Francisco, impressions of, 172
Schlipf, Fred, 161
Schneider (coworker at OEEC), 84
scholarship, future of, 206
Sebestyén, Geza, 133, 143
serials, indexes to, 113
Sharp, Katharine, 159, 216n
Silkin, Jon, 92
Six-Day War, effect on MG, 124
Sklar, Terry, 162
Smith, Jean, 64, 65, 66, *67*
Smith, Vincent, 22–23, 36
Smith family, 22–23
Spalding, Sumner
    in bar in Lisbon, 140
    editor of AACR, 193–94
    opposition to Lubetzky, 165–66
    and reactionaries at LC, 200
    resignation from CCRC, 185
The speaker (film), controversy over, 187
Spender, Stephen, 122, 214n
St. Alban's Catholic Preparatory School, Finchley, London, 21–22, 23–24
St. Edward's Catholic Church, 44
St. Mary's School, London, 19–20
Staley, John, 56
standards for cataloguing
    meeting with Dorothy Anderson, 132
    as MG responsibility at Bibliographic Standards Office, 151
    MG's first interest in, 110
    need for, debated at ALA conference, 188
    See also cataloguing codes
Standley, Albert, 150
Stevens, Rolland, 161
Stevenson, Gordon, 199
Stone, Eric, 109, 110, 113
subject cataloging, 110, 193
Sullivan, Maxine, 178–79
superimposition policy, 200
Switzerland, visit to, 106

T

Tait, Elizabeth, 178
Tallahassee conference (1979), 201
Taylor, Arlene, 200
Taylor, Harry, 120
technology
    as hindrance to interlibrary cooperation, 110
    use of at BNB, 145
    See also library automation
Terry, Richard, 162
Thanksgiving, 167
Thatcher, Margaret, 22, 104
Thomas, Alan, 109, 110, 113, 161
Thompson, Anthony, 131, 132, 134, 195
Thomson, Isabel, 58–59
Thorould, Dorothy, 53
Toufar, J. A., 107
transaction cards, 59

U

UNESCO/IFLA report, 131–32, 134, 136, 195
United Kingdom as heading for government, proposed, 186, 217n
University of Illinois at Urbana-Champaign library
    as head of Technical Services, 183–84, 188–89
    history of library, 158–59
    Technical Services Department, 184–85
University of Illinois at Urbana-Champaign library school
    accepts job at, 151, 153
    Clinic on Library Applications of Data Processing, 179
    friends on faculty, 164–65
Urquhart, Brian, 145–46
user-friendliness of catalogues and AACR2, 200

V

values of librarianship
   and bookbinding class, 111
   not taught in library schools, 109
Vangelatou, Natasha (paying guest), 41
Velasquez (coworker at OEEC), 85
Verona, Eva, 136

W

Wales, trip to, 124
war, fears of, 123–25
The war game (film), 123
Warmind, Inger, 140
Wedemeyer, Mogens, 140
Weihs, Jean, *202*
Wells, A. J. "Jack"
   at BNB, 117, 118, 126, 130
   at British Library, 145
   character of, 127
   and UNESCO/IFLA report, 134, 195
Wembly, 100
Wesemael, Guust van, 136
White, Lucien, 159
Williams, Diana, 113–14, 133, 150
Wilson, Colin, 71
Wilson, Harold, 175
Windsor, Phineas, 159
Winkler, Paul
   and AACR2 Part 2, 185, 197, 199–200
   increasingly untenable draft of, 178
   at JSC/IFLA meeting on ISBD(G), 176
   and reactionaries at LC, 200
   at tripartite meeting, 152
   work with on AACR2, 165–66
World War I, influence on MG, 72–73
World War II, effect on Gorman family, 7, 8–9